A volume in the
DOUGLASS SERIES IN EDUCATION,
edited by HARL R. DOUGLASS, Ph.D.,
DIRECTOR OF THE COLLEGE OF EDUCATION,
UNIVERSITY OF COLORADO

VOLUMES IN

DOUGLASS SERIES IN EDUCATION

STUDENT TEACHING

in the

SECONDARY SCHOOL

By

WILLIAM T. GRUHN

DIRECTOR OF PRE-SERVICE TEACHER EDUCATION
UNIVERSITY OF CONNECTICUT

THE RONALD PRESS COMPANY · NEW YORK

Library of Congress Catalog Card Number: 54–7616

PRINTED IN THE UNITED STATES OF AMERICA

It is the purpose of this book to provide the student teacher with a better understanding of his responsibilities. It is hoped that it may be used to advantage in a number of ways. It should be helpful as a textbook in courses that lead directly to student teaching, as a basis for conferences and discussions preparatory to student teaching and during the teaching period, and as a general guide to which the student may refer for help in all his teaching activities. It is designed particularly for use by student teachers in senior high school, junior high school, or the seventh and eighth grades of elementary school.

A straightforward, practical approach is used throughout the book. It is directed at the specific problems faced by the student teacher from the time that he begins his student teaching until he is ready to seek a teaching position. It is intended to help the student teacher to understand his professional relationships with the principal, other teachers, pupils, and parents; to plan his work for the classroom; to participate in guidance and extraclass activities; and to work effectively in the school and the community. It also offers suggestions on locating, applying for, and obtaining a teaching position.

In addition to background information for the student teacher, there are numerous suggestions of practical activities which will prepare him for his work as a beginning teacher. These activities are varied enough in content and purpose to make them suitable to many different teaching situations. It is not expected that the student will complete all of them. He should select those which are most appropriate and helpful for his particular needs.

It is important that students should be prepared to employ effectively the newer approaches to teaching. For this reason much attention is given to student teaching in core-type classes, using the experience-centered approach, group activities, and other new methods. At the same time it must be recognized that many student teachers will work in cooperating schools and with teachers whose approach may be conservative. Throughout the entire text student teachers are urged to adapt themselves to the school situations in which they are placed, using the newer approaches as much as possible, but recognizing the preferences of the principal and teachers in the cooperating school.

It is recommended that the student read the book from cover to cover before making a start on actual student teaching. During the student-teaching period he should refer to it constantly as particular problems arise, use it as a basis for discussions with his cooperating teacher and college supervisor, and carry out as many as possible of the practical activities suggested. It is the author's hope that after the training period is completed the new teacher will find it a continuing source of fresh ideas and practical information during his first year or two in an independent teaching position.

WILLIAM T. GRUHN

Storrs, Connecticut
February, 1954

CONTENTS

PART V

After Student Teaching

PART I

Looking Ahead to Student Teaching

Chapter 1

STUDENT TEACHING IS IMPORTANT

The Thrill of Teaching

Student teaching is the most important phase of your teacher-education program. It is at this point that you begin to experience the thrill of working with children and youth, the satisfaction of assuming professional responsibilities, and the joy of successes—or the discouragement of failures—in teaching activities.

The success you achieve will depend largely on your preparation for and your attitude toward these professional responsibilities. You should have some perspective of the total responsibilities of the student teacher, of the preparation that the various activities require, and of the various approaches to successful teaching. These chapters are intended to help you gain that perspective.

You Are Prepared

You are no doubt prepared for assuming student-teaching responsibilities. All the professional courses, the subject matter preparation, and even the general education background which you have had in the past have in many ways pointed toward student teaching. The professional courses have given you an overview of the American school system and the philosophy and organization of the elementary and secondary school; they have helped you understand children and youth—how they develop, their emotional makeup, their interests and needs, the way in which they learn; and they have given you an understanding of the methods and procedures for working with children, planning for learning experiences, and carrying on effective learning activities. The courses in your subject matter areas have provided you with background in your teaching fields—background for preparing adequate teaching plans and for assisting pupils with preparing and carrying on worth-while learning activities.

Student teaching is the culmination of all these teacher-education activities. It is in student teaching that you implement the philosophy and theory, apply the psychology, employ the methods, and use the subject matter backgrounds which you have previously studied. With the backgrounds gained in the teacher-education courses you should be well qualified to work with boys and girls in the student-teaching program.

Various Approaches

There are several different approaches to student teaching in teacher-education institutions throughout the country. One plan is to have a school for student-teaching purposes organized and administered by the teacher-education institution itself. These schools, called laboratory, practice, or demonstration schools, are more common at the elementary than at the secondary level. A second plan is to provide student-teaching opportunities in a limited number of public or private schools, usually by contract arrangement, in the immediate vicinity of the teacher-education institution. Under this arrangement, a considerable number of student teachers are placed in a given school, the same teachers serving as critic or supervising teachers year after year. A third plan is to place student teachers on an individual basis in schools that are not too far away from the teacher-education institution. Under this plan, such placements are made in terms of the needs of the individual student in selected cooperating schools, with the number of students assigned to a given school being definitely limited.

Whatever approach may be employed in your institution, there are certain values to be gained from it. If there is a laboratory school, the student teacher is likely to have contact with superior teachers who have special preparation in teacher education. If other public or private schools cooperate in the teacher-education program, the student teacher will probably observe and participate in a school situation more like the one in which he will begin his professional work. If student teachers are assigned on an individual basis to a school which takes only a few students, they are likely to receive more individualized help than in either the laboratory or contract school. In fact, some institutions employ more than one of these plans so that student teachers may have as broad experience as possible. You should study the peculiar values of the student-teaching arrangement in your institution and profit from it accordingly.

Time for Student Teaching

The time arrangements for student teaching differ as widely as the plans for placing students in various schools. In some schools, the observation and student teaching is divided so that it will come at several places in the teacher-education program. For instance, some institutions provide observation experiences in the sophomore year; in the junior year they have students assist with teaching activities; while in the senior year they have students assume major teaching responsibilities. If such extended experiences can be arranged, this plan for observation and student teaching is a very desirable one because it gives the student contact with pupils in learning situations throughout much of his teacher-education program.

A more common plan is to have the student teacher concentrate this experience in his senior year or, in a few institutions, a fifth year. The advantage of this plan is largely administrative, since the student-teaching period can, as a rule, be more easily arranged late in the student's program. It is true, also, that the student is better prepared to assume teaching responsibilities once he has completed other phases of the teacher-education program.

There are different practices, also, in the manner in which student teaching is included in the student's daily schedule. Specialists in teacher education tend to favor a plan which provides for full-time student teaching, so that the student may become in effect a member of the teaching staff, working with pupils from the time they arrive at school in the morning until they leave at the end of the day. Such full-time student teaching gives the student an opportunity to observe and participate in all phases of the life of the school, both in class and out. Furthermore, it affords the student much greater professional satisfaction to be, for even a brief period, a participant in an all-school program on a full-time basis.

In many institutions, however, student teaching is on a part-time basis, with the student meeting some college classes during the day. If that plan is in effect in your institution, you should make every effort to observe and participate in as much of the school program as possible. Where the part-time plan is used, some initiative on your part will help considerably in giving you a well-rounded teaching experience.

A Well-Rounded Teaching Experience

In the secondary school today, the teacher's responsibilities extend far beyond the classroom. He usually has a home room, serves as sponsor of a school club, assists with assembly programs, supervises school parties, serves on faculty committees, and attends PTA meetings. These activities, and many others, constitute the professional work of the teacher in the modern school. It is for these responsibilities that you are preparing yourself. You should plan your activities as a student teacher so as to gain a well-rounded experience in all the duties and responsibilities that are ordinarily assumed by the regular teachers.

The supervisor at the teacher-education institution will, no doubt, have discussed with the cooperating teachers the advisability of having you gain a complete, well-rounded professional experience. The success you have in achieving this goal will depend largely upon your own initiative. You should volunteer to assist pupils after school; indicate a willingness to meet with faculty committees and attend faculty meetings; attend and observe pupil club activities; go to PTA meetings; and attend pupil functions after school and in the evening. It may appear that attendance at activities such as these is very time-consuming. It is—but it is essential for you to participate in this way if you are to have a well-rounded student-teaching experience.

Terms That Are Used

Different terms are used for the teachers and the schools participating in the student-teaching program. The schools may be called laboratory, demonstration, model, practice, or cooperating schools. In these chapters, all schools in which student teaching is done will be referred to as cooperating schools. The teachers with whom students work, sometimes called critic or supervising teachers, will be called cooperating teachers. The representative of the teacher-education institution who supervises the student teacher will be referred to as the college supervisor or just the supervisor. It is not intended to suggest that these terms are more appropriate than others, but they seem to serve the present purpose.

Do Your Best

This may be superfluous—but a word should be said about the importance of student teaching to your professional future. Up to this point in your college work, you have been acquiring professional and subject-matter backgrounds that are exceedingly worth while. In that work, however, attention was not focused directly on your success as a teacher. It may be that shortcomings in your early professional and subject-matter courses can be overlooked, but your successes —or failures—in student teaching will be scrutinized carefully by prospective employers. This is true because in student teaching you have an opportunity to show what you can do in learning situations with boys and girls—how well you understand them and their problems, how thoroughly you prepare your work, how much originality you have in developing learning activities, and how well you get along with teachers, supervisors, and administrators in a school situation.

Soon you may be seeking your first position as a teacher. The effectiveness of your student-teaching experience will be the best present indication of your future success. You will be observed closely by the college supervisor, by the principal and teachers of the cooperating school—and perhaps by a principal or superintendent seeking a new teacher. Need it be said that you should *do your best?*

Chapter 2

BEFORE YOU BEGIN

You can do a number of things to get ready before your student-teaching work begins. First of all, you should have well in mind the objectives of student teaching and how it fits into your total program of teacher education. The previous chapter has given you some suggestions on this point. You should also develop some understanding of your relationship with the school and the teachers with whom you are going to work. Then, too, there are a number of specific things that you can do to plan for student teaching, to become acquainted with the school, to know the community, and other things that will make your student-teaching experience more worth while. This chapter suggests some of those things.

The School and You

The School's Point of View

Although your college supervisor will place you in the best school available, you may find that this school is not outstanding in all respects. This is difficult for some student teachers to understand. In their education courses they hear so much about the outstanding practices and points of view in modern education that they develop an enthusiasm for observing these things in actual school situations. There is no school, however, that is outstanding in all aspects of its program. Furthermore, if a few such schools could be found,

9

the large number of student teachers would make it difficult to place students only in those schools.

You should not be unduly critical of the program of the cooperating school. Give particular attention to the forward-looking features in the program, rather than its shortcomings. You should find much that is helpful in preparing you for the responsibilities of a beginning teacher.

The Cooperating Teacher

Likewise, you will find great differences among the teachers in a school. One may be very forward looking in his educational thinking, and consequently will employ many of the newer teaching practices. Another may be conservative in his classroom approach and use rather traditional teaching methods. Obviously, you must accept the cooperating teacher as he is.

You should not feel that you must conform in every respect to the practices employed by the cooperating teacher. Most teachers are willing to give the student some freedom to try out his own ideas. Be sure to discuss with the cooperating teacher any plan you have in mind which deviates considerably from the usual classroom practice in that room, and then plan that activity with the utmost care to assure its success. The freedom which the cooperating teacher gives you is likely to increase as you demonstrate your effectiveness in teaching.

Early in your student-teaching period you should have an understanding with the cooperating teacher concerning the time and manner in which he would like to study your plans. Since he is responsible to the parents and the community for the achievement of his pupils, he will want to examine your plans carefully. Keep in touch with him as you develop your plans so that you may profit from his suggestions. Be sure that he reviews and approves the final plans day by day before you teach.

Visit the School

A visit to the cooperating school before your student-teaching period begins may prove helpful. Your college supervisor should be consulted before you make such a visit. In fact, the arrangements for the visit might well be made by him. In any case, make an appointment with the persons you want to see before visiting the school. In order that your visit may be most profitable, make some definite plans for it, such as making a list of those you want to see, formulating questions you want to raise concerning your work in the school, and having in mind the materials about the school which you would like to obtain. Some of the specific values of such a visit include getting acquainted with the principal and the cooperating teacher, becoming familiar with the building and the classrooms where you are going to work, and obtaining a definite statement concerning your teaching assignment.

The principal or cooperating teacher may have materials which will help you get acquainted with the school. The following are some materials that you might request: (1) a teachers' handbook, (2) a pupils' handbook, (3) mimeographed or printed materials describing the program of the school as a whole, (4) courses of study or curriculum guides, and (5) the textbooks or other basic study materials. Perhaps the teacher can give you some idea of the work that will be covered while you are student teaching, and perhaps tell you what units you are to teach.

Your Place in the Community

Know Your Community

It will be helpful in your teaching if you have some understanding of the community in which the school is located. This background will be useful in planning your work, in understanding the pupils, and in relating the work of the classroom to the life needs of the pupils. You should have such information as the following: (1) what the local people do for a living, (2) the cultural, racial, and nationality backgrounds of the pupils, (3) the cultural and recreational opportunities in the community, and (4) the organization of the community government. For instance, in an Eastern state the school may be located in a rural community where dairying is the predominant industry; not many miles away there may be another high school located in a small factory town; and within the same state there may be high schools in large industrial centers. In every subject, the examples that you use, the activities that you carry on, and the materials that you make avilable to the class should reflect the type of community in which the school is located.

It may not be easy, in the brief period you spend in the community, to obtain much information about it first hand. Some of it you may gather on your visit to the school before your student-teaching period begins. The principal and the teachers in the cooperating school may be of help. The Chamber of Commerce, local trade associations, the public library, and similar agencies may be sources of information concerning the community. The school librarian may have a file of materials dealing with the history, cultural backgrounds, the government, and the economic life of the community. In any case, become as familiar as you can in the time that you have available with the type of community in which you are to do your teaching.

Participate in Community Life

The satisfaction which a teacher gains from teaching in a community is greatly enhanced through participation in the activities of a local church, the YMCA or YWCA, service clubs, and other community organizations. As a student teacher, you should approach as much as possible the professional and community participation of a teacher in service. If your student teaching is being done in the community where the college is located, such participation will be relatively easy. If you are going to a new community, your participation in the various activities obviously must be limited.

Even so, there are a number of things which a community-minded student teacher may do. The easiest is perhaps attendance at the church of your choice. As the guest of the principal or teachers in the cooperating school, you may also attend meetings of various service clubs and other community organizations. A suggestion of interest on your part is quite likely to lead to an invitation for such attendance. Although community contacts of this kind may be relatively limited, you will enjoy your stay there much more if you have such participation.

Finding a Place To Live

The student teacher in a strange community should give considerable time and attention to locating a suitable place to live. Your experience in this respect will be much like that of a teacher in his first position. The place where you live will not only have a bearing on your pleasures away from school, but it will also influence considerably your success as a student teacher. For instance, you may be unfortunate enough to live in a place that is not conducive to effective study; the home you have chosen may be that of the village gossip; or your rooming place may be the home of one of your problem pupils.

An unfortunate experience in your living place may be avoided if a little care is taken. First, discuss rather fully with your college supervisor how to locate a place to live. Second, ask the principal of the cooperating school to suggest rooming places. Frequently there is a list of suitable places in his office or in the office of the superintendent of schools. Third, ask the cooperating teacher for information and advice about a place to live. It may be that you can find a room in a home where other teachers are now staying. In any case, the experiences of teachers in the community will be helpful in locating an appropriate home during your student-teaching period.

The College Supervisor and You

Know Your Supervisor

It is exceedingly important for you and your college supervisor to know each other sufficiently so that the two of you may work well together during your student-teaching period. You should be familiar with his philosophy of education, his point of view on teaching methods, and any suggestions that he may have for student teaching. There are these ways of getting acquainted with the supervisor's point of view: (1) through individual or group conferences with him, (2) through materials on student teaching prepared by him, and (3) through materials on teaching methods and on student teaching which he may suggest to you.

If your college supervisor does not suggest either individual or group conferences before your student teaching begins, you are urged to take the initiative in this matter. Do this fairly early so that time will permit several conferences with him if that appears advisable. Ask for specific suggestions concerning the approach that he would like to have you take in your student teaching, suggest that he give you references that you may study, and inform him of your availability for either individual or group conferences at any convenient time.

Responsibility to the Supervisor

Although the cooperating principal and teacher are usually in direct charge of your work as a student teacher, a college supervisor usually represents the teacher-education institution in directing your work. The relationship of the student teacher with the college supervisor will vary, of course, from one institution to another. There are certain responsibilities to your supervisor, however, which are common to most institutions.

For instance, it is your responsibility to keep your supervisor informed concerning your activities as a student teacher and the progress you are making. Although you may feel that he should keep in touch with you, you must realize that he probably has a considerable number of students to supervise. Let him know when you are likely to teach, difficulties that you have in your schedule, matters that are not clear in your relationships with the cooperating principal and teachers, difficulties that you have in preparing teaching plans, problems that you face in locating source materials, and any other matters that may affect your success as a student teacher.

College supervisors want to be fully informed about your activities as a student teacher, although they have different ways of getting the information. Some are satisfied to observe your activities as they develop when they make periodic visits. Others like to have the student teacher keep a day-by-day diary of the activities in his classes, particularly those for which he was responsible. Some supervisors also like to have the student teacher keep a complete file of his teaching plans to be turned in periodically or at the end of his student-teaching period. Even though your supervisor does not require a diary or other record of your activities, you may find it helpful to keep such a record. In any case, be sure that you are properly informed concerning the records that the college supervisor expects you to keep.

The Supervisor and the Cooperating Teacher

Although the relationship between the college supervisor and the cooperating teacher varies greatly from one institution to another, each one usually has certain responsibilities. The supervisor usually informs the cooperating teacher concerning the background of the student, his preparation for student teaching, his peculiar interests, his skills and talents, and any significant shortcomings that he may have. The supervisor is also responsible for helping the student teacher meet the requirements of his college and those for certification. Consequently, he usually develops the over-all plan for the total student-teaching experience.

The cooperating teacher is more directly responsible for your work from day to day. He must be sure that his pupils make normal progress in their subjects while you are there, and that the usual requirements of the school are met. This means that the cooperating teacher is usually the one who gives approval concerning the time when you are to teach, he may help you with your plans, and he is responsible for those things that affect the immediate progress of the class. Both the college supervisor and the cooperating teacher are greatly interested in your success and will do everything they can to be of assistance.

Make Some Plans

Review Teaching Methods

If you have taken your course work in methods recently, that information should be sufficiently well in mind to necessitate little review. If a semester or more has passed since you took this work, a rapid but intensive review of teaching methods is urged. In any case, be sure to have well in mind such things as the following before your student-teaching period begins:

1. Have an over-all philosophy of teaching methods.
2. Understand how to work effectively with boys and girls.
3. Have well in mind what should be included in a unit plan, as well as a procedure for developing unit plans.
4. Know how to prepare plans for the day-by-day work of your classes.
5. Know how to organize and administer a class for various types of learning activities.
6. Be able to evaluate, record, and report the progress of pupils.
7. Understand some of the responsibilities that you may assume for the total administration of the school.
8. Understand the responsibilities for the home room and guidance which you may be called upon to assume.
9. Be able to assume responsibility for certain extraclass activities, such as clubs, assemblies, and social functions.

This list of suggestions may seem to cover almost everything that was included in your previous study of methods. It does suggest, however, a good review list of things that a student teacher is likely to be called upon to do. Later chapters in this book will be of help in that review.

Study Subject Content

The student teacher who is well prepared in subject matter will not only find that his teaching is easier, but he should also be more successful in it. Because secondary school courses are often of a survey nature, they may cover a broad field of subject matter. Even though you are well prepared in your major subject, there may be certain areas in which you have had little work at the college level. That is particularly true of teachers in such broad fields as the social studies, general science, and the language arts. For instance, one well-prepared teacher of social studies was assigned as her first unit one that dealt with the local government, an area in which she had little work at the college level. Another student teacher of biology was asked to teach a unit in botany, whereas his college major was in zoology. These student teachers found it necessary to do a tremendous amount of background reading in preparation for their work in these units.

On your preliminary visit to the cooperating school, it might be well to find out what units you are likely to teach. If there are some in which you feel inadequate, it is best to be frank about it. In most cases, however, you may have sufficient time to do some background reading in areas where you are deficient. The college library and some of the teachers in the subject matter departments of your college will prove helpful.

Locate Reference Materials

From the day that you begin your teacher-education program, you should accumulate a variety of reference materials in your subject area. In some instances these may be the materials themselves, such as booklets, pamphlets, pictures, cartoons, newspaper clippings, magazine articles, and similar materials. For other types of materials such as library books, films, film strips, recordings, and similar teaching aids, it may help to prepare a bibliography on small index cards. Since most students do not have suitable filing space for such materials or reference cards, large manila envelopes may be a convenient way to keep them.

When you know more definitely what your student-teaching assignment will be, spend some time to locate and organize the study materials for the units that are to be covered. The following suggestions may be helpful for this purpose:

1. Select from the teaching materials you have accumulated those which may have a bearing on your student-teaching assignment.
2. Consult your college supervisor and teachers in the subject matter departments for suggestions of materials that

are appropriate for the units you are to teach at the secondary school level.

3. Consult the lists of free and inexpensive teaching materials which are prepared by various agencies in most subject fields. Your college supervisor may be of help in suggesting such sources.

4. Examine magazines of various kinds for leads to materials that you might use. Current magazines often list publications by commercial, historic, civic and government agencies in various advertisements. *School Life*, a monthly publication of the United States Office of Education, lists government publications.

5. Obtain catalogs of audio-visual materials from nearby libraries and go through them to check those films, film strips, radio transcriptions, and recordings which have a bearing on your teaching assignment.

6. Arrange these materials in some well-organized fashion so that they will be more usable when you do your student teaching. An easy way is to place both the reference cards and the related materials in large manila envelopes by units of study.

Sometimes the cooperating teacher will give the student a definite statement of units for which he will be responsible. If that is done, you may do some definite planning before the student-teaching period begins. Obviously, such planning must be tentative because you do not know the school, the materials that will be available there, the approach that the teacher has been using, and the pupils that you will have. Then, too, it is hoped that there may be some cooperative planning by you as a student teacher with the pupils in your classes.

Even so, it will be to your advantage to organize subject matter backgrounds, to begin a list of activities that might be employed, and to organize the study and reference materials. Then, too, you will be able to obtain suggestions from the college supervisor and from other persons on the college campus concerning possible approaches to teaching these units. This preliminary planning may save you much time later on and result in more effective teaching.

Things for You To Do

These, then, are some of the things that you may do to get ready for student teaching:

1. Visit your cooperating school to meet the principal and teachers, to obtain materials about the school, to obtain courses of study and textbooks, and to find out about your teaching assignment.

2. Find a place to live, if the school is located some distance from the college. Obtain suggestions from the college supervisor, the cooperating principal or teachers, and college friends who live in the community.

3. Get acquainted with the community in which the school is located—the people and their backgrounds, the industries, cultural advantages, and recreational opportunities.

4. Have conferences with your college supervisor concerning your student teaching, discussing such matters as the ethics of student teaching, your relationships with the college supervisor and the cooperating principal and teachers, the planning of your work, the location of reference materials, and similar matters.

5. Review your teaching methods, especially if some time has elapsed since you studied them.

6. Review your subject backgrounds in terms of your student-teaching assignment.

7. Accumulate reference materials of various kinds that may have a bearing on your student-teaching assignment, and organize them by units so that you can locate and use them readily.

8. Get an overview of the courses you are to teach by reading, in advance, the textbooks, basic references, curriculum guides, and courses of study for your classes.

In Summary

The things that a student can do before he begins his student-teaching period will, of course, vary greatly from school to school. The suggestions given in this chapter are those which pertain to most situations. You should consider them only as suggestions, and go far beyond them in exploring the possibilities of preliminary work that will make your student teaching easier and more successful.

Chapter 3

GETTING STARTED

How To Get Acquainted

Observation Is Important

It is important that the student teacher observe intelligently during the first few weeks he spends in a school. That is true whether it is a separate observation period or a part of the student-teaching experience. Intelligent observation means that the student teacher has definite things in mind that he wants to observe and a well-organized plan for observing them. Suggestions for helping you observe the program of a school intelligently will be given in this chapter.

Plan Your Observation

The time that you are able to devote to observation is likely to be all too limited. You can use that time most efficiently by making careful plans for it. The following suggestions may serve as guides in preparing an observation plan:

1. Make a list of the major areas of the program of the school that you should observe, such as the subjects, the extraclass activities, the services, and the administrative organization.
2. In each of these areas prepare a list of questions that should be answered as you observe the program of the school.
3. Make a list of the sources of information in the school

which will help you gain a better understanding of its program.

4. Plan a time schedule for your observation so that you may cover the various areas in the time you spend in the school.

5. Prepare the observation plan after consultation with your college supervisor and the principal and teachers of the cooperating school.

Sources of Information

The cooperating principal and teacher will be able to suggest sources of information concerning the program of the school. In most schools these sources include (1) the faculty and staff, particularly the principal, assistant principal, director of guidance, director of curriculum, department heads, and key teachers, (2) the teachers' handbook for the system, as a whole as well as the handbook for the school, (3) the pupils' handbook, (4) printed administrative forms such as pupil progress reports, cumulative records, guidance records and home room records, and (5) printed and mimeographed bulletins describing various aspects of the program of the school.

If these materials are not provided in your initial conference with the cooperating principal and teacher, do not be hesitant about requesting them. The cooperating principal and faculty will be glad to furnish any materials that will help you become acquainted with the program of the school.

Keeping a Record

The information that you obtain through observing the program of the school should prove helpful not only during your student-teaching experience but also later on as a beginning teacher. Although practices in no two schools are identical, familiarity with the program of one school should help you understand that of another more readily. It is suggested, therefore, that you keep some kind of record of your observation. The college supervisor may suggest the form this record should take. A simple device for this purpose is to divide a notebook into sections, with the headings for your observation plan to designate various parts of it. Under each heading give the questions you had in mind during your observation, and briefly summarize the information that you have gained.

If you have the opportunity to observe or to do student teaching in more than one school, the observation record will prove helpful in making a comparison of practices. Retain the observation record as part of the material that you may use as a beginning teacher.

Knowing the School

The Faculty and the School

The first step in getting to know the school is to become acquainted with members of the staff. Perhaps you can get a list of the teachers and the administrative and supervisory staff, to help you learn their names. Staff members whom you should know particularly include the principal, the assistant principal, the attendance officer, the counselors, the dean of boys, the dean of girls, the director of audio-visual aids, the librarian, the director of student activities, and key individuals in charge of various other activities. It is with these staff members that you are most likely to have some contact. You should also know the teachers of the various subject areas, particularly those who teach subjects related to your own.

Then, too, it is important that you understand the teacher's relationship to the administration of the school as a whole. In most schools the student teacher is expected to observe the same policies and regulations as regular staff members. For instance, you need to have such information as the following:

1. What hours are teachers expected to be at school?
2. What should teachers do if they find that they are unable to come to school because of illness or some other reason?
3. Are teachers expected to report to the office' upon arrival at school?
4. What arrangements should teachers make if they need to leave the building during the regular school hours?
5. What are your responsibilities as a student teacher with respect to faculty meetings and other professional staff meetings?

The School Day

One aspect of the school day with which you must be familiar is the bell schedule. That is, you should know when pupils are admitted to the building, when they are considered tardy, whether there is a home room period, when classes begin and end, what the arrangement is for lunch, when school closes for the day, and at what hours pupils are expected to be out of the building. It is essential that you memorize this schedule immediately because you must follow it closely when working with a group of pupils. It may spoil the teaching period if you run over for even a minute or two. Be certain the clocks in the classroom are accurate.

The daily schedule varies considerably from one school to another. One practice, for instance, is to begin the day with a home room period when attendance is taken and announcements are made. Following the home room period, the pupils usually proceed to their first period classes, and then continue with their other classes throughout the day. Some schools have a daily activities period for club meetings, home room activities, and assemblies. Pupils who are not in an activity during this period usually return to their home room or go to a study hall.

The noon hour is another time of day that may, at first, be a bit confusing to you. Although in some schools pupils go home at noon, it is a common practice to have a cafeteria where many or all pupils eat their lunch. Usually there are several cafeteria periods, which may necessitate some adjustment in the class schedules during that part of the school day. Find out what the policy is with respect to having pupils remain in the school building or on the grounds during the lunch period, as well as your responsibility for the supervision of the pupils during the noon period.

Some schools also have a period late in the day for makeup work, special help, and conferences with pupils. Usually pupils are dismissed at the beginning of that period unless they have some responsibilities for which they are expected to remain. Where there is such a period, teachers are usually expected to be in their rooms so that they can help pupils who need it.

Pay particular attention to the policy for keeping pupils after regular school hours. In schools where pupils are transported, it may be unwise to keep them after school except by special arrangement with the principal or the pupils' parents. Obviously, transported pupils must leave with the bus, unless they have made other arrangements.

In a few schools, there are double sessions because the building is not large enough to accommodate the entire pupil body at one time. Sometimes teachers divide their time between the two sessions, but usually there are separate faculties and administrative staffs, except for the principal who is responsible for the total program. Although teachers may have classes in only one session, they frequently direct extra-class activities for the entire student body. If you are teaching in a school that has two sessions, inform yourself concerning your responsibilities throughout the day.

Buildings and Grounds

During the first few days you should become thoroughly familiar with the buildings and grounds. For instance, you need to know the location of the administrative offices, the nurse's office, the attendance office, the offices of the counselors, the school library, the audio-visual aids rooms, the teachers' rooms, and the classrooms where you are to work. Sometimes there is a floor plan for the school in the pupils' handbook or in the teachers' manual. If one is not available, the cooperating teacher may be willing to assign a student to help you become acquainted with the building.

Sometimes there are special policies and regulations concerning the school building which you should know. For instance, you should know the hours a teacher is expected to be in the building, and what other hours the building is open to them. Then, too, there may be special rules about locking classroom doors and the doors to the school building. Study with particular care the regulations for fire drills, air-raid drills, and other disaster drills.

Teachers also have responsibility for protecting pupils against accidents while they are under the supervision of the school. Some schools have a carefully developed statement of regulations on the use of the buildings and grounds by the pupils. As protection against accidents it is usually required, for instance, that pupils be supervised by a teacher at any time that they are engaged in a school activity, and that the teacher remain until all pupils have left the building and grounds. Teachers are also expected to be on the alert for accident hazards anywhere in the school program. This concerns such things as broken furniture, the safeguarding of equipment in shops and homemaking laboratories, the use of gymnasiums, and other places in the program where hazards may exist. Become familiar with any statement that the school may have on accident protection so that you may better discharge your responsibilities in this respect.

The Pupils and the School

In most schools there are rules and regulations concerning the relationship between the pupils and the school. Although as a student teacher you may have responsibility for enforcing only a few of them, it will help you as a beginning teacher later on to know what such rules are like. Your first concern should be with those rules that you may have to enforce. This information may be obtained from the pupils' handbook, the teachers' manual, mimeographed material in the office, or the cooperating teacher. The answers to questions such as the following will be helpful:

1. What are the rules concerning the tardiness and absence of pupils?
2. What is the policy and what are the rules for the readmission of pupils who have been absent because of illness?
3. What should be done with pupils who become ill or are injured while at school? What reports need to be made for such pupils?
4. What are the rules for keeping pupils after school for special help or for any other reason?
5. Are there any special rules for excusing pupils from class, the use of the library by pupils, and similar matters?

The Library and Other Facilities

Most secondary schools today have a library and similar facilities that are used by teachers and pupils in preparing for their learning activities. Pupils usually are assigned to the library for certain study periods daily or several times weekly. Frequently teachers make arrangements to have a special shelf in the library for their classes or to bring library books to their classrooms for use in connection with certain units. Become well acquainted with the library, particularly with the books and reference materials that have a bearing on your subject. Furthermore, become informed concerning the manner in which you may use the library for your classes, how pupils may be sent to the library, and how they may check books out for use at home. In some junior and in a few senior high schools there are arrangements for taking entire class groups into the library for study purposes. Where that is done, the librarian needs to be informed some time in advance so that he may schedule the use of the facilities for your group and have materials available for the work you are doing. When the entire class goes to the library as a group, the teacher and the librarian usually work together in helping the pupils with their study.

In many schools today, there are audio-visual aids facilities that are of great help to teachers and pupils. Large schools usually have an audio-visual aids director who is in charge of assigning the equipment, seeing to it that it is properly used, and ordering the materials for the teachers. Audio-visual aids facilities usually include a variety of equipment, such as sound and silent movie projectors, opaque projectors, film strip projectors, record players, and tape and wire recorders. In the audio-visual aids office you will find catalogs that list available films, film strips, recordings and radio transcriptions. Inform yourself concerning the policy and practices that govern the use of these materials and equipment.

In large school systems, libraries of films, film strips, slides, recordings and transcriptions are now being acquired. Even where there are such local libraries of audio-visual materials, there must be preplanning on the teacher's part so that he can be reasonably sure that the materials will be available when they are needed. If it is the policy to obtain films from rental libraries, teachers in the various departments are usually limited by a budget for this purpose.

There are also other special facilities in most schools

that affect the work of teachers with their classes. Some schools have a book room with a clerk or faculty member in charge where you obtain the various textbooks and other materials that are issued to pupils. A few schools have a store where pupils may purchase books, notebooks, papers, pencils, and other supplies and materials. In some schools this store is operated cooperatively by a student association or council, while in others it may be sponsored by the school administration. A school bank is another similar service. Where there is a school bank, it is usually the place where pupils make payments for class dues, tickets for school events, cafeteria tickets, club dues, towel fees for physical education, and other materials and supplies that are issued by the teachers. If you are teaching in a subject such as homemaking, industrial arts, physical education, or art, where supplies are issued to the pupils and paid for by them, you need to know the policy and regulations governing the payment for such supplies.

Administrative Policies and Practices

A number of administrative policies and practices that may affect you as a student teacher have already been discussed. There are others, however, that you should know if you are to function effectively as a student teacher. Although these practices and policies vary greatly from school to school, such questions as the following ordinarily need to be answered:

1. What is the marking policy of the school?
2. Are there all-school policies concerning tests and examinations for each marking period and for the semester?
3. What are the practices and policies regarding pupil-progress reports to parents?
4. For what attendance records are teachers responsible?
5. How are marks and attendance records placed on the re-

ports that are sent home to parents and on the permanent records in the school office?

6. What records should be kept of textbooks, materials, supplies, and equipment that are issued to pupils?

7. Is there any all-school policy concerning home work for pupils?

8. What are the policies and regulations governing field trips of pupil groups during the school day as well as similar activities outside school hours?

9. What is the policy concerning the discussion of controversial issues in social studies, science, English, and other subjects?

These are some of the general administrative policies and practices that may concern you as a student teacher. Consult the pupils' handbook, the teachers' manual, and the cooperating principal and teachers for information about such policies and regulations.

The Curriculum

Observe the Total Program

Every teacher should understand the total curriculum of the school and the place which his subject has in it. The total curriculum includes the philosophy of the school, the all-school objectives, the curricula that are offered, the program of studies in each curriculum, and the required and elective courses in the various curricula. In many schools a printed leaflet or bulletin gives the program of studies, while in others it is included in the pupils' handbook. A more complete statement of the philosophy and objectives of the school, as well as the organization of the curriculum, is usually found in the teachers' manual.

If the student-teaching time permits, arrange visits for observation purposes to as many of the departments in the school as possible. For instance, you might use one week for visits to all subject departments, including homemaking, industrial arts, physical education and health, business education, and the various academic subjects. Perhaps group conferences can be arranged between a representative of each of the departments and all the student teachers in the school. In any case, make some attempt to observe the total school program in action, as well as to study that program through the various publications of the school.

Furthermore, it is important that you be well informed concerning those subject areas that are related to your own. The teacher of English, for instance, should be familiar with the work in other subjects that may have oral and written activities, such as social studies and science. The homemaking teacher should know about the program in art and the sciences, while the industrial arts teacher should be informed about the work in art, the sciences, and mathematics. Such understanding of related subject areas is especially important today because of the current emphasis on integration between the various subject fields.

Extraclass Activities and Guidance

Although later chapters will deal more fully with the student teacher's place in the activities and guidance programs of the school, some suggestions may be appropriate at this point concerning things that you may do early in your student-teaching experience to become oriented in the school. For instance, you should have a good understanding of the total program of extraclass activities and the relationship which they bear to the rest of the school program. Get all the information you can concerning the philosophy of the activities program, the objectives for the program, the policies and practices concerning pupil participation, and the types of activities that form a part of the total program. The pupils' handbook, the teachers' manual, and similar publications will be helpful in giving you that information.

Many secondary schools have a director of guidance or a head counselor who devotes considerable time to planning and directing the guidance program. Home room teachers also have some responsibility for guidance activities. These persons may help you get acquainted with the guidance activities of the school. Early in your student-teaching experience, have a conference with the director of guidance or a counselor, spend some time in the guidance offices observing the activities there, examine the records of information about pupils that are available, and study the files of occupational and educational information in the counselor's office or in the school library.

Questions such as these concerning the guidance program may give you pertinent information:

1. Where is group guidance carried on in the school?
2. What responsibility has the director of guidance or counselor for the total guidance program?
3. What responsibility do the home room and classroom teachers have for guidance?
4. Under what circumstances are conferences with the director of guidance, the counselor, or other specialists arranged for the pupils?
5. What information about pupils is available for guidance purposes?
6. What occupational and educational files are available to pupils?
7. What specialists are available to pupils for guidance on problems of health, emotional adjustment, social adjustment, and similar problems?

Knowing Your Classes

Observe the Cooperating Teacher

Although it is to be hoped that you may use your own ideas in teaching in so far as possible, your approach must be in harmony with that employed by the cooperating teacher.

You need to be thoroughly informed about how the co-operating teacher plans his work, the classroom methods he employs, the relationships which he has with his pupils, the types of learning activities he prefers, how he evaluates pupil progress, his use of library, audio-visual, and similar reference materials, and other matters that bear upon the teacher's approach to classroom work. Although much of this information may be obtained by observing the cooperating teacher at work, some of it will need to be gained through conferences with him.

Get Acquainted with the Pupils

You should begin to get acquainted with the pupils in your classes and home room as soon as you arrive. Learning their names is the first step in making their acquaintance. In classrooms where pupils are assigned regular seats, the easiest way is to prepare a seating chart. In many classrooms today pupils work informally in groups, thereby making a seating chart ineffective as an aid to memorizing their names. Obtain a list of the pupils' names the first day, learn how to pronounce them, and become familiar with them by keeping the list constantly before you while you observe the class at work.

You should have much other information about the interests, the achievements, the strengths and weaknesses, and the personality and character qualities of the individual pupil. The cooperating teacher may suggest ways of getting that information. Please remember that all such information must be kept confidential. More detailed suggestions for getting to know the individual pupils in your classes are given in a later chapter.

Examine Study Materials and Equipment

During the first few days, spend much time studying the textbook, the reference materials in the classroom, and the supplies and equipment that are used in teaching the subject. In such subjects as homemaking, industrial arts, science, art, and business education, supplies and equipment are especially important, while in the language arts and social studies certain reference materials usually are a part of the regular classroom facilities. For instance, you should be familiar with the dictionaries, the encyclopedias, the maps, the newspapers, magazines, and leaflets, and other similar materials.

It has already been suggested that you should study the library, the audio-visual aids department, and the bookroom for other related study materials. Materials that are available outside the school, such as those in the public library, a local museum, and other community agencies, may also be used in your subject. Prepare a list of all available materials both in the classroom and elsewhere that have a bearing on the work you are to do.

Begin To Participate Early

The best way to become acquainted with your classes is to participate immediately in the learning activities. In industrial arts, homemaking, art, and physical education, where there is much individual and small group work, the student teacher can begin to participate in the learning situation the day he arrives. Although the situation is different in such subjects as the language arts, social studies, science, and mathematics, even there the alert student teacher may participate in some ways as an assistant to the cooperating teacher. For instance, in mathematics there is always a need for individual pupil help; in social studies, pupils frequently work on activities as individuals, in small groups, and in committees; and in language arts, pupils need individual help with their written and oral work. Such participation is of great help in getting acquainted, in establishing rapport with the pupils, and in developing poise and self-confidence in the classroom. In some classes the cooperating teacher will suggest to the student teacher how he may be of help. If that suggestion is not made, you should take the initiative in offering your services to the cooperating teacher and the class.

Planning Your Student-Teaching Program

Approach to Planning

Frequently a student teacher proceeds with his work without preparing an over-all plan of the activities for his student teaching. The result is that his student-teaching experiences are not always so effective and satisfying as might be desired. That is particularly true in situations where the length of the student-teaching period is too brief to engage in more than a few of the activities of an in-service teacher.

You are urged, therefore, early in your student-teaching period to discuss with the college supervisor and the cooperating teacher the preparation of an over-all plan of the activities in which you should engage. This plan for your student teaching must obviously be a flexible one, so that changes may be made for various situations as you go along. It need not be elaborate, but it should provide a specific statement of the activities you hope to perform and the sequence of those activities. In some schools the college supervisor, the principal, or the cooperating teacher may suggest the formulation of a plan for your student-teaching activities and the form in which it should be prepared. If they do not do so, you should take the initiative in this respect. In any case, the college supervisor and the cooperating teacher should participate in the preparation of your over-all student-teaching plan.

What to Include in Your Plan

It has already been suggested that the plan for your student-teaching activities should include everything in which you may engage during the student-teaching period. In that plan, you should answer questions such as the following:

1. What are the objectives for my student-teaching program?
2. What should I observe in the program of the school as a whole, particularly in subjects other than the one I plan to teach?
3. What should I observe in the classes that I am to teach?
4. How should I become acquainted with the library, the book room, the audio-visual aids center, and other agencies in the school that have a bearing on my teaching?
5. What responsibilities should I assume for the home room?
6. What responsibilities do I have in my classes when the cooperating teacher is in charge?
7. What units am I likely to teach during the time that I am here?
8. What responsibilities should I assume for such administrative activities in my classes as marking, recording tardiness and absences, and similar matters?
9. What responsibility should I assume for such extraclass activities as clubs, assemblies, and social functions?
10. What should be my participation in community activities?
11. How and when should I come in contact with the work of the director of guidance, the nurse, the principal, and other administrative and supervisory personnel?
12. What plans should I make for a periodic evaluation of my work as a student teacher, including evaluation by the cooperating teacher, the principal, the college supervisor, and myself?

It is usually best for student teachers to begin gradually in assuming professional responsibilities. For instance, instead of taking full responsibility for a total unit of work as your first teaching activity, it may be better to teach for a day or two in a unit for which the cooperating teacher is responsible. In an English class, a spelling lesson is a good way to begin; in a science class, you may prepare a demonstration; in a social studies class, you may assume the responsibility for a current events lesson; and similarly in other classes, you may take charge of some activity that carries on for only part of a class period or only a day or two rather than for an entire unit. This approach will help you gain confidence and poise before the group.

Things for You To Do

In the preceding discussion on getting started with your student teaching, some suggestions have been given of things that you can do to become oriented in the school, to get acquainted with the pupils, and to get ready for teaching. The following is a summary of such activities:

1. As a basis for any observation that you do in a school, either separate from the student-teaching period or as part of it, prepare a plan of the things you expect to observe and the way you intend to proceed with your observation.

2. Obtain copies of the pupils' handbook, the teachers' handbook, mimeographed materials about the school, record and report forms, and similar materials from the cooperating school. Study these materials to become acquainted with the program and the organization of the school.

3. Have a conference with the principal, the assistant principal, or some other staff member to obtain a picture of the total program and organization of the school.

4. Become thoroughly familiar with the floor plan of the en-

tire school, especially the location of the library, the audio-visual aids center, the nurse's office, and other places with which you may need to have contact.

5. Study carefully the policies and regulations of the school that apply to teachers, such as teachers' hours, what to do in case of illness, and similar matters.

6. Study those pupil policies and regulations which you may need to apply or enforce, such as attendance, tardiness, fire drills, home work, and after-school activities.

7. Make a list of important materials in the library and audio-visual aids center that have a bearing on the units you are going to teach.

8. Introduce yourself to members of the staff whom you need to know, such as the librarian, the audio-visual aids director, the nurse, the counselor, and others. The cooperating teacher may be helpful in having you meet these persons.

9. Place orders for audio-visual aids and materials for all units you plan to teach. This should be done early so they will be available when you want them.

10. Make a list of all the community agencies that may have a bearing on your subject, especially on the units you plan to teach.

11. Study the information the cooperating teacher has about pupils in your classes, so that you may know the home backgrounds, previous achievement, interests, and abilities of each one.

12. Study cumulative records for the pupils in your home room and classes.

13. Have conferences with pupils in the home room to get better acquainted with them. Prepare for these conferences with the help of the cooperating teacher.

14. Memorize the names of all pupils you expect to teach. Be sure you can pronounce them correctly.

15. Prepare an over-all plan of all the things you expect to do during your entire student-teaching period, including the sequence of those activities, and the way in which they may be carried on.

In Summary

In this chapter suggestions have been given for getting started with your student-teaching activities. It is not intended that these suggestions should be anything more than a brief overview of things that you might do during the first few days. More detailed suggestions as to how to proceed with your student-teaching activities will appear in later chapters. Use the material in this chapter as a guide for getting started with your student-teaching work.

PART II

At Work in the Classroom

Chapter 4

PREPARING TEACHING PLANS

Different Approaches to Planning

Why You Must Make Plans

Some student teachers are not enthusiastic about spending many hours in planning for instruction. It sounds like fun to be with a class and to work with pupils, but it may not be much fun to spend hours preparing unit plans, gathering study materials, and developing ideas for learning activities. However, the success of your teaching and the pleasure you have in the classroom depend more than anything else upon the thoroughness with which you prepare. It will be rare, indeed, for you to have a successful classroom experience except after a very thorough period of planning.

It is particularly difficult to impress some student teachers at first with the importance of planning because the cooperating teacher may seem to spend comparatively little time in preparing teaching plans. You must remember, however, that the cooperating teacher is able to draw upon years of experience. He may have teaching plans that he has prepared and used previously with some degree of success, and he already has in mind numerous activities and resource materials that he can employ. Furthermore, because of his experience he is able to adapt himself more readily to the many unusual classroom situations that arise when one works with secondary school pupils. You must expect to spend much more time in the preparation of teaching plans than the cooperating teacher.

You need to inform yourself about the approach to planning that is employed by the cooperating teacher. It may not be necessary that you use precisely the same approach, but at least you should be informed about it so that you may fit into the type of preparation that the cooperating teacher ordinarily makes for his classes. Early in your student-teaching experience, have a discussion with the cooperating teacher concerning the form in which you should prepare teaching plans.

Program for the Year

The first concern of the in-service teacher with respect to planning is to make preparation for the work of his classes for the entire year. That is, he needs to know what units of work should be covered, what basic study materials he needs to have in the classroom, the related materials that should be available in the library, the audio-visual materials for which arrangements should be made, and work materials and equipment that should be obtained. Furthermore, he will have to prepare some kind of a time allotment for the various units of study so that there may be some assurance that, at the close of the year, the program in the subject will have been completed.

In some subjects there may be considerable flexibility with respect to the work that needs to be covered, but in such subjects as mathematics and the foreign languages it may be necessary to adhere to a program for the year which has been agreed upon with other members of the faculty. Whether the plan is a flexible or a rigid one, the important thing is that the successful teacher needs to have an over-all plan for the year's work.

If you do your student teaching at the beginning of the year, you may have a part in planning the year's program.

This will be excellent experience as you look forward to your first year as an in-service teacher. If the program for the year is already planned when you arrive, you should inform yourself about it so that you may fit more satisfactorily into it. Discuss with the cooperating teacher how he proceeded to prepare the year's plan. Inform yourself concerning the extent to which there must be group planning with other teachers in the department and with teachers in other departments of the school. Find out if the department head, the supervisor, or the principal reviews the over-all program for the year. In other words, inform yourself as best you can concerning the approach that is used to plan the year's work.

Long-Term Planning

Most teachers in the secondary school today plan their work for several weeks ahead. Such long-term planning is desirable for a number of reasons, among them the following:

1. The work for the entire year is more likely to be covered satisfactorily.
2. Plans for instruction are likely to be prepared more thoroughly and with more imagination.
3. The material and equipment needed for the learning activities can be made more easily available.
4. Plans will be available for a substitute in case of the absence of the regular teacher.

In a few schools, teachers are required to submit plans to the supervisor or the principal for a period of a week or more ahead so that the administrative and supervisory authorities may be assured of plans in case the regular teacher is unexpectedly absent. Although the advisability of such a requirement may be questioned, you will need to observe that requirement if it is in effect in your school.

The most common approach to long-term planning today

is the unit plan. This approach lends itself well to most subjects, particularly to the language arts, social studies, science, homemaking, industrial arts, physical education, music, art, and some of the business subjects. In mathematics, the foreign languages, shorthand, and similar skill subjects, it is not as frequently used. The unit approach to planning is ordinarily distinguished by the following characteristics:

1. It is built around one central theme, objective or activity.
2. It is clearly related to other units of work covered during the year.
3. There is a clear relationship from one part of the unit to another as the teachers and pupils proceed to work with it from day to day.

The length of the unit will vary with the subject and the interest span of the pupils. In the secondary school one may find units that are only a week or so in length, and others that may carry on for as long as six or eight weeks. Although it is impossible to prescribe an ideal length for a unit, it should not continue so long that pupils lose interest in it. It is much better to divide a unit into two parts so that pupils may have the satisfaction of completing one, and then proceed with the other. In any case, there should be a clear relationship from one unit to the next.

Planning Day by Day

There are some teachers who do their planning day by day without reference to some such long-term plan as the unit. Even though the cooperating teacher does not use the unit approach to planning, there is no reason why you should not suggest to him that you would like to plan your work in this way. If he prefers that you do not use a long-term plan, obviously you should follow his wishes.

Where the daily lesson approach to planning is used, you may find that it can be effective if you think in terms of long-range learning outcomes. Project your daily plans into the future much as you do in planning a unit. For instance, develop objectives covering the work of several weeks; look ahead with the activities that you expect to have; locate reference materials and equipment that you intend to use; and in other ways look ahead with the preparation of your daily plans. By looking ahead you can have that overview of the work that is to come which is essential in helping you and the pupils see the relationship in the learning activities from day to day.

Helps for Planning

In some schools materials have been developed by the supervisor or teachers to aid in planning instructional activities. These materials include courses of study, curriculum guides, and source units.

Courses of study, the oldest of these planning aids, ordinarily give a statement of the objectives of the course, a subject matter outline, study materials that are available, suggested activities, and other suggestions for teaching the course. Usually they indicate the requirements of the course, as well as optional content and materials. Curriculum guides are much like courses of study, except that they give suggestions for the course in broad outlines rather than in specific terms. Curriculum guides, like courses of study, give the objectives for the course, content to be covered, reference materials, and suggestions for teaching the work effectively. The source unit ordinarily deals only with the unit of study, outlining in much detail the many materials, the activities, and the suggested approaches one might employ in working with pupils on the unit. As its name implies, it is a source of information and ideas for teaching the unit. If materials such as these are available, the student teacher will find them helpful in planning a unit of study.

Some secondary school teachers use a basic textbook as a course of study. That is most often true in such subjects as mathematics, science, and the foreign languages, but it is sometimes the practice in other subjects as well. Where a textbook is closely followed by the cooperating teacher, the student teacher should use it as a basis for planning units of study. In this respect, it serves to some extent the same purpose as a course of study except, of course, that the suggestions that one may find in a course of study are missing. Even though you begin with the textbook as a basic guide, you are urged to go beyond it to locate other reference materials and to develop activities for the unit. If you are expected to adhere closely to the textbook, do not hesitate to bring in related materials that contribute to the teaching of the unit.

Types of Unit Plans

Subject-Centered Units

There are several different types of units. The oldest of these is the subject-centered unit. In this approach to unit planning, the major emphasis is placed on the organization of subject matter for teaching purposes and on the development of plans for helping pupils gain the most effective mastery of that subject matter. The reference materials, pupil activities, methods of evaluating pupil growth—in fact, everything included in the unit plan is directed toward helping pupils with the acquisition of subject matter skills and backgrounds.

In the subject-centered unit, there may be various types of pupil activities, but these activities tend to emphasize drill on subject matter skills, information, and understandings. The unit is usually planned by the teacher with little participation by the pupils. If provision is made for individualized activities, this again is done primarily to help individual pupils study subject matter more effectively. In other words, the primary purpose of the subject-centered unit is to help pupils gain a mastery of the subject matter concerned.

The subject-centered unit is widely employed by teachers in the secondary school, particularly in the senior high school grades. In the junior high school, some teachers are using other approaches to unit planning. The subject-centered unit is also emphasized more often in the older studies in the curriculum, such as science, mathematics, the foreign languages, English, and history, while it is used less frequently in industrial arts, homemaking, art, physical education, music, and other newer subjects.

Activity-Centered Units

An approach to unit planning which has come into extensive use in the last two decades is the development of the unit around pupil activities. In the activity-centered unit there is much subject matter, often more than in some subject-centered units, but the emphasis in the unit is on pupil activities rather than on subject matter. The distinct characteristics of the activity-centered unit are usually obvious to the observer. The traditional recitation, for instance, is much less in evidence than in the subject-centered unit. Instead, the class period is frequently used for various kinds of pupil activities—oral and written, group and individual.

The learning activities in this type of unit may be grouped into two classes. First, there are the major activities which involve a number of pupils and extend over a considerable period of time. The field trip in the science class, the mock trial in the social studies class, the dramatization in the English class, the tea for mothers in the homemaking class, and the hobby show presented by the industrial arts group, are examples of major activities. Sometimes the major activity becomes the focal point for the entire unit, with all subject matter, class discussions, minor activities, reference materials, and evaluation activities pointing toward its development. The second type of activities may be referred to as minor activities since they are ordinarily confined to one or two pupils and are completed in a limited amount of pupil time. They include oral reports, bulletin board activities, brief written projects, and similar activities that bear on a relatively small part of the unit. In the activity unit, minor activities usually grow out of and are centered around the major activities which serve as the focus for the entire unit.

The activity-centered unit is used much more extensively in the junior than in the senior high school. Furthermore, it lends itself particularly well to certain subjects, such as the language arts, the social studies, science, homemaking, industrial arts, and similar subjects. Although some teachers have used it with considerable success in mathematics and the foreign languages, it is employed less frequently in these subjects. The activity-centered unit generally requires much more resourcefulness and skill on the part of the teacher than the subject-centered unit. It demands broad background in the subject matter concerned, familiarity with a wide variety of reference materials, and ideas for challenging pupil activities. When it is employed effectively, it becomes an interesting approach for both teacher and pupils.

Experience-Centered Units

A recent development in unit planning is to center the units around the interests and experiences of boys and girls. This approach does not minimize the importance of subject matter or the use of pupil activities. In fact, it emphasizes both of these, at the same time that it is oriented much more around the interests of pupils. The more significant characteristics of the experience-centered unit are these: (1) it is developed around interests that are of real concern to the pupils, (2) the pupils have a major part in planning the unit, (3) it transcends the limits of a given subject field if that is necessary for the development of the unit, and (4) it is centered around activities that are planned and carried on by the pupils.

The experience-centered unit has been employed most often in schools where some form of the core approach to curriculum development has been introduced, and it is more common in junior than in senior high schools. The experience-centered approach need not be confined, however, to core-type programs. It may also be used in such subjects as English, social studies and science. If it is to be most effective, however, the experience-centered unit should not be confined too much to a narrow subject area, but should give opportunity for correlation with related subjects.

A word should be said about the place of subject matter in the experience-centered unit. Some teachers feel that, since the emphasis is on pupil experiences and interests, subject matter becomes of little importance. That is certainly not true. In the experience-centered unit there is a need for much subject matter, perhaps more than in any other approach to unit planning. Broad subject backgrounds and competence in subject skills are essential for the wide variety of activities in which pupils are likely to engage. In the experience-centered unit, subject matter is a means to an end rather than an end in itself. Furthermore, subject matter is not thought of as existing in narrow compartments. Rather, the teacher and pupils may draw upon several subject areas for the materials they need in developing the unit. Much subject matter is indeed necessary for the successful development of an experience-centered unit.

Select the Appropriate Approach

You should keep a number of things in mind in deciding upon the approach to unit planning which you use in student teaching. In the first place, be sure that you are qualified to employ the approach that you select. Your choice should depend largely upon your previous secondary school experience and upon the professional courses that you have had. Second, you must be governed in part by the approach which is employed by the cooperating teacher. If he has been using the subject-centered approach, you may indeed have difficulty in developing an experience-centered unit with the group. Third, the organization of the curriculum in the school and the various instructional facilities which are available will also be factors to consider. A subject-centered unit may be out of place in a school with a core-type program. Likewise, it might be difficult to develop an experience-centered unit in a school with meager library facilities, few audio-visual materials, and little cooperation among teachers in the various subject areas.

You should discuss your approach to planning with both the college supervisor and the cooperating teacher. With their help you may develop teaching plans that are somewhat different from those which have been used by the cooperating teacher. If the departure from that which the classes have been using is not too great, your approach should have every opportunity of success.

What the Unit Plan Includes

It is the purpose of the next section in this chapter to give you an overview of the contents of a unit plan and the procedure you may employ in planning a unit. Some parts of the discussion may appear at this point to be inadequate for your needs. In most cases, they will be taken up again in succeeding chapters and be developed there in more detail.

Formulating Objectives for the Unit

In developing a plan for a unit of study, you should decide first upon the objectives the unit is to achieve. The objectives give direction to the entire unit—to the subject content, the materials, the activities, and the methods of evaluation. They are the goals which the pupils, with the help of the teacher, should achieve. These suggestions may help you in formulating unit objectives:

1. The objectives for the unit should clearly grow out of the objectives for the course as a whole.
2. The objectives for the unit should preferably be stated in terms of pupil growth or behavior.
3. There should be a limited number of objectives for a unit, probably one or two general objectives and not too many specific objectives.
4. The general objectives should be such that they can be realized in the limited time devoted to the unit.
5. The objectives for the unit should be stated in simple terms which can easily be understood by the pupils and will be accepted by them.

Be sure that you use the objectives as guides in planning the entire unit. Everything that you include in the unit— the subject content, the study materials, the activities— should make a direct contribution to achieving the objectives.

Deciding upon the General Approach

Early in planning the unit, you need to decide upon the general approach that you will use in working with the pupils. That is, you must decide how this unit fits into the work of the course as a whole; how it is related to the unit that has gone before and those that are to follow; whether it should be developed as a subject-centered, an activity-centered, or an experience-centered unit; what part the pupils are to play in planning and carrying on the unit; whether the unit is to be built around a major project, a problem, or other activity; and other matters concerning the general approach for developing the unit. The various aspects of this approach should be discussed with the cooperating teacher before you go far with your plans.

Subject Matter To Be Included

Student teachers frequently do not see the importance of preparing a well-organized outline of subject matter that is to be covered in the unit. They often comment that they know their subject matter well, and therefore feel that such an outline is unnecessary. It is one thing, however, to know one's subject, and it is another thing to have it well organized for teaching purposes. No matter how confident you are in your subject, you should organize it in outline form under several general headings so that the significant points will stand out clearly in your mind. It is only in this way that you can be sure of helping the pupils in your classes gain an understanding of the significant subject matter content that is essential in the study of the unit.

There are various ways of organizing subject content for a unit. Usually a simple outline with the major ideas to be covered, and a statement of details under each heading, will be sufficient. The less confident you are of your subject, the more thorough and detailed should be your outline. Furthermore, if the subject content is being drawn from a number of different sources rather than from one textbook alone, it is helpful to be more detailed in your plan.

A detailed outline of subject content is desirable in every type of unit plan. In activity- and experience-centered units, as well as in those that are subject-centered, the activities in which pupils engage demand much background in subject matter. Whatever your approach to planning, a thorough understanding of your subject is essential to the success of your work.

Planning the Activities

By activities we mean all the things that the teacher and the pupils may do to achieve the objectives of the unit. This includes teacher activities, pupil activities, and co-operative teacher-pupil activities. Your unit plan should include many types of activities, such as projects and problems, oral reports, written activities, bulletin board displays, panel discussions, debates, class discussions, skits and dramatizations, exhibits, drills and reviews, field trips, interviews, and a host of similar things in which the group might engage. Use all available sources to get ideas for activities for a unit. The best sources include the cooperating teacher, the pupils in your classes, lists of activities in textbooks and reference books, and the course of study and source units provided by the school. It is the activities in which teacher and pupils engage that give motivation to the unit and the best assurance of success in achieving unit objectives.

Locating Study Materials

The nature of the study materials for a unit will differ greatly from subject to subject. In mathematics and the foreign languages, the textbook may be the chief source of study materials. In the language arts, social studies, science, homemaking, and industrial arts, a variety of study materials should be available. Particularly in activity- and experience-centered units, you will need many different types of materials. Besides textbooks, you should locate such study materials as pictures, pamphlets, movies, slides, film strips, recordings, charts, magazine and newspaper articles, encyclopedias, and library materials. Various community resources may also be used in teaching a unit, such as local business, professional, and industrial leaders, civic and historic places, and business and industrial establishments.

The cooperating teacher may be of considerable help in suggesting sources of study materials. In some schools certain staff members such as the librarian and the director of audio-visual aids are available to assist you in locating study materials. Prepare as complete a list as possible of the available study materials for the units you are to teach.

Introducing the Unit

The introduction to the unit should (1) develop interest on the part of the pupils, (2) help them see the relationship between this unit and the rest of the course, (3) formulate the objectives which the unit is to achieve, and (4) help pupils gain an overview of the content and activities to be covered. Give thought particularly to some way of gaining enthusiasm among the pupils for studying the unit. If the unit is developed cooperatively by the teacher and pupils, an effective beginning for the unit is often more readily achieved. The manner in which the unit is initiated will have a considerable bearing on the enthusiasm with which pupils engage in it.

Helping Pupils with Spelling and Vocabulary

Many secondary school teachers today assume a definite responsibility for helping pupils improve their spelling and vocabulary as they work on a unit of study. That is true not only of English teachers, but of teachers of social studies, science, mathematics and other subjects as well. Usually spelling and vocabulary lists are prepared to include those words which are peculiar to the unit being studied. As a student teacher, you should prepare such word lists for the units you are to teach. In this preparation study carefully the subject matter to be covered to locate words which may be new to pupils at this grade level. The lists for any one unit should not be long. In planning the unit, provide for activities to teach the spelling and vocabulary lists.

The Unit Day by Day

Whatever approach to planning the unit is employed, the plan must ultimately be translated into activities that the pupils may engage in day by day. This means that daily lesson plans need to be developed from the subject content and activities that are to be included in the unit. Suggestions concerning the nature of the daily lesson plans will be made later in this chapter.

Bringing the Unit to a Close

The effectiveness of a unit of study will depend to a large extent upon the manner in which the work is brought to a close. If possible, there should be a culminating activity which leaves pupils satisfied with their study of the unit. Furthermore, there should be provision for summarizing the more important skills, information, understandings, and attitudes which the pupils have gained from the unit. Try to develop activities which will help bring the unit to a satisfying and effective conclusion.

Evaluation of Learning Outcomes

As pupils work on a unit, you need to know how well they are achieving the unit objectives. This means that you must plan ways for evaluating the progress which pupils are making. The most common method of evaluation is to give various kinds of tests, since they are particularly helpful for measuring the skills which pupils have developed and the information they have acquired. Tests are not especially effective for measuring such learning outcomes as the abilities of pupils to work together, their skill in oral

58 STUDENT TEACHING IN SECONDARY SCHOOL

activities, and their attitudes, understandings, and apprecia-
tions.

The pupils themselves should have some part in evaluating
their progress toward the objectives of the unit. Although
some evaluation by the pupils may be based on the tests that
are given, they may also use some evaluation techniques
which are more subjective. For instance, the pupils may
periodically center a class discussion, panel discussion, or
committee presentation around the question: "What progress are we making?" They may prepare written evaluations of their own progress, with leading questions given by
the teacher or developed by the class as a guide. On some
occasions, pupils may be asked to evaluate the work of one
another. The cooperating teacher may help you develop
effective ways for having pupils participate in evaluating
the progress they are making in their work on a unit.

Outline for a Unit Plan

The preceding discussion gives a brief overview of what
may be included in a unit plan. In summarizing the above,
it might be suggested that most unit plans should include
the following:

1. *Title of the unit:* What is the topic or theme to be covered in the unit?
2. *Time allotment:* How much time in terms of class periods
   may be devoted to the unit?
3. *General objectives:* What purposes or goals should the
   pupils achieve through their study of the unit?
4. *Overview:* What should be the general approach of the
   teacher and the pupils as they study the unit?
5. *Subject content:* What subject matter should be included
   in the unit?
6. *Teacher and pupil activities:* What problems, projects,
   reports, bulletin board displays, dramatizations, debates,
   class discussions, and other activities may be included as
   part of the work on the unit?

7. *Study materials:* What books, pictures, pamphlets, movies, slides, recordings, charts, magazine and newspaper articles, lectures by local persons, interviews, and other materials may be used to advantage in the study of the unit?

8. *Introduction:* How should the unit be initiated so as to obtain the interest, enthusiasm, and cooperation of the pupils from the first day?

9. *Daily lessons:* How should the teacher and the pupils proceed from day to day so that the time devoted to the unit will be employed most efficiently?

10. *Spelling and vocabulary lists:* What words and terms that are peculiar to the unit should pupils learn to spell and to use as a part of their oral and written work?

11. *Culminating activity:* How should the unit be brought to an interesting and effective conclusion?

12. *Evaluation and tests:* How may the progress of the pupils toward the objectives of the unit be evaluated from time to time?

What the Daily Plan Includes

Need for Daily Plans

The effectiveness with which the work of the unit proceeds is determined by the way in which the unit develops from day to day. This means that there must be good preparation for the learning activities of each class period. In order that the daily plans may contribute most fully to the achievement of the unit objectives, they should clearly grow out of the plan for the entire unit. Ordinarily the plans for daily work cannot be prepared for more than two or three days in advance. If the daily plans at any time are more than tentatively planned several days ahead, it probably means that the work is highly regimented and planned entirely by the teacher. It is exceedingly important, however, that as a student teacher you do not fail to have well-prepared plans every day for the classes that you meet.

Formulating the Daily Objective

There should ordinarily be one or two objectives for each day's work. If you have more than one objective, be careful that you do not divide your efforts so much that none of them is realized. The objective for any given day should grow out of the objectives for the entire unit, and may be formulated either by the teacher or cooperatively by the teacher and the pupils. In either case, the objective should be one which is readily understood and accepted by pupils.

As compared with the unit objectives, which are broad and general, the daily objectives usually are specific. They may deal with a specific skill, an understanding, or an attitude, or with some information that is essential to the development of the unit as a whole. Preferably, daily objectives should be stated in terms of changes in pupil behavior, and in terms that they will readily be understood. The daily objectives become the focal point around which the activities for the daily lesson are developed.

Materials To Be Used

There should be a brief statement of all the study and reference materials, the equipment, and the construction materials that are necessary for the day's work. It includes those things which are to be provided by the teacher as well as others that pupils are to bring. The statement of materials for the daily lesson ordinarily is taken from the longer list of such materials in the unit plan. The list of materials for the English and social studies class may include such things as sets of reference books, library books, maps, charts, films and film projectors, tape recorders, record players, rulers, and construction materials; for the mathematics class, drill materials, workbooks, rulers, protractors, compasses, and supplementary books; for the science class, reference books, charts, display materials, and laboratory equipment; and for the physical education class, the sports equipment that is to be used. Whatever the subject, the list of materials used for the day's work should be prepared in sufficient detail to assure efficient procedure for the activities of the class.

Introducing the Day's Work

Your pupils may have had many contacts and experiences since they left your class yesterday. This means that they are not likely to have immediately in mind the objective or objectives for today, nor have a strong interest in it or them. You should therefore be prepared with a way of interesting them readily in the work to be done during the period.

A simple technique for introducing today's work is to begin with a review of what was accomplished yesterday. The teacher, some pupil, or the two cooperatively may assume the responsibility for such a review. Other devices for initiating the day's work are an appropriate story, an anecdote, and a demonstration. This introduction should not take much time. In any case, be sure that you have thought through the manner in which you plan to begin the work for the class period.

Activities for the Period

You should have a well-organized plan of the various activities in which you and the pupils will engage during the period. This should include a statement of what you and the class plan to do, as well as how you may proceed to do it. Whether it be a class discussion, a test, a skit or dramatization, a committee presentation, or a work period for the class, the teacher should have in mind an efficient plan of procedure so that as much progress as possible can be made toward the objective for the day.

It is always best that the plan for class activities be exceedingly flexible because you will not know precisely how the work may develop. A good daily plan is one that includes preparation for the various developments that may arise. For the cooperating teacher this is not a serious concern because he may draw on past experience to make adaptations in his plans. Without that experience, the student teacher should try to anticipate changes that may have to be made in the class activities, and prepare for them.

Summarizing the Day's Work

Usually, it is helpful if, at the end of the period, you bring together in a brief summary the significant things that have been accomplished. This must necessarily be brief. The teacher may develop such a summary, he may ask some pupil to do it, or it may be developed cooperatively by the teacher and the class. The summary may begin with the objectives which you and the class set up at the beginning of the period, and it may well be used to direct the attention of the class toward the activities of the next day.

Looking Ahead to Tomorrow's Work

In the unit plan, the daily assignment is not particularly common. Rather, activities are agreed upon by teacher and pupils which are to be developed over a period of several days or weeks. Although that is often true when the unit approach is used, you will find that many teachers give definite daily assignments as well. When such an assignment is given, you should develop it so that the results may be as worth while as possible. In developing daily assignments, it is suggested that you observe the following:

1. Pupils should recognize and accept the objectives for the assignment.

2. They should understand clearly what is to be done.
3. They should be aware of study materials that will help them complete the activities in the assignment.
4. Suggestions should be given for doing the assignment as effectively and as efficiently as possible.

Pupils Participate in Planning

Trend Toward Cooperative Planning

The older approach to planning consisted of unit and daily plans prepared entirely by the teacher. In recent years educators have come to believe that there is much value in having pupils participate in preparing the plans for learning activities. The values of such participation include the following:

1. Pupils gain skill and experience in organizing learning situations which will be helpful in group activities outside the school, both now and in adult life.
2. Pupils are likely to have greater interest in the learning situation if they have had a part in developing it.
3. Pupils will understand the learning activities much better, and consequently will profit more from engaging in them.
4. Pupils can make a contribution to the unit plan through suggesting activities that are of particular interest and concern to them, with the result that the unit is more likely to meet the individual interests and needs of all pupils.

Some teachers misunderstand the meaning of pupil participation in planning. It should not mean that the teacher gives up his position of leadership in the class. He is still the one who is responsible for stimulating the interest of pupils, for suggesting different learning activities, and for providing leadership in the development of the learning situation. The teacher consequently continues to have an important part in the development of the unit plan, but the pupils also share in it. It should be emphasized that the cooperative plan is developed neither by the teacher nor by the pupils, but by the two working together.

How to Plan Cooperatively

There is no specific formula as to how you should proceed to plan learning activities cooperatively with pupils. Certain units may be planned cooperatively as a whole, with teacher and pupils formulating the objectives, developing the outline of subject content, deciding upon activities, locating study materials, and participating in the evaluation of learning outcomes. Other units lend themselves to cooperative planning in only some of these respects. The extent to which pupils may participate in the planning of a unit depends upon such factors as the teacher's skill in cooperative planning, the previous experience of the pupils in planning, the working relationship that exists between teacher and pupils, and the familiarity of the pupils with the subject to be studied. You should engage in cooperative planning only to the extent that it seems advisable in view of these factors.

You may also find that it is easier to do cooperative planning in some subjects than in others. For instance, in social studies, the language arts, and science, it may be relatively easy for teacher and pupils to work together in developing a unit plan. In mathematics, the foreign languages, and similar subjects it may not seem appropriate to have pupils participate as much in planning. It is true, however, that in all subjects there are some occasions when it is desirable to have pupils help in deciding what should be studied, what activities are most appropriate, and how those activities may be carried on.

Just remember that cooperative planning means that you raise questions with your pupils such as these: How important is this work? What should be our more immediate objectives? What subject matter should be included in this unit? What study materials would be helpful? What activities would be appropriate? How well are we proceeding toward our objectives? How should we evaluate what we do? By helping you answer questions such as these, the pupils may make a significant contribution toward the development of a unit plan.

Avoid Certain Mistakes

There are certain errors that you may avoid in cooperative planning. For instance, you should not devote too much time at the beginning of the unit to preparing a detailed plan with the pupils. It may be better to prepare an over-all plan, and then begin to make some progress toward realizing the unit objectives. The pupils may lose interest in the unit if you spend too much concentrated time at the beginning on cooperative planning. Much of the detail with respect to materials, activities, and evaluation techniques may be planned as the unit develops.

Then, too, you should not expect all pupils to help decide every detail in connection with the unit plan. It may be best to have the class assist in developing the outline for the unit as a whole, but that either you alone or cooperatively with a small group of pupils will give attention to the details. The time available and the interest of the pupils should determine how far you may go in planning the details of the unit cooperatively with the class.

As a teacher, you have to do much more thorough planning in advance if pupils participate in developing the unit than if it is planned by you alone. You should be ready with many suggestions for activities, be thoroughly familiar with the subject matter concerned, know what study materials are available in the school and the community, and have in mind some way of maintaining interest on the part of the pupils as you move along. Be ready to proceed in any one of several ways with the plan for the unit.

Be sure that the cooperatively planned unit is well organized. This is one of the serious dangers to this approach. Properly done, teacher-pupil planning should lead to a much better understanding by the pupils of the work that lies ahead. This means, however, that you must see to it that the plan developed cooperatively is logical and well organized in every respect.

The Teacher's Responsibility

The teacher has much greater responsibility in the cooperatively prepared plan than in those which he develops alone. The following suggestions may help you as you work with pupils to plan learning activities together:

1. You should be respected by the pupils as a democratic leader. They must respect you as a person, as one who is competent in teaching methods, and as one who knows his subject.
2. You should develop a thorough but flexible plan in advance. The plan should emphasize ways of working with pupils in developing a unit as well as the content of the unit.
3. You should prevent a few aggressive pupils from dominating the development of the unit. As much as possible, every pupil should contribute in some way to the plan as it is developed.
4. You should be sure that progress toward the achievement of the unit objectives will proceed smoothly and without undue loss of time. Needless delays and waste of time frequently impede the work on units that are planned by teacher and pupils together.
5. You should give assurance that the plan which is developed for the unit is in harmony with the long-term objectives of the course.

Suggested Steps for Planning the Unit

There is no one way for proceeding with the preparation of a unit plan which is better than any other. Furthermore, the procedure may vary with the preference of the individual teacher, the nature of the subject, and the particular unit with which you are concerned. You need to develop a procedure for planning a unit which suits your individual preference. If you have not had much experience in developing a unit, the following procedure may be helpful:

Step 1. Examine the objectives for the course as a whole, the units which have already been covered, and those which are to follow, so that you may see how the unit under consideration fits into the work for the entire year.

Step 2. Examine the course of study or curriculum guides, the source units, the basic textbook materials, and other materials which may give suggestions for developing the unit. The cooperating teacher is the source of such materials.

Step 3. Formulate the general objective or theme around which the unit as a whole may be developed.

Step 4. Develop the basic approach for the unit as a whole, including the answers to such questions as these: Would a problem or other major activity be a good focal point for the unit? How may pupils participate in developing the plan for the unit? How much time should be devoted to the unit?

Step 5. Prepare a list of all the reference materials that you are able to locate, including those in the possession of the cooperating teacher, in the school library, in the audio-visual aids center, in the community, and elsewhere.

Step 6. Prepare a well-organized outline of the subject matter which you think may be appropriately included in the study of the unit.

Step 7. Prepare a list as detailed as you can make it of the activities that might appropriately be included in the unit.

Step 8. Prepare a spelling and vocabulary list of words that are new to the pupils and are frequently used in the unit.

Step 9. Develop some way of initiating the unit so as to gain the interest and enthusiasm of the pupils.

Step 10. Prepare tentative plans for the first three or four days so that you may have well in mind how the unit may develop in its early stages.

Step 11. Develop a plan for evaluation and tests which may be carried on from time to time as work on the unit progresses.

Step 12. Develop a summarizing or culminating activity for bringing the unit to an effective conclusion.

Things for You To Do

You will gain much experience in planning when you are student teaching, through the preparation of units and daily lessons. You can do a number of things to make your experiences in planning more meaningful. The following activities are suggested as possibilities:

1. Examine the courses of study, curriculum guides, or source units, if any of these are provided in the cooperating school, for information such as this: (1) to gain an overview of the course for the entire year, (2) to see how these curriculum guides are organized, (3) to gain a better concept of unit planning, and (4) to obtain ideas for the units you are to teach.

2. Prepare an over-all plan for an entire year for one of the classes that you are to teach, giving the titles of the units to be included and the general objectives for each unit. If the cooperating teacher has such a plan, compare your plan with his.

3. Ask the cooperating teacher to suggest different teachers

in the school who use the subject-centered, activity-centered, and experience-centered approaches effectively. See if the cooperating teacher can arrange visits for you to these classes to observe the way in which these approaches are used.

4. Work closely with the cooperating teacher in developing unit plans that he expects to use, taking the responsibility for preparing certain parts of these plans, such as the lists of study materials, the spelling and vocabulary lists, and the materials and techniques for evaluation and testing.

5. Prepare a detailed statement of the things you may do in your subject to develop a unit plan cooperatively with the pupils. It would be best to apply this to a unit plan which you expect to teach.

6. Prepare different types of unit plans when they are appropriate in your subject, including subject-centered, activity-centered, and experience-centered plans.

7. Take a unit in your subject, and outline briefly how you would plan and teach it as (1) a subject-centered, (2) an activity-centered, and (4) an experience-centered unit.

In Summary

In this chapter, emphasis has been placed upon unit planning because that is the approach which is at present most often suggested to beginning teachers. You should accept the contents of this chapter in the nature of broad suggestions. You need to do much to clarify your own thinking and procedure through experience. The material provided here should be helpful as you gain that experience.

Chapter 5

METHODS NEED ATTENTION

What Approaches May We Use?

Have a Basic Point of View

In the previous chapter reference was made to the importance of having a basic point of view on planning learning activities. This is likewise true with respect to the teaching methods that you employ. In your professional courses you probably have formulated what might be called your "philosophy of methods." That philosophy will be reflected in the way you work with boys and girls in learning situations.

As with unit planning, so with methods—we may classify them as subject-centered, activity-centered, or experience-centered. Although it is not likely that you will use only one approach to the exclusion of the others, you will probably emphasize one particularly in your teaching methods.

Methods That Are Subject-Centered

If you employ the subject-centered approach, the methods you use will be pointed largely toward helping pupils accumulate subject matter, with emphasis on the acquisition of information and the traditional skills. In the classroom, you will use such techniques as the recitation method, frequent drills, subject matter tests, considerable memorization, and emphasis on a basic textbook.

The subject-centered approach is dominated largely by the teacher. The classroom from day to day is characterized by having the teacher in the front of the room; the teacher leads the discussions which are usually based on reading done in study hall or out of class since the previous day; and there is little emphasis on group activity, oral reports, committee work, and other similar activities. In the subject-centered approach, the class activities are centered around the teacher rather than the pupils.

Methods That Are Activity-Centered

The methods used in the activity-centered approach will be very different from those just described. In the activity-centered approach there are many activities with pupils in charge and the teacher in the background. There are such oral activities as panel discussions, oral reports, skits and dramatizations, and committee discussions, as well as a variety of written activities. Although class discussions and recitations are used, these do not predominate to the same extent as in the subject-centered classroom. Another characteristic of this approach is the use of a variety of teaching materials, including audio-visual materials, library books, reference books, and community resources. However, attention to subject matter skills and knowledge is not neglected. In fact, there is much subject matter in an activity-centered unit, but it is studied through pupil activities rather than the traditional teacher-led recitation.

Methods That Are Experience-Centered

The methods that are employed in the experience-centered classroom resemble those in the activity-centered approach. It is characterized by pupil activities with the teacher definitely in the background, the use of a variety of instructional materials, and a minimum of teacher-led discussions and traditional recitations. There is, however, one basic difference between the two approaches. Whereas in the activity-centered unit the work is planned largely by the teacher, in the experience-centered unit it is developed from the interests of the pupils and with their participation. Thus cooperative teacher-pupil planning becomes an essential part of the teaching method in the experience-centered classroom.

Using Activities in the Classroom

General Suggestions

Much has been said in the discussion of the activity- and experience-centered approaches about the use of different kinds of pupil activities. If activities are to be used effectively, it takes considerable skill to plan them and carry them to successful completion. A few general suggestions may be helpful as you plan and carry on various class activities, such as the following:

1. The activities should clearly contribute to the objectives of the unit.
2. The activities should be of interest to the pupils. Pupil participation in selecting and planning the activities contributes to pupil interest.
3. The activities should be at the ability level of the pupils so that they may engage in them successfully.
4. The activities should approach real-life situations in so far as that is possible.
5. The activities should not be unduly time-consuming. The time devoted to them should be in proportion to their value in achieving the objectives of the unit.
6. The activities should be of a type for which appropriate facilities are or readily can be made available.

Pupil Discussions Can Be Effective

The class discussion in one form or another continues to be the most frequently employed activity in social studies, science, the language arts, and many other subjects. All too often it is a subject-centered activity with little purpose to it. If it is well planned and effectively used, however, the class discussion can make a considerable contribution to the realization of unit objectives. That is true in the activity- and experience-centered units as well as in the subject-centered approach. It seems appropriate, therefore, to discuss this type of activity first.

You may be interested in some of the abuses of the class discussion method. The most obvious one is that the class-discussion approach is used too frequently, sometimes to the exclusion of other types of activities. Furthermore, much of the time it is little more than a recitation of information that pupils have read in the textbook, with little attempt to add new generalizations or understandings. Then, too, teachers often fail to plan the discussion adequately, with the result that it leads to no significant learning outcomes. Finally, one of the most serious abuses of this method is that the discussions are dominated all too much by the teacher rather than being pupil-centered.

In planning a class discussion, the teacher should have in mind an objective or problem around which the entire activity may be developed. This problem should be presented to the pupils or should be developed cooperatively by pupils and teacher several days before the discussion is to take place. There should be three or four leading questions or issues that grow out of the problem, and these should be recognized by the pupils as they begin their preparation for the discussion. The main problem and the related questions, therefore, serve as guides to the pupils in their reading and study. The leading questions will also serve as guides for carrying on the discussion effectively.

It is particularly important that the discussion be as pupil-centered as possible. This does not necessarily mean that a pupil needs to be the discussion leader, since there are other ways of making it pupil-centered. In fact, a skillful teacher can do much to lead the discussion in such a way that all members of the group have an opportunity to participate, that their views are respected, and that any conclusions are accepted by them. Such ways as the following may be helpful in achieving better pupil participation:

1. An informal debate by two pupils on one of the leading issues of the problem under study may be used to get the discussion started.
2. Individual pupils may be asked to make a particular study of certain issues related to the problem, present their views on these issues, and then lead a discussion on it.
3. The class may be divided into groups, each group being urged to study some particular aspect of the problem, thereby serving as specialists on that part.
4. A panel of pupils may be used to begin the discussion, with the rest of the class participating later in the period.

In carrying on the discussion, the leader should be sure that progress toward the objective is made and that some conclusions are reached in the time available. It is the leader's responsibility to help the class give consideration to all the major issues involved, instead of limiting discussion to one or two. Although some conclusions are desirable, it is not necessary always to arrive at a definite decision. For instance, the group may conclude that further information is necessary or additional discussion is desirable before reaching a decision. At the end of the discussion period it is helpful to have a summary. Sometimes it is helpful to have a summary put on the blackboard by a pupil secretary as the discussion proceeds. In other cases, one or two pupils may be asked to prepare a brief summary which they present at the close of the period. Whatever the plan for the summary, it is helpful to bring the discussion to a close with some restatement of the more significant ideas that were developed.

Finally, there should be occasional evaluation by the group of the effectiveness of the discussion as a step toward developing skill in this type of activity. Although the teacher may take an important part in this evaluation, it is likely to be more effective if pupils participate in it. Some techniques for evaluation are (1) appointing a pupil observer to present an evaluation at the end of the period, (2) having a pupil prepare a "flow chart" to show the extent and nature of participation by other pupils, (3) having a class discussion for evaluating the activity, and (4) having the teacher make an evaluation of the way in which the activity was carried on. Questions such as the following should be considered in an evaluation of a class discussion:

1. Was it well planned by the teacher and the pupil participants?
2. Did it center around an objective which the group kept in mind throughout the entire discussion?
3. Was a reasonable amount of time devoted to each major issue?
4. Was there participation by all or most members of the group, without domination by the teacher or the pupil leader?
5. Did pupils show consideration for the opinions of other pupils which were different from their own?
6. Were conclusions reached and were these effectively summarized at the end of the discussion?

Panels Are Helpful

One interesting variation of class discussions is a pupil panel. This type of activity is particularly appropriate in such subjects as the language arts, social studies, and science. It can be used effectively either to clarify information and understanding or as a basis for the discussion of a controversial issue. In a panel discussion, there is ordinarily a pupil chairman, three or four other panel members, and a summarizer. The most common practice is to have each member of the panel make a brief presentation; usually this is followed by a general group discussion with all members of the class participating.

In planning a panel discussion with a group of pupils, the following suggestions may be helpful:

1. The entire class should understand the procedure which is to be followed in the discussion.
2. The chairman should understand his responsibilities as a discussion leader, including his responsibility both to the panel and to the class as a whole.
3. The discussion should center around one major problem which is clearly understood by both the panel and the class.
4. The problem should be agreed upon several days in advance, and both panel members and other pupils should make adequate preparation to participate.
5. Near the end of the period, there should be a summary of the discussion in which the significant points covered and apparent conclusions reached are briefly stated.
6. As with class discussions, there should be provision for an evaluation which points toward more effective panel discussions in the future.

Group Activities Are Common

In recent years, much emphasis has been placed upon group activities in the secondary school. This is due in part to the recent attention to group dynamics. In these activities, cooperation among small numbers of pupils or among those in the entire class may be emphasized. Having pupils work in committees is the most frequent expression of the emphasis on group activities.

When group activities are emphasized, the unit is built largely in terms of those activities. This means that early in the unit the major activities are agreed upon and groups of pupils take the responsibility for them. It is expected that each group will make some contribution to the other members of the class by bringing them information, clarifying important issues, and adding interest to the study of the unit. Usually a considerable part of the preparation by pupil committees needs to be done in class so that the teacher may be of help. The activities with which the various pupil groups concern themselves vary greatly. Some committees may gather information concerning some aspect of the unit problem, others may prepare bulletin board displays, while still others may present skits or dramatizations appropriate to the unit.

Because group activities involve considerable skill in classroom organization and administration, the beginning teacher frequently has difficulty with them. As a student teacher, you are urged to discuss such activities thoroughly with the cooperating teacher. Pay particular attention to such matters as the selection of pupils for these groups, the way in which pupil committees organize their work, the importance of bringing materials that will be of use to them, and the progress that each group is making. Be sure also that each group keeps in mind the particular contribution that it is expected to make to the class as a whole. If you give careful attention to matters such as these, you should have success with group activities.

Dramatizations Add Interest

Various types of dramatizations may add interest to the work on a unit, as well as contribute to the achievement of the unit objectives. There are many different kinds of dramatizations, from formal ones like those which grow out of the study of drama in an English class to informal skits that may be developed by pupils in language arts, social studies, science, homemaking, business, and other subjects.

You will probably use many more informal skits and dramatizations than formal ones.

Except for the formal dramatizations, it is not wise to devote much time to memorizing parts and to the preparation of scenery and stage settings. Although there should ordinarily be thorough preparation by the participants, it may contribute much to the child's learning experience if activities at times are spontaneous. In planning and presenting dramatizations, it is suggested that you observe the following:

1. Help pupils plan their dramatization in terms of a clearly defined objective that bears on the work of the unit.
2. Give them an opportunity for a rehearsal or two, even though the dramatization is an informal one.
3. Give attention to staging, being sure that, no matter how informal it may be, the details are taken care of before the beginning of the class period.
4. Guests will always add interest when the dramatization is presented. The principal, a teacher, or another class are appropriate guests.

Bulletin Board Displays Are Appropriate

Some pupils who have little enthusiasm for other types of activities will find an interest in preparing bulletin board displays. Such displays are particularly appropriate in the new secondary schools which have ample bulletin board space. Obviously, they contribute more to the work of some subjects than others. Whenever bulletin board displays may be helpful in the learning situation, make plans for them. It may add interest if the displays are changed frequently, with each one developed around a different theme or objective. Materials appropriate for displays include newspaper and magazine materials, pictures, diagrams, cartoons, and materials prepared by the pupils themselves.

It is important, of course, that the pupils themselves assume responsibility for preparing the bulletin board displays. They should be neatly arranged, preferably with a title to indicate the objective or topic around which the display is centered. It may be appropriate to have the pupils responsible for the display explain it to the class, as well as to allow time for the class to study it. Wider pupil participation may be gained by having several pupil committees prepare different displays for a unit. Effectively used, bulletin board displays may contribute a great deal of interest and information to the development of a unit.

Have Some Written Activities

In most subjects it is important to have some written activities in order to give pupils experience in written expression. That is particularly true in language arts, science, social studies, and business. Written activities present a problem for the student teacher because it is difficult to develop these activities in such a way that pupils may be interested in them. If those activities are to be most effective, however, pupils must have some enthusiasm for them.

There are several reasons why written activities are not popular with pupils, such as the fact that they usually have no part in planning them, they are often unrelated to the interests of pupils, and they must be prepared according to some formal pattern which may seem unduly stiff and limiting to the pupils. There is the English teacher, for instance, who requires a theme a week whether there is pupil interest in it or not, or the social studies teacher who demands a five-hundred-word paper of every pupil on some topic with each unit of study. Written activities such as these elicit little enthusiasm because they do not develop from the real concerns of pupils.

When you plan written activities for your classes, it is suggested that you try to find some purpose that will appeal to the pupils around which the activity may be developed.

If pupils participate in developing the plan, this should give more assurance of their interest in it. For instance, one class in English prepared a little magazine composed of stories, poems, informative details, and book reviews written by the pupils. In a certain social studies class, each pupil prepared a small advertising circular concerning his home town in connection with a unit on the study of the local community, of which the best ones were presented to the local Chamber of Commerce. In another English class, as part of a unit on business letter writing, the pupils selected a vocation in which they were interested and wrote letters to colleges, supply houses, and local business and professional firms to obtain information about it. These are a few examples of written activities that were developed with the participation of the pupils and centered around their interests.

Teach Spelling Efficiently

Beginning teachers frequently neglect the teaching of spelling, or when they do teach spelling, they sometimes do not do it efficiently. In every subject, the teacher should assume responsibility for teaching the spelling of those words that are peculiar to his subject. This needs to be done regularly, but it should not take so much time that it deprives the pupils of other valuable learning experiences. If you have not had experience in teaching spelling, this brief statement of suggestions may prove helpful:

1. Develop a list of words which may be new to the pupils and which they use in the unit. Add to this list other words used by the pupils which they seem to misspell frequently. Do not make the list too long.
2. Divide the longer list into spelling lessons consisting of ten to twenty words each, the length of the list depending on the maturity and ability level of the pupils.

3. Give a pretest on this list in order that pupils may find out which words they do not know how to spell.

4. Suggest that pupils study those words that they have misspelled on the pretest, writing each misspelled word correctly ten or fifteen times daily.

5. Several days after the pretest, give a spelling test to see which words the pupils still cannot spell correctly.

6. In a notebook, have each pupil keep a list of the words that he continues to misspell.

7. Add the words which have been misspelled by a number of the pupils in each test to the next spelling list.

8. Continue this procedure until the pupils in the class as a whole can spell all the words.

9. Encourage pupils to spend a few minutes of free time now and then on their list of spelling errors.

Oral Reports Can Be Interesting

Beginning teachers frequently formalize oral reports just as they do written activities, with the result that secondary school pupils often dread oral report day. If oral reports are developed in terms of an objective, a topic, or a problem that is related to the work of the unit as a whole, and are built around the concerns of pupils, they can be both interesting and worth while. A short time ago when the writer was working with student teachers in a certain school, he visited one social studies class where a teacher was having oral report day. Apparently each Monday was set aside for that purpose. On this particular day, the reports that were given seemed to bear no relationship to each other nor did the pupils in the class seem to feel that they were of any value. The pupils presenting the reports merely went through the formality of fulfilling a requirement.

About the same time, the writer observed oral activities in a social studies class of another school, where a totally different approach was used. In this class, the unit was concerned with the history of ancient Athens. The reports were developed around the problem, "What contribution did the ancient Greeks make to our Western civilization of today?" One pupil discussed the contributions of the Greeks in literature, another their contributions in art, still another their contributions in architecture, and so on. At the close of the period, the significant contributions of the ancient Greeks presented in the reports were summarized in five or six statements which the pupils could take down in their notebooks for later use. There was also a brief evaluation of the way in which the reports were given, with the entire class participating. In this class, the pupils seemed to have a great deal of interest in the reports because they were centered around a topic which grew out of the objective for the unit as a whole and therefore made some contribution to the work on the unit.

Interest may also be added to oral reports through ingenious ways of having them presented in class. For instance, two pupils may present a report by having one interview the other on the subject at hand. Other interesting ways of presenting reports are informal debates between two pupils in which they present opposite aspects of a question, a presentation by a pupil committee, and a symposium of talks on various aspects of a topic.

The effectiveness of oral reports depends to a large extent upon the help that you, as a teacher, give the pupils in preparing them. You may help them understand the purpose that the report is to serve, suggest material for their reports, suggest ways of organizing notes and how to use them, and give them suggestions concerning the way to present the report in class. If a pupil lacks confidence before a group or for some other reason is concerned about giving a report, have him practice it with you alone once or twice so that he may have the benefit of your help.

The student teacher sometimes fails to realize that time is necessary to gather information and to organize the material for oral reports. It is rare that pupils should be asked one day to give a report a day or two following. If the pupils are to have sufficient time to prepare adequately for them, such activities should be made a part of the long unit assignment and should be given early in the development of the unit.

Drills Have a Place

In the subject-centered class, drill on specific skills, facts, and information is a common teaching practice. Drills also have a place for certain purposes in the activity- and the experience-centered units as well. For instance, drills in the mathematics class may help pupils gain specific mathematics skills, while in the social studies and science classes they will help pupils retain basic information essential for further study of the subject. Similarly in other subjects, drills may be used to gain mastery of basic skills and essential information.

Avoid drill on insignificant or nonessential skills and information. Study carefully the significance of those materials which you incorporate into drill activities, and include only those which are essential either for the study of the present unit or as a basis for further study in the subject. It is important also that pupils understand the significance of the skills and information they are expected to master.

In planning drill activities, you may develop a learning cycle similar to that suggested for spelling. In brief, it may include a pretest, a drill period, a test, a review period, and a retest, with this cycle being continued until the pupils have mastered the subject satisfactorily. The cooperating teacher may be able to help you develop drill techniques and devices which will be effective and avoid undue monotony for the pupils.

Developing the Culminating Activity

The culminating activity for a unit differs from other activities in two ways: first, much of the work of the unit is developed around it, and second, it serves as a high point of interest in the study of the unit. This means that, as a rule, the culminating activity should be planned early in the work of the unit. The pupils should have a part in deciding upon the activity, in planning the way in which it is to be developed, and in carrying it to completion. Ordinarily, the culminating activity comes at the close of a unit.

Things for You To Do

The best way of learning to use pupil activities effectively in a class situation is, of course, to plan and carry on such activities again and again with a group of pupils. There are some things you may do before and during your student teaching which will make your experience with pupil activities more profitable. The following are some suggestions:

1. Analyze various types of oral activities which are being carried on by the cooperating teacher to see precisely how he (1) initiates the activities, (2) plans them with the class, (3) assists pupils in preparing for participation in them, (4) plans the physical arrangements in the classroom, (5) assists pupils if they encounter difficulty, and (6) evaluates the activity with the class.
2. Assist the cooperating teacher in helping pupils prepare for an activity by working closely with a pupil committee or a key participant. For instance, work with the chairman of a panel discussion concerning his responsibility as a leader, assist a pupil preparing a report, or help one side on a debate.
3. Help a group of pupils prepare a skit or dramatization on some aspect of a unit being taught by the cooperating teacher.

4. Prepare detailed suggestions for helping pupils plan and present oral reports, with suggestions for (1) finding material, (2) organizing the material, (3) preparing notes, (4) appearing before the class, and (5) presenting the report in class.

5. Prepare detailed suggestions for the part that each of the following is to take in a panel discussion: (1) the chairman, (2) the panel members, (3) the class, and (4) the summarizer.

6. Prepare a spelling and vocabulary list for a unit being taught by the cooperating teacher and request permission to teach the spelling for that unit.

7. Assist a pupil committee in taking care of bulletin board displays for a unit being taught by the cooperating teacher.

8. Make a list of all the ways that are used by the cooperating teacher and the class to evaluate the effectiveness of activities.

Using Study Materials

General Suggestions

Much time and thought need to be given to locating and selecting the variety of study materials to be used in a unit, especially in such subjects as science, social studies, homemaking, and business. The library should be searched, audio-visual aids catalogs examined, community resources studied, magazines, newspapers, and pamphlets checked, and a host of other sources studied for materials that may help pupils with the subject content and the activities of the unit. Not only should the materials be selected for their appropriateness, but their use should be so planned that they may be most helpful.

In locating and using various types of study materials, the following suggestions may be helpful:

1. The materials should make a definite contribution to the objectives of the unit.
2. There should be many different types of study materials, including books, pamphlets, audio-visual materials, community resources, and others, depending upon the subject and the unit being studied.
3. There should be a variety of materials so that some may be used to advantage by pupils at different ability levels.
4. There should be materials to satisfy the various interests of individual pupils.
5. The materials should be used as aids in developing the unit and not as ends in themselves.
6. Pupils may assist in locating study materials, especially pamphlets, pictures, newspaper and magazine articles, and community resources.

Using the Textbook

The textbook continues to be used as the basic reference in most secondary school classes. In such subjects as mathematics, this practice is no doubt appropriate. It is to be hoped, however, that in social studies, science, the language arts, business, industrial arts, and homemaking, you will not confine your study materials to one basic text. Rather, you should consider a textbook, if one has been issued to the pupils, as only one of a variety of study materials. Used in this way, the textbook may serve a worth-while purpose by giving continuity to the subject content of the course and tying together in the pupil's thinking the many ideas and the information obtained from all the other study materials.

The greatest abuse of the textbook is making it the chief basis for all learning activities, and particularly for the daily assignments that are so generally given. For instance, some teachers give assignments primarily in terms of pages to be read in the textbook or textbook exercises to be completed. If daily assignments are given, it is much better to develop them in terms of the objective to be achieved and to suggest textbook readings as one source of information in preparing for the activity that has been agreed upon. The textbook thus may become a valuable aid to instruction, but it does not serve as the sole source of information, nor as an end in itself.

The Library

The way in which you and your classes use the library as a source of study materials will depend upon the library arrangement in your school. The most common practice is for pupils to have a library period some time during the day. If that is the practice, you should arrange with the librarian to have appropriate study materials available for the unit which your class is studying. It should be emphasized that the librarian needs to be informed concerning the work that you are doing if he is to be of the most help to you and your pupils.

In some schools it is possible to take class groups into the library for a full period or more so that they may have the help of their teacher as well as the library staff. Where that is done, you need to make arrangements with the librarian well in advance to reserve the library for your group and to give the librarian time to locate materials that bear on the work of your class. You and the librarian should organize carefully the plans for using the library during the periods that your class is to be there.

Another way of using the library is to send pupil committees from your classroom to the library to study special problems. The committee members should have clearly in mind the objectives that they are to achieve and the contribution that they are to make to the rest of the class. Before they go to the library they should have their problem clarified, they should know the types of materials that will be helpful, and they should have a plan in mind for organizing the materials that they are to use. If the librarian has been informed that the committees are to come and of the nature of their assignment, he may be of considerable help in locating materials that will be of use to them. You need to keep closely in touch with such committees to be sure that they are using their time efficiently and will be able to make a contribution to the work of the rest of the class.

A few schools have arrangements for teachers to take appropriate books from the library to their classrooms while they are working on a unit. Under this plan, the materials are more readily available to the pupils and their use may be supervised better by the teacher. If you plan to use the class period frequently as a supervised work period, it is a good plan to have library books placed in your room. Since you become responsible for these materials, develop a plan for checking them at the close of each period so as to avoid losing them.

Audio-Visual Materials

Some student teachers do not make the best use of audio-visual materials. Because these materials are more interesting to pupils than books, pamphlets, and other reading materials, there is a tendency to use them without planning as well as might be desired. In order that audio-visual materials may be most effective in contributing toward the objectives of the unit, it is suggested that you use them as follows:

1. The material that is used should be more appropriate than any other type of material that is available for the purpose at hand.
2. The material should be previewed by the teacher to be sure that it is appropriate and so that the best plan may be made for its use.
3. Pupils should be prepared for the particular contribution that the material should make to the development of the unit.

4. There should be a definite plan for using the information and background presented in the material, either through a discussion or some other appropriate activity.
5. Audio-visual materials of any one type should not be used too frequently lest they lose their effectiveness.

Field Trips Must Be Planned

If you plan to take a field trip as part of the unit, you are urged to make careful preparation for every detail. Certainly, you should consult the cooperating teacher before you go far with your plans. You will need to do such things as the following:

1. Inform yourself concerning the policy of the school with respect to field trips, including such matters as transportation of pupils, supervision of pupils, conflicts with other classes, and the cost of the field trip.
2. Make arrangements well in advance with any out-of-school persons who may be concerned with the field trip.
3. Prepare your pupils for the field trip so that they will be well informed concerning the information that they are to gain, the use that is to be made of that information in developing the unit, and the details of taking the trip.
4. Make arrangements within the school by discussing your plans with those persons who are concerned by the trip, such as the principal and other teachers.
5. Make plans for adequate supervision on the field trip so that the danger of accidents and unfortunate incidents will be held to a minimum.
6. Have a well-prepared plan for using the information and ideas gained from the field trip once you return to school.
7. Perform such courtesies as writing letters of thanks to those who assisted in making the field trip possible.

One cannot urge too strongly the importance of arranging carefully all the details of a field trip. The fact that pupils are away from school invites a variety of hazards. Since the school authorities are responsible for the safety and welfare of the pupils in any school activity, you as the representative of the school must share that responsibility.

Using Other Community Resources

The field trip provides one means of using community resources in developing a unit. There are other ways which may be employed to advantage, such as having pupils go into the community to interview appropriate persons, having them come into the school to talk to the classes, and obtaining films, film strips, pamphlets, and other materials from various community agencies that explain their activities. If these methods are skillfully employed, they may provide splendid learning experiences for the pupils.

The interview approach gives pupils worth-while experience in itself, as well as providing a means of obtaining helpful information for the unit they are studying. Pupils need help in preparing for such interviews. For instance, if pupils in a social studies class interview the mayor or some other city official, they should know how to make arrangements for the interview, how to plan for the interview, how to introduce themselves to the mayor, how to raise questions concerning the work of their unit, how long to remain, and how to thank the mayor for his time. It might be helpful to stage a mock interview in class to give pupils some idea of how to carry on this type of activity. Usually it is best to have more than one pupil go for the interview, because two or three pupils give each other confidence and support.

If local citizens are invited to speak to a school group, the pupils likewise should learn certain details concerning this type of activity. The pupils should invite the speaker, they should inform him concerning the work of the class and the contribution that he may make to it, they should introduce him to the group, they should be ready to raise questions if a discussion is permitted, and they should thank him for his help after the talk. The pupils should also be prepared for their responsibility as hosts, such as greeting the visitor when he arrives, introducing him to the teacher and other pupils, taking his coat and hat, escorting him to the cafeteria for lunch, showing him the school building, and other details which pupils may neglect if not properly informed. It is obvious that, in an activity such as this, the experience that pupils have in making the arrangements and serving as hosts is fully as important as the information which the speaker brings to the group. Furthermore, it should contribute to the pupils' interest in the subject.

Other Resources and Reference Materials

Such materials as pamphlets, booklets, bulletins, pictures, newspapers, and magazines are used in the classroom much in the same way as the materials that have just been described. It is important to keep in mind that these materials should be selected because of their peculiar contribution to the development of the unit. Sometimes these materials become useful by placing them on tables or shelves in the classroom where pupils may select those that they find of interest and value. In other cases, however, such materials should be obtained in sufficient quantities for a considerable number of pupils to use them at the same time. Frequently, industrial and business firms, civic agencies, and historical societies make materials available in sufficient quantities for school use at little or no charge.

Things for You To Do

The following are some activities that may help you learn how to use various types of instructional materials effectively:

1. Prepare a statement of suggestions for helping pupils use the textbooks as effectively as possible, including

suggestions on (1) the place of the foreword and preface, (2) the place of the table of contents, (3) the purpose of section headings within a chapter, (4) the help given by footnotes, (5) the use that may be made of the index, and (6) the purpose of bibliographies.

2. Have a conference with the librarian concerning ways in which a teacher and the librarian might work together more effectively in using library facilities.

3. For a unit that is being prepared either by you or the cooperating teacher, study the library thoroughly for all the materials which may be helpful to either teacher or pupils as they work on the unit, and arrange these materials in a well-organized list.

4. Prepare a list of all the catalogs, bulletins, and other publications that give classified information on various types of audio-visual materials. Obtain copies of the publications which are free or inexpensive. Study all the publications which are available so that you may know how to use them readily in locating materials in your subject.

5. Make a list of the audio-visual aids libraries located sufficiently near your community so that it is practicable for you to obtain materials from them.

6. If the school system where you do your student teaching has an audio-visual library of its own, visit the library, have a conference with one of the staff members concerning its use, and examine its listings and services.

7. Take the responsibility for one day's work in a unit being taught by the cooperating teacher for which some audio-visual material is the center of the activity. Make the arrangements for the material and the equipment, plan the learning activity, and take charge of the class for that day.

8. Make a thorough study of the policy of your school concerning field trips. With the help of the cooperating teacher plan all the details for a field trip which is to be taken by the class, including (1) arrangements with the administration of the school, (2) arrangements with

out-of-school agencies involved, (3) transportation, (4) cost, (5) supervision of pupils, (6) preparation of pupils for the field trip, and (7) the use that is to be made of the information and ideas gained.

Keeping Pupils Interested

Get Started Right

Student teachers ordinarily are much concerned, and rightly so, about keeping pupils interested in their work. Although skill in motivating pupil interest may be the result of much experience, there are a number of things that you can do as a student teacher to maintain the interest of the pupils in the unit that is being studied. Of first importance is the way in which you get started with a unit. Try to do something that will gain the interest and enthusiasm of the pupils the very first day, through a demonstration, a story, a movie, or an anecdote. Another approach is to suggest to the class an activity or two to be included in the unit which might have a particular appeal to the pupils. If you can find some way of developing enthusiasm during the first day or two, it should help greatly to maintain pupil interest as the unit develops.

Let Pupils Participate

One of the most effective ways of motivating pupil interest in a learning situation is to give them a prominent part in planning it. They are much more likely to feel that the unit is theirs if they help to formulate the objectives, suggest study materials, develop activities, and have a part in evaluating the results. Such participation gives them a stake in the work of the unit which is impossible if it is developed largely by the teacher. Then, too, if pupils participate in planning the unit, it is much easier for the teacher to be aware of their individual interests and to develop activities that appeal to this particular group. The more prominent is the part pupils have in developing and carrying on the activities of a unit, the more likely they are to have enthusiasm for it.

Make Progress Steadily

Another factor in motivating pupil interest is the feeling that they are making progress toward a goal which they have accepted. This means that they have the objectives of the unit well in mind, they have accepted these objectives as being significant to them, and they have the feeling that steady progress is being made toward achieving those objectives. The summary that is made at the end of a day's work is an especially appropriate place to review the progress that the class is making toward the unit objectives. In this way pupils will get the feeling that they are getting somewhere. Without that feeling, interest in the work at hand is likely to lag.

Help the Individual Pupil

Reaching the individual child is one of the most important ways of keeping pupils interested. If each child feels that he is recognized by the teacher and that special attention is being given to his individual interests, problems, and needs, he will have a feeling of belongingness and loyalty to the group that cannot come in any other way. You should explore every means of personalizing the work of your class so that it may reach each individual child. Know his out-of-school backgrounds, his interests in pupil activities, his hobbies, and his educational and vocational interests. Try to keep informed about his concerns both in and out of school, such as honors he achieves, difficulties he encounters, illness or death in the family, activities of parents, brothers, and sisters, and the host of other things that bring joy or concern to all of us as individuals. Be informed especially of his strengths and weaknesses in your subject, so that you may help him succeed as well as possible. Your ability to understand the individual pupil and to personalize the work of the class for him will do more than anything else to keep individual pupils interested in their work.

Show Confidence in Pupils

The interest which pupils maintain in your class will depend in large part upon the confidence that you have in them as individuals, the respect you have for their opinions and judgment, and recognition by you that they are reasonably mature. It may not be easy for you to give pupils this feeling of respect and confidence because you may not realize how mature secondary school pupils really are. Because of this, beginning teachers often talk down to secondary school pupils, as if they were children whose judgment is unsound and whose conduct is unpredictable. Pupils will be sensitive indeed to your attitude toward them and will respond accordingly. If they are respected by you, they will have a greater feeling of security in your class and keener interest in their work may be the result.

If pupils are to remain interested in their work, they must also feel that they are making a worth-while contribution to the class. More than anything else they need encouragement when they participate in the activities of the group. That is especially true of pupils who are shy, have some physical defect, or have limited ability. Nothing generates greater satisfaction for either child or adult than the knowledge that he has made a contribution to his group, which it has in turn recognized and appreciated. Try to find ways of having all pupils participate in the activities of the class as another means of motivating and maintaining a high level of pupil interest.

Motivation Is Not Easy

You will not find it easy to motivate interest in your class on the part of all pupils. That is difficult even for an experienced teacher. You should, therefore, not become unduly discouraged if you fail to generate enthusiasm in the learning activities every day. As you gain experience in working with pupils, you will develop confidence in yourself, you will understand adolescent youth better, and you will develop techniques for attracting their attention and interest. This should lead to better motivation of interest in the work of your pupils.

Things for You To Do

It will take much experience before you have great skill in motivating pupil interest in your subject. These activities may prove helpful in gaining such experience:

1. Try to analyze and list all the different ways which the cooperating teacher employs for the purpose of motivating interest in the work of the class.
2. Select several pupils in your classes who do not appear particularly enthusiastic about their work. Study the complete backgrounds of these pupils thoroughly to see if you can locate the reason for their lack of interest. On the basis of your investigation, try to develop an approach for each one which may lead to better interest on his part.
3. Have a conference with the cooperating teacher about motivating pupil interest. Ask him to help you develop techniques for motivation which may be appropriate for a beginning teacher.
4. Have conferences with several pupils to find out what makes them have interest or a lack of it in their work. These conferences need to be carefully planned if you are to obtain information that will help you. The co-

operating teacher should approve these conferences and should assist you in planning them.

In Summary

In this chapter, some of the important considerations in teaching methods have been reviewed. Although there are many others that might be mentioned, it is these which are of most concern to the student teacher. Study your teaching methods carefully, use those in which you have a feeling of confidence in terms of your ability and experience, and adapt them to the peculiar needs and interests of the pupils. The methods of teaching which you use will have a great bearing upon the success of your work with the pupils.

Chapter 6

MEETING PUPIL NEEDS

Knowing the Pupils

This Is Important

If you are to work effectively with pupils, it is important that you know each one as an individual—his needs, his abilities, his out-of-school backgrounds, his personality and character qualities, his previous achievement in school, his vocational and avocational interests, and other characteristics and qualities. If you are well acquainted with the characteristics and backgrounds of each one of your pupils, you will be able to help them more effectively with their school work and assist them with adjustments, decisions, and personal problems. You should begin to become acquainted with the pupils as soon as you arrive in the school, and continue to obtain information about them as long as you are there.

Any information that you gain about your pupils should be considered highly confidential. Not only should you refrain from discussing this information with any one else, but the records of pupil information which you may have should be placed where pupils cannot possibly have contact with them. It would be unfortunate, indeed, if these records should get into the hands of any of the pupils.

Psychological Backgrounds

The teacher should have information about the psychological backgrounds of his pupils, including their mental abilities, aptitudes for school and out-of-school activities, and their emotional and social adjustment. In most secondary schools, there are records of the mental age and the intelligent quotient for all pupils. These are one indication of the child's capacity to do work in school. Beginning teachers frequently attach too much importance to mental test records, since they may assume that this information alone provides an accurate measure of the child's academic ability. That is, of course, not true. The mental age or intelligence quotient should be used as only one part of a total picture of information concerning the child's ability to do school work. Other information which bears on a pupil's ability to succeed in school includes his health backgrounds, aptitude test records, his interests, previous achievement in the basic subjects, and home background. A teacher should withhold his judgment of the child's potential success in any subject until he has gained a thorough understanding of the pupil and his total background.

In some schools, tests are given to help ascertain the child's aptitude for various school subjects, particularly in the foreign languages, science, and mathematics. This information is frequently used by the counselor or the home room teacher to help the pupil plan his educational program, but it is helpful also to teachers who are working with pupils in the various subjects. It is one measure of the pupil's probable success in a subject. The child's previous achievement in the subject or closely related subjects provides additional information which may be used for predictive purposes.

Teachers should know something about the emotional and social problems that face individual pupils. Although tests of emotional and social adjustment are not as satisfactory as some other types of tests, such information has value especially if it is used with a record of the pupil's previous adjustment problems. The records in the guidance office or the cumulative records in the principal's office usually provide such information.

Achievement Backgrounds

As a basis for helping the individual child, the teacher should be informed about his previous achievement in school. In some subjects, such as English, social studies, and science, information about the pupil's skill in reading, spelling, composition, arithmetic, and similar fundamentals may be of value. For instance, teachers of social studies, science, and other subjects, may do as much as the English teacher to help a pupil improve his language skills.

It is, of course, important to know how well pupils succeeded in your subject in previous years. There are several sources of such information, the most common ones being marks in the subject, records of standardized achievement tests, and the results of diagnostic test records of pupils. The cooperating teacher may also have retained materials prepared by the pupils which you may examine, such as their test papers, samples of their written work, and projects and other materials they have prepared. As you study the achievement backgrounds of individual pupils, try to analyze the specific difficulties of each one, and the reasons which may account for them. Study all information which may bear on the pupil's achievement, such as his health records, his home backgrounds, and his school citizenship record. Such information often reveals the reasons for a pupil's learning difficulties. For example, a child's reading difficulties may be traced to a sight problem; poor participation in class activities may be due to a hearing problem; and low achievement in general may be the result of an adjustment problem. As a student teacher, you need to discuss with the cooperating teacher your analysis of the work of individual pupils in your subject, and the remedial activities you have planned for them.

Health Backgrounds

The extent to which you should be informed about the health backgrounds of individual pupils and the information you need is determined in part by the subjects you teach. In physical education, for instance, it is absolutely essential that you have detailed information regarding the health backgrounds of the individual pupil. That is important for two reasons: (1) in order that you may protect the pupil with physical handicaps from engaging in activities that may prove harmful, and (2) so that you may help individual pupils plan remedial activities. In subjects other than physical education, there is not the same urgency for having complete information immediately about the physical and health condition of pupils. Even so, it is desirable for teachers of all subjects to have such health information as the following about individual pupils:

1. Defects in sight or hearing, which may have a bearing on the place where pupils should be seated.
2. Left-handedness of pupils so that they may be placed in left-handed seats or in seats where there is ample light.
3. Physical defects that may have a bearing on posture or the type of seats pupils should have.
4. Emotional or nervous conditions which need to be taken into consideration in protecting pupils against undue pressure from home work, marks, examinations, or certain class activities.
5. Speech problems, such as stammering and stuttering, which may need sympathetic understanding by the teacher to avoid embarrassment to the pupils concerned.
6. Cardiac, circulatory, orthopedic, and other problems that may limit the movement of pupils on stairways, in crowded corridors, and in such activities as fire drills.

If you do student teaching early in the school year, you may have a part in studying the health information about pupils and making plans to adapt the work of the class to their needs. Discuss with the cooperating teacher the approach that should be used in working with various pupils, the classroom arrangements that might be appropriate for them, and the adaptation that should be made in various activities. The first day of school, for instance, pupils who are on crutches or walk with difficulty need to know what to do in fire drills or in going up and down stairs. In some cases, it is advisable to discuss the health needs of individual pupils with the school nurse, the physician, the counselor, or the parents. It is best to proceed cautiously with pupils who have unusual physical and health problems until you know what is best for them.

Experience Backgrounds

Information concerning the experience backgrounds of individual pupils is helpful to the teacher in capitalizing on them for various learning activities in school. You should know about their participation in extraclass activities, including sports, dramatics, clubs, journalism, music organizations, and student council; the offices they have held or now hold in student organizations; the school honors they have earned; and the athletic teams on which they play.

The out-of-school experiences of pupils which may prove helpful in school are work experiences during vacations and after school hours, travel experiences, membership in the Boy Scouts, Girl Scouts, YMCA and YWCA, and 4-H Club, camp experiences during the summer, and church and community activities. It is easier to converse with individual pupils if you are informed about their experiences, and that information will be useful in planning pupil participation in learning activities.

The Interests of Pupils

In the preceding paragraphs, several types of information have been suggested which will help teachers become informed about certain interests of their pupils. There are a number of other interests, however, which also are of concern to the teacher, such as the educational goals of pupils, their present vocational interests, and their recreational and hobby interests. Interest inventories, which are administered in some schools, give useful information about the interest which pupils have in a variety of activities. Other techniques for finding out about the interests of individual pupils are informal questionnaires administered by teachers, conferences with pupils, study of cumulative records, conferences with the home room teacher or teachers of previous years, and observation of the pupils in your classes and about the school.

Because a pupil's interests at the secondary school level may change rapidly, information about them needs to be obtained periodically. For instance, in the seventh grade a pupil may want to be a professional baseball player, in the eighth grade a farmer, and in the ninth grade a coach of athletics. But by his senior year he may decide on one of the professions, such as dentistry, medicine, or law. Similarly, his educational goals may change several times during his secondary school career. At one time he may look forward to leaving school as soon as the law permits, at another he may want to complete only the secondary school, while later he may decide to go on to college. It is important, therefore, that the teacher keep up to date the information which he has about the interests of individual pupils.

The hobbies which pupils have are so helpful in individualizing learning activities that they deserve special mention. These interests are of particular value in the English class, where they may serve as the basis for oral and written activities. They may also be useful in other subjects. For instance, the photography fan can make a contribution to a science class; the stamp collector may provide an interesting period in social studies; and the amateur mechanic may be of help to a shop class. You will find numerous opportunities to capitalize on the hobby interests of your pupils if you are informed about them.

Home Backgrounds

The teacher should have some information concerning the home backgrounds of individual pupils, including the occupation of parents, the social and economic status of the home, the language that is spoken, the educational background of parents and older children, and similar information. Because pupils and their parents may resent giving information about home backgrounds which seem rather personal to them, teachers need to be exceedingly tactful in the manner in which they solicit such information. You may have little part in obtaining such information from pupils because it may already have been accumulated by the cooperating teacher, the home room teacher, or the counselor before you arrive. You should be aware, however, of the need for discretion in soliciting information about home backgrounds from the pupils or their parents.

The teacher needs to be aware also of problems that may develop from using such information as he works with pupils. Because pupils may be sensitive concerning such facts about their home situations as divorced parents, recent foreign background, the occupational status of parents, the neighborhood in which they live, or other matters, it is best to refrain from reference to them in the presence of other pupils, or with the pupils themselves unless it is necessary. Then, too, teachers sometimes attach too much importance to specific facts about a child's home background. Because a foreign language is spoken in a pupil's home, his parents are separated, or he lives on the "wrong side of the tracks," does not necessarily explain pupil maladjustments in school. Information about a pupil's home and family status should be studied as only part of a total picture as the teacher becomes acquainted with a pupil so that he may work with him more effectively.

In Summary

As a student teacher, you should have as much information as possible about your pupils so that you may better meet their needs, interests, and abilities. The information that will be most helpful may be summarized briefly as follows:

1. The psychological backgrounds of pupils, including results of intelligence and aptitude tests, tests of emotional and social adjustment, and the previous adjustment records of pupils in school, the home, and the community.
2. The achievement backgrounds of pupils, including previous achievement in your subject and related subjects and results of diagnostic and achievement tests in such basic skills as language arts and arithmetic.
3. The health backgrounds of pupils, such as sight and hearing problems, orthopedic defects, cardiac and circulatory ailments, and nervous disorders.
4. The experience backgrounds of pupils, including work experience, participation in extraclass activities, travel, and membership in out-of-school organizations.
5. The interest backgrounds of pupils, including educational, vocational, avocational, cultural, and social interests.
6. The home backgrounds of pupils, including social and economic status, educational backgrounds of parents and other children, cultural interests, occupational status, and parent relationships.

Getting Information About Pupils

The Teachers Will Help You

Most of the information that you need about individual pupils in your classes and home room will be in the possession of the cooperating teacher. In some schools, duplicates of the cumulative records, certain guidance records, a health record, and a summary of test information are given to teachers for all pupils under their supervision. In other schools, the teachers themselves must summarize the information about pupils from the records in the various offices. Then, too, teachers should obtain much information from the pupils themselves, information about their work in school, their school and out-of-school activities, and their hobbies and interests. With the understanding that this information is to be kept strictly confidential, the cooperating teacher usually will make it available to the student teacher.

It is a good thing for you to know the sources of information about pupils which are available in the school. In some schools the principal, the counselor, and other staff members give student teachers an opportunity to study the records of individual pupils, and to summarize that information which you can use. In the next few paragraphs some of the sources of information about pupils commonly used in secondary schools are described.

The Offices Have Records

In medium-sized and large schools there may be several offices in which records of information about individual pupils are kept. In the principal's office, one usually finds the cumulative records, which carry a complete statement of the child's progress through school. In some systems the cumulative record includes only information about the pupil in the secondary school, but in others it is a complete record of the child's work from the time that he entered school. Cumulative records vary greatly from school to school, but they most often include such information as the child's home background, certain test scores, achievement marks, the attendance record, the schools the pupil has attended, and similar information. In some secondary schools, cumulative record forms have been expanded to include much additional information, such as a citizenship record, an inventory of pupil interests, character and personality ratings, anecdotal information, a record of vacation and after-school employment, information about adjustment problems, and a record of honors, awards, and participation in pupil activities.

The guidance office also has information concerning individual pupils. In some schools the cumulative records are located there. More particularly, the guidance office usually has information concerning the pupil's interests, educational goals, vocational interests, social and emotional adjustment, and other information that may have a bearing on the child's educational program and his success in school. The office of the school physician or nurse, like the guidance office, also has certain specialized information. There you may find a detailed record of the physical examinations for each pupil, the illnesses that he has had, and recommendations concerning educational activities that bear on his individual health problems. Some schools have an attendance officer, visiting teacher, school dentist, and a psychologist, who also maintain in their offices records of appropriate information about pupils. Sometimes all the information about pupils is accumulated in one central office, but more often you must obtain it from the various offices where it was originally recorded.

Pupils Will Provide Information

Teachers frequently get much valuable information from the pupils themselves, using individual conferences, auto-biographies, and questionnaires for this purpose. Informal contacts with pupils throughout the year in classes, school activities, and out of school also provide the teacher with much information. If you do your student teaching at the beginning of the year, you may assist the teacher in obtaining such information from the pupils.

Individual conferences with pupils are one of the more effective ways of getting to know the members of your groups, because it gives you an opportunity of establishing good rapport with them, as well as providing you with valuable information. Individual conferences are most satisfactory if they are conducted as informal visits for the purpose of getting acquainted, rather than as formal situations in which a planned list of questions is asked to solicit specific information. The conference should be private, it should have no connection with any problem the pupil may have had, and it should not be too limited in time. Immediately following the conference, the teacher should make a record of the impressions and information that he would like to retain.

The chief limitation of the individual conference is that it is time-consuming and difficult to arrange. In core programs, where teachers may have fewer pupils, individual conferences are fairly common. In other schools, some teachers have individual conferences with their home-room pupils, but because of the number involved, not with pupils in their classes. When it can be employed, the individual conference with pupils is an effective technique for establishing good rapport and getting acquainted with them.

Because it is more easily administered, the questionnaire prepared by the teacher is more frequently used than the individual conference. The questionnaire should be concerned with information about pupils that has a bearing on your subject, without duplicating too much the information in pupil records in the school offices. Pupil skills, abilities, experiences, and interests should have a prominent place in your questionnaire. It may be mimeographed, or the questions may be read by the teacher, with the pupils giving the information on appropriate sheets of paper.

In addition to such informal questionnaires prepared by the individual teachers, more formal ones are sometimes developed in the office to obtain general information from pupils for records in the central office. The formal questionnaires are usually administered through the home room. The informal questionnaire which the teacher develops for his own classes should request information from the pupils which is not included in the more formal one from the central office.

Teachers of English, core classes, and home rooms often use autobiographies prepared by the pupils as a means of getting acquainted. In English it serves as an excellent written activity early in the year. You should explore with your pupils their interest in preparing an autobiography, lest they already have had a similar activity too often in the past. The autobiography can be a useful device for obtaining information about your pupils, as well as an appropriate learning activity.

Teachers Should Know the Home

In small communities the teacher ordinarily knows the parents of his pupils and has some contacts with their homes, but in larger communities that is obviously difficult. In some school systems, contact with the home has been considered so important that teachers are encouraged to visit the homes of all their home room pupils. Then, too, in some subjects, particularly home economics, home visits by teachers are considered highly desirable. In communities where it is practicable, home visits are an excellent means of becoming better acquainted with your pupils.

It is not likely that you can do much home visiting during your student-teaching period. Then, too, in some city neighborhoods you should not visit homes except in the company of another teacher, unless you are familiar with the home situation. If you plan to make home visits, be sure to explore fully in advance with the cooperating teacher whether such visits are advisable, how to arrange them, and what to do on such a visit. Better yet, accompany one of the regular teachers on home visits to gain some experience.

Teachers have an opportunity to become acquainted with the parents of pupils at meetings of the Parent-Teacher Association. Since PTA meetings will probably be held during your student-teaching period, you should have an opportunity to attend some. You may also be able to meet parents through attendance at church and other community organizations. In a few schools, parents are encouraged to visit occasionally during the school day. Recently, a number of schools, particularly junior high schools, have provided school time for the counselor or the home-room teacher to have conferences with pupils and parents. If that is the practice in your school, it should be an interesting and valuable experience for you to participate in such teacher-parent conferences. Whether you meet the parents in their homes, at school, or through a community organization, this contact is a splendid one for helping you gain insight into the nature and backgrounds of your pupils.

Things for You To Do

There are many things that you can do to gain experience in learning about individual pupils, as well as becoming informed about the pupils who are now in your classes. Some things have been suggested in the preceding discussion. Such activities include the following:

1. Obtain copies of all the record forms used in the school for keeping information about individual pupils, such as cumulative, guidance, health, attendance, and anecdotal forms. Find out the following: (1) how information is placed on the forms, (2) how changes are recorded, (3) how teachers may use them, and (4) what is done with them after pupils withdraw from school or graduate.

2. Select a number of pupils from your home room or classes, and prepare a detailed summary of all the information you can obtain about them which would be helpful in meeting their individual needs. Group this information under these headings: (1) psychological, (2) achievement, (3) health, (4) experiences, (5) interests, and (6) home.

3. On the basis of the information obtained above, prepare a statement of things that you can do to meet better the individual needs of each of these pupils in your classes.

4. Have a conference with the school nurse or physician for the purpose of studying the following: (1) the physical defects and health needs of individual pupils that should be of particular concern to a teacher of your subject, and (2) things that you should do to meet these health needs.

5. Have a conference with the director of guidance concerning the way in which you may use results of mental, aptitude, and personality tests in getting to know your pupils and adapting learning activities to their individual needs.

6. If you do student teaching early in the year, prepare a questionnaire to obtain information from pupils which will help you individualize instruction in your classes. With the help of the cooperating teacher, administer the questionnaire, study and summarize the results, and

decide how you may use the information as a basis for work in your classes.

7. If you are a teacher of English, develop a series of learning activities in written expression around the preparation of pupil autobiographies. This should be a worth-while experience in written expression for the pupils as well as a source of information about the pupils for the teacher.

8. Assume the responsibility for accumulating anecdotal information about pupils in one of your classes for your student-teaching period, these items to be placed in the cumulative files of the pupils.

9. Make home visits with one of the teachers, with the following in mind: (1) planning the visit, (2) arranging the visit, (3) making the visit, and (4) recording the results of the visit.

10. Select a number of pupils with whom you plan to have conferences to get acquainted. These conferences should be held soon after you arrive at the school. In planning the conferences, give attention to such things as these: (1) the purpose of the conference, (2) the place and time for the conference, (3) arranging the conference with the pupil, (4) conducting the conference, and (5) recording the results of the conference.

11. Select some pupil in your classes with a serious physical handicap, such as a polio victim on crutches. Plan the consideration there must be for such a pupil throughout the entire school program, including protection in corridors, on stairways, what to do during fire drills, his problems in physical education, industrial arts, and similar subjects, and special consideration in your classes.

Individualizing Through Methods

There Are Many Methods

There are many different ways of individualizing instruction through the teaching methods that are used. The methods which you use will depend in part upon your own interests and skills, the peculiar needs of your pupils, and the instructional materials and facilities available. Then, too, for the sake of variety, you will want to use a number of different ways of individualizing instruction. A few of the more common methods for individualization will be presented here.

Unit Approach to Teaching

If it is effectively employed, the unit approach to teaching is probably the most appropriate means of meeting the different needs, abilities, and interests of pupils in your classes. The unit approach lends itself readily to individualized instruction because it is a long-term teaching plan, because pupils may participate in developing it, and because it encourages the use of a variety of instructional activities and materials. Then, too, the flexibility in teaching methods which is essential if you are to meet the needs of all the pupils is an inherent characteristic of the unit approach.

Reference has already been made to the fact that there are a number of different types of units, such as the subject-centered, the activity-centered, and the experience-centered unit. Although all three types of units provide much opportunity for individualizing instruction, the experience-centered unit is especially appropriate for this purpose because it is built around the interests and needs of the pupils. This means in effect that the unit deals with the concerns of the pupils, they have a part in planning it, and they play a prominent part in carrying on the various activities.

It is a mistake to assume that, just because you are using the unit approach, you will naturally meet the needs of individual pupils. Effective individualization of instruction does not come that easily. The best one can say is that the unit method lends itself readily to individualized instruction. The extent to which it achieves that purpose is determined largely by the imagination and skill of the teacher in planning the unit and the participation of the pupils in developing it and carrying it to completion.

Pupil Participation in Planning

It should be obvious that if pupils participate in planning a unit, the needs of the individual pupils in the group are more likely to be recognized. If there is pupil participation in planning, they can suggest an approach to the unit which they like, they may indicate activities that are of concern to them, and they should enter into the study of the unit with more enthusiasm and understanding. It should be made clear to the pupils, however, that as they participate in planning and developing the unit, they should study their own individual needs and interests, and should select activities that are likely to meet those needs. Pupils should realize that they have an opportunity to plan activities that will be of value to themselves, as well as some which they may enjoy. An understanding on their part of the importance of meeting individual pupil needs should contribute greatly to the effectiveness with which they participate in planning individualized activities for a unit. A more effective approach to individualized instruction is one of the significant values of pupil participation in planning.

Engaging in Many Activities

It is largely through the learning activities in which pupils engage that their individual needs will be met. In other words, your classes should have many different types of learning activities, some that will provide a place for the needs, the abilities, and the interests of each individual child. Individual and group activities, oral and written activities, formal activities that are carefully preplanned and spontaneous ones, are all helpful for this purpose.

Pupils should have a wide choice of the individual activities in which they engage, and should complete them with all of the resourcefulness, skill, and thoroughness at their command. In such subjects as social studies, the language arts, science, and industrial arts, it is comparatively easy to prepare a comprehensive list of individual activities from which pupils may choose. In the skill subjects, such as mathematics, reading, typewriting, and foreign languages, this must be accomplished in part through developing a variety of drill materials, providing problems and exercises at various ability levels, and having pupils proceed at different rates of speed. In some subjects, grouping within a class may be necessary for certain purposes to achieve the most success in meeting pupil needs through individual activities.

In planning group activities, much attention should also be given to the individual needs, interests, and abilities of students. Most group activities lend themselves especially well to this purpose because they can provide a variety of ways for individual pupils to participate. For instance, a mock court trial in a social studies class will include a judge and attorneys who need considerable creative skill and oral ability, but there is also need for jurors, a sheriff, a bailiff, and a court clerk, parts that do not demand much creative talent. Dramatizations in an English class usually have one or more major parts, but they also include minor parts, prompters, costume makers, and scenery helpers. An assembly program presented by a foreign language class, a science fair sponsored by a science group, a hobby display from an industrial arts class, and an exhibit by an art class—activities such as these provide many different types of opportunities for pupil participation. In other words, if group activities are properly planned, there can be a place in those activities for pupils of different abilities, interests, and talents.

Using a Variety of Material

One effective means for meeting the needs of individual pupils is to use a variety of instructional materials in the classroom. In some subjects, such as English and mathematics, different basic textbooks and reference materials are used for different classes, particularly in schools that have some type of homogeneous grouping. Sometimes several sets of reference books are provided, each one suited to pupils with different interests, backgrounds, and ability levels. The effective use of library books is another way of meeting individual pupil needs. The free and inexpensive bulletins, pamphlets, and pictures which may be obtained from business and industrial firms, civic and historical societies, and government agencies also provide a splendid variety of study materials for meeting individual interests.

You need not limit yourself to providing a variety of reading materials in trying to satisfy the interests of individual pupils. Audio-visual materials of various kinds are also exceedingly helpful for this purpose, the visual materials being especially effective with slow learners and poor readers. The more able pupils, on the other hand, may find various types of community resources challenging, including persons in the community who may be interviewed or brought to school to address the class. Whereas the average and the slow pupils need materials that are presented in concrete terms, the superior pupils may use materials of a more abstract nature.

Having pupils participate in locating various types of reference and study materials is an effective way of meeting individual interests. Obviously, pupils are likely to bring in materials of all kinds which appeal to them. Furthermore, the fact that they are suggested by the pupils tends to create more interest in these materials. Pupil participation in this way should lead to more effective individualization of learning activities.

Methods for Different Ability Levels

One of the biggest difficulties you may have as a student teacher is that of adapting your teaching methods to the various ability levels of pupils—the superior, the average, and the slow. Of these three groups, it is the slow-learning pupil who is likely to give you the most concern. It does not follow, of course, that you are challenging the superior pupils as much as you should, but at least they perform better on the minimum essentials you have in mind for your course. As for the slow-learning pupil, we do know that certain methods are more effective than others in meeting his needs. The following are some methods appropriate for slow-learning pupils:

1. Because their interest span may be shorter, it may be desirable to have units of study and learning activities that can be completed in a shorter period of time.
2. They should engage in activities that are simple rather than involved and complex. It is important, however, to remember that they, like the average and superior pupils, will profit much by having many different types of activities.
3. They need more help and supervision from the teacher.
4. They should engage in activities of a concrete rather than an abstract nature.
5. They tend to prefer oral to written activities, but these activities should be kept simple.
6. For the various skill subjects, they need much drill work, but the drill periods should be of shorter duration. It is not possible or necessary, however, to maintain the same standard of achievement in the basic skills for these pupils as with the more able ones. Some teachers tend to overemphasize drill on information and basic skills with these pupils.

7. Visual and audio materials are particularly appropriate for slow-learning pupils.

8. Attention needs to be given to the development of character, personality, and citizenship qualities, since these pupils have rights, privileges, and responsibilities as citizens in their communities. Methods of teaching which develop such qualities therefore need much emphasis with these pupils.

Things for You To Do

There are a few things that you may do to help you understand better how to meet individual differences through the methods of teaching which you employ. The following are suggested:

1. Take several major activities which are appropriate for your subject, preferably ones that either you or the cooperating teacher may use during your student-teaching period. Plan the activity so as to meet individual differences as follows:

    a) For each activity, list all the different parts that pupils may take in it.

    b) For each part, select a pupil who would be particularly well suited for it in terms of ability, interest, and experience.

    c) Try to include pupils of various ability levels in each activity.

    d) Give pupils an opportunity to participate in developing the activity and choosing the part they want to take in it. Use the preplanning which you have done to help pupils select parts that are appropriate for them, to suggest participation by the less aggressive pupils, and to distribute participation among all pupils.

2. Analyze the textbooks and reference materials which are available in your subject in terms of the reading and ability levels of the pupils. Group these materials as

appropriate for superior, average, and slow-learning pupils. In making your analysis, consider such things as the following:

  a) The vocabulary level of the material.
  b) The pictures, diagrams, and arrangements of the text.
  c) The backgrounds required in the subject for using the reference effectively.

3. For a given unit in your subject, examine the materials available in the library, and group them according to:
  a) The ability levels for which they are appropriate.
  b) The pupil interests they might satisfy.
  c) The maturity level for which they might be used.

Administrative Approaches to Individualization

Grouping Helps Individualization

In some secondary schools, particularly in junior high schools, some form of homogeneous or ability grouping is used as an administrative aid to individualization of instruction. In ability grouping, pupils are arranged into classes on the basis of their ability to do school work, as measured by such factors as the intelligent quotient, marks in previous semesters, and ratings by teachers. The purpose of ability grouping is to place pupils of similar abilities together so it will be easier for the teacher to meet individual differences. In class groups arranged according to ability, there is still a great variety of pupil needs, interests, and abilities, but the range of differences among individual pupils is usually much smaller than in heterogeneous groups.

You should inform yourself soon after you arrive about the plan of grouping that is used in the cooperating school. Find out how pupils are placed in class groups, whether course of study materials are arranged for different ability levels, what textbooks are used for the different groups, whether the marking system is modified for different group levels, and other information that may affect your work with the various ability groups.

It is important to remember that the effectiveness of homogeneous or ability grouping depends largely upon the way in which the teacher adapts instruction from group to group. Grouping in and of itself does not lead to better individualized instruction, but it may make it easier for the teacher to meet individual differences. It is suggested that you consider the following in planning work for the various ability levels:

1. Inform yourself concerning the abilities, needs, and interests of the various ability groups. The types of information about pupils suggested earlier in this chapter should help you. Try to find out especially what differences there are among pupils within a given ability group.

2. Examine the course of study materials, textbooks, and reference materials that are used in the different groups, to find out whether the basic course requirements are differentiated for them. For instance, in such subjects as English and mathematics, the course content is frequently very different for the high as compared with the average and slow-learning groups.

3. Prepare different plans for the various ability groups. Sometimes it may be the same basic plan with adaptation of materials and activities, but in other cases the plans from group to group may be totally different.

4. Study especially the activities that may be appropriate for the abilities, needs, and interests of pupils in the various groups. Pupil participation in selecting and planning the activities will be helpful for this purpose.

5. Locate all the study materials that are available in the classroom, the library, audio-visual aids libraries, the community, and elsewhere, and arrange them in terms of their appropriateness for the various groups.

Pupils Elect Curricula and Courses

The oldest administrative device in the secondary school for meeting the individual needs, interests, and abilities of pupils is the offering of a number of different curricula on an elective basis, such as the college preparatory, commercial, general, industrial arts, homemaking, and others. Within each curriculum, some elective courses may also be offered. When pupils enter the secondary school, particularly the four-year and the senior high school, they choose a curriculum in terms of their educational and vocational objectives. The course requirements differ from one curriculum to another.

In some schools, pupils are grouped according to the curriculum they have chosen so that such basic courses as English, mathematics, and science may be adapted to the needs of each curriculum. As an example, mathematics for the college preparatory curriculum may be algebra; for the commercial curriculum, it may be primarily business arithmetic; for the industrial arts curriculum, it may emphasize mathematics related to shop activities; and for the general curriculum, it may be general mathematics. If that is the practice in your school, inform yourself concerning questions such as these:

1. How does the content in your subject differ from one curriculum to another? For instance, are the courses in English, mathematics, and science different for the college preparatory, commercial, and general curricula?
2. Is there any difference in the abilities of pupils enrolled in one curriculum as compared with another? For example, is the average ability of pupils in the college preparatory curriculum higher than that in the general curriculum?
3. Is the same basis for marking employed in the various curricula? If not, how is the marking system differentiated? How does this affect marking in your subject?

4. Do teachers vary the methods of instruction from one curriculum to another? If so, what are the differences in your subject?

5. In your subject, are different textbooks and other study materials used in the different curricula? If so, what textbooks are used in each one?

It might be appropriate to point out that, in a number of schools today, pupils are not arranged in class groups according to the curriculum in which they are enrolled. That is true particularly in the Middle West and the Far West. In these schools, it is believed that you have a more democratic learning situation if pupils are placed in class groups in such basic subjects as English, mathematics, and science without reference to their educational and vocational goals. In the Northeast particularly, however, pupils are generally arranged in groups according to the curriculum which they are taking. Naturally, as a student teacher, you must adapt yourself to the thinking that pertains in the school where you are teaching.

Some Schools Have Remedial Classes

In a few secondary schools, there are remedial classes for pupils who have difficulties with certain basic subjects, particularly in English and mathematics. For instance, pupils who have reading difficulties may be placed in remedial groups where special attention is given to their reading problems. Some schools also have remedial classes in speech, arithmetic, and spelling. Usually a teacher with special training in remedial work is in charge of these classes.

Although it is not common to place a student teacher in remedial groups, there is some value in giving you contact with the work that is done there. From such a contact, you may develop an interest in remedial work. Furthermore, in schools that do not have remedial classes, you may be expected to provide some remedial instruction in the regular classes. If you have an opportunity to observe and participate in remedial work, it may prove helpful for you to do so.

Special Help After School

An old approach to individualizing instruction is to provide special help after school hours for those pupils who are having difficulty with their work. In some schools, there is a regular period at the close of the school day when teachers are available for such help. For instance, in one school there is a regularly scheduled period from 2:15 to 3:00 o'clock when teachers are in their rooms to help pupils either on a required or a volunteer basis. Those pupils who do not need special help are permitted to leave at 2:15. In most secondary schools, however, after-school help is left to the judgment of individual teachers.

As a student teacher, you should make yourself available for such after-school help. Not only should this be a part of your regular responsibility as a student teacher, but it is excellent experience for you to work with pupils in this way. You will get to know the pupils better, it will help you understand their difficulties, and you can make a real contribution to their progress in your classes. You should study the approach that the cooperating teacher uses in organizing such after-school help. By some teachers, it is conducted on a rather formal basis, whereas by others it is entirely informal, with the teacher working with individual pupils as they come on their own initiative. Whatever the approach that is used, after-school help continues to be one of the ways in which teachers meet the needs of individual pupils.

Individualizing Marks

One of the most serious problems in individualizing instruction is the giving of marks for pupil achievement. The usual marking system requires that the work of pupils be evaluated and marked on the basis of a standard which is uniform for the entire class or grade. In other words, the mark is based very largely on a group standard, rather than on the potentialities of the individual child. Where a group standard based on the mastery of subject matter exists, the marking system makes it difficult indeed to individualize the content, the activities, and the methods of instruction. You should discuss this problem with your cooperating teacher so that you may understand the policy of the school with respect to individualizing marks.

In recent years, some schools have changed their marking system so that it is based primarily on the potentialities of the individual child and includes the progress of the child in areas other than subject matter. In other words, a pupil is not compared with his classmates on some arbitrary subject matter standard, but his work is evaluated in terms of his individual abilities and talents. If the pupil has made considerable growth as an individual, the marking system recognizes that fact irrespective of how he stands in comparison with other pupils in the group. The new marking system frequently provides for the evaluation of pupil progress in citizenship, personality, and character development, as well as in subject matter achievement.

The new-type marking systems have been introduced in a number of junior high schools and in a few senior high schools. If you should happen to do your student teaching in one of these schools, you must inform yourself concerning this approach to evaluation and marking because it is not as easily administered as the older one. However, the new approach should make it easier for you to meet the individual needs and abilities of the pupils.

Things for You To Do

The things which you can do to learn about administrative approaches to individualized teaching will depend upon the practices employed in your cooperating school. For instance, if pupils are grouped according to ability you may engage in certain activities which may be difficult or impossible if there is heterogeneous grouping. From the following activities, select those which are appropriate in your situation:

1. If the cooperating school has ability grouping, discuss with several of the teachers the problems they encounter with it, such as these: (1) attitudes of pupils, (2) attitudes of parents, (3) methods appropriate for various ability levels, (4) maladjustments of pupils in certain groups, (5) discipline problems that may develop, (6) problems of marking pupils, (7) the materials appropriate for the different groups, and (8) difficulties in placing pupils in the appropriate group.

2. Study the pupils in the ability groups that you are observing to see if you can locate some who appear maladjusted. Try to find out what might be done to help such pupils.

3. If pupils are shifted from one group to another at the end of the term, locate the pupils in your groups who should be shifted, using the bases for grouping employed in the school. Compare your judgment with that of the cooperating teacher.

4. On the basis of your observation of ability grouping in the cooperating school, develop a policy concerning grouping that (1) makes it easy to individualize instruction, (2) is democratic, and (3) is conducive to good mental health.

5. Study the policy of the school with respect to the placement of pupils in the various curricula to find out what bearing pupil abilities have on the choice of curricula.

6. Discuss with teachers who have pupils in your subject in the various curricula the different approaches they use in teaching these pupils, particularly with reference to (1) the basic textbooks, (2) the content of the course, (3) the reference materials, (4) the learning activities, (5) the standard of achievement, and (6) the marking of pupils.

7. If there is a remedial class in your subject, observe that class to find out what methods of teaching are used there, including (1) the content, (2) the learning activities, and (3) the study materials. Find out how pupils are selected for the remedial class and when they are removed from it.

In Summary

In this chapter, some suggestions have been given to help you, as a student teacher, work with individual pupils in your classes. It is important to remember that you can do a great deal to help the growth of each child by becoming acquainted with him as an individual. Inform yourself fully about him, learn about his individual interests and problems, and let him know that you are concerned about him as an individual. Always think of your class not as a group, but as twenty-five or thirty individual boys and girls, no two of whom are alike. That is the essence of individualized instruction.

Chapter 7

EVALUATING, RECORDING, AND REPORTING PUPIL PROGRESS

Evaluating Pupil Progress

Purposes of Evaluation

Beginning teachers, and perhaps experienced teachers too, frequently think of evaluation as having one purpose only, namely, to provide the basis for giving pupils marks on achievement. Although evaluation may be necessary as a basis for marking, this should be considered as only one of the purposes which it may serve. The various purposes which should be served by the periodic evaluation of the progress which pupils are making in your classes include the following:

1. It should give the teacher and pupils information of the progress which the pupils are making as individuals toward the objectives which have been set for the learning activity concerned.
2. It should give the teacher and pupils information which can be used to develop further learning activities, both for the class as a whole and for the pupils individually.
3. It should provide information which can be used by both teacher and pupils to analyze the progress of each individual, to ascertain his strengths, and to locate his difficulties, as a basis for remedial activities.
4. It should be used as a basis for motivating further learning by encouraging pupils through a recognition

of the progress they have made and by stimulating them to improve where they have fallen short.

5. It should provide information on all aspects of a pupil's progress, not on subject matter achievement alone, so that the teacher may help the child grow more effectively as a citizen and as a person.

Suggestions for Evaluation

With the above statement of purposes in mind, the following general suggestions may guide you in developing ways of evaluating pupil progress for your classes:

1. Evaluation should be made in terms of progress toward some goal. The goal may be the objectives of the course, the unit, the daily lesson, or the activity concerned.
2. Evaluation should be made in terms of some starting point, from which the progress of the child is measured. That point is the achievement level of the individual pupil when he begins work on a learning activity.
3. Evaluation should recognize the backgrounds and potentialities of the individual pupil. The superior pupil with favorable backgrounds should proceed more rapidly and more completely in the fulfilment of the recognized objectives.
4. Evaluation should be continuous throughout the entire learning situation. In a unit of study, the evaluation should be so planned that teacher and pupils are continuously informed of the progress that the group as a whole and each individual child is making toward the objectives.
5. Many techniques and devices for evaluation should be employed, of which tests and examinations are only one. These devices should be made as objective as possible, but some of them may of necessity be highly subjective.
6. There should be self-evaluation by the pupils as well as evaluation by the teacher. Since the pupils are participating in the learning activity, they can contribute much to an evaluation of their progress. Furthermore, they

should gain experience in evaluating themselves and their own individual growth.

7. The evaluation should be of a constructive nature, emphasizing ways in which the pupil might improve his progress. It should locate pupil shortcomings, not to pass judgment, but to suggest ways for improvement.

Informal Evaluation by the Teacher

Much of the evaluation of pupil progress is made informally by the teacher from day to day. Such informal evaluation may contribute as much information about the child's growth in school as the formal tests and examinations. The teacher's informal evaluation usually follows directly any participation by the pupil in a learning situation. The informal evaluation by the teacher should bear on questions such as the following:

1. What things has the pupil done well that should be continued?
2. What weaknesses in his work might be improved?
3. What suggestions may help him overcome those shortcomings?

The manner in which the results of the teacher's evaluation is presented to the pupils needs to be considered as carefully as the evaluation procedure itself. If it concerns a number of pupils, it may be made to the entire class, either in a presentation by the teacher or in a discussion with the pupils participating. For an individual pupil, the teacher's evaluation may be presented as a written comment or in an individual conference.

The teacher's effectiveness in using such evaluations as a means of improving the work of individual pupils depends to a great extent on how well he knows their abilities and their backgrounds. If he knows their previous achievement in his subjects, their personality qualities, attitudes toward school and school activities, and their out-of-school backgrounds, he can make a better analysis of their progress and offer more appropriate suggestions for improvement. Furthermore, if he has good rapport with his pupils, he may be able to present his evaluation results more tactfully and expect a better response to his suggestions.

Self-Evaluation by the Pupil

Educators today believe that it is good for pupils to learn to evaluate their own progress. Not only is this appropriate because it prepares the pupil for self-evaluation both now and in adult life, but it may also contribute greatly to improving his work in school. Self-evaluation by the pupil does not mean that he is expected to mark himself. Where there is a formal mark which is based on competition with other members of the class, this would hardly be appropriate. Self-evaluation does mean, however, that the pupil is encouraged to ask himself these questions: "How well have I been doing? How can I improve?"

Most self-evaluation by a pupil is made following a specific learning situation in which he has participated. He is encouraged to analyze his participation, to see his strengths, and to locate his weaknesses. With the teacher's help he develops ways of improving himself for future similar participation. This approach is used for group activities in which the pupil has had a part, for oral and written activities, and for achievement in basic skills and subject content.

Self-evaluation by the pupil should not be limited to specific activities such as these. Occasionally it is helpful if he examines his progress toward the objectives of the unit being studied and also those for the entire course. Periodic evaluation of progress toward such long-term objectives is essential if pupils are to have a sense of direction for their learning activities and have the satisfaction of knowing that they are making progress in the course. In evaluating his progress toward the objectives of the unit or the course as a whole, the pupil should be encouraged to raise questions such as these about his work:

1. What are the objectives toward which I have been working?
2. What progress in general have I made toward achieving those objectives?
3. What things have I done and what progress have I made that has been particularly good?
4. What deficiencies or shortcomings are there in my progress as I have engaged in this work?
5. Has my attitude toward my work been wholesome and has it contributed toward the better realization of my objectives?
6. Have my work habits and procedures been most effective for the activities in which I have engaged?
7. What reading, drills, and other activities might I engage in which will improve my work?

Up to this point, our discussion of self-evaluation has been concerned with the study which the pupil may make of his own progress. There is also some value in having pupils evaluate each other's work. This must be done with extreme tact so as not to offend or embarrass anyone. If such an evaluation is well supervised by the teacher, that is not likely to happen. The group should understand the purpose of their evaluation, they should realize the value of emphasizing constructive suggestions, and they should be aware of the need for tact and good taste in their comments. The group should avoid faultfinding and petty criticism. Instead, its comments should emphasize positive suggestions which may help the individual pupil improve his work. The evaluation of an individual pupil's work, carried on in this way, may be exceedingly helpful for improving his progress in school.

There are times when it may be desirable for a class to evaluate its progress as a group. That is especially true when the group has taken a prominent part in planning and carrying on a learning activity or a unit of work. In fact, the full values of pupil participation in planning are not likely to be achieved without some self-evaluation by the group of the progress it has made toward accomplishing what it set out to do. Group self-evaluation may be made periodically as work on a unit proceeds and again more extensively at the close of a unit. Like the evaluation by individual pupils, it should help the group examine its progress and develop suggestions for improvement.

There are various ways in which the group may evaluate its own progress. There may be a discussion of progress led by the teacher; a pupil observer or two may present progress reports from time to time; a pupil committee may present a report and lead a discussion on the progress of the group; or individual pupils may write their evaluations of the work of the group as a whole, these comments to be summarized for the benefit of all. The teacher and the group should develop an approach to self-evaluation of progress which is appropriate for the learning situation concerned.

Evaluation by Tests and Examinations

The most common means of evaluating the progress of pupils is to give tests and examinations. No doubt you will give a number of these during your period of student teaching. Give much thought to planning the tests, the time when they had best be given, and the use that is to be made of the results. The following suggestions may be helpful in planning tests for your classes:

1. The tests should be developed in terms of the objectives of the unit and the particular learning activity concerned.
2. Several short tests at various times in the unit are more satisfactory in evaluating pupil progress and for improving the work of the pupils than one large test at the end. Both short periodic tests and longer review tests may, however, be desirable.

3. The tests should be so developed that they cover all aspects of the learning situation concerned, including pupil growth in attitudes, personality and character qualities, citizenship qualities, human relations, and leadership skills, as well as achievement in subject matter skills and knowledge.

4. The teacher should give pupils help in preparing for tests through suggestions of the significant things to be covered and the best way of studying for them.

5. The tests should be used as a basis for helping the class as a whole and individual pupils locate their shortcomings and develop ways for overcoming them. It is the use that is made of the tests for improving the progress of the group that is most important.

6. Tests should be recognized as only one device for evaluating pupil progress. For any unit, their use should be planned as part of a broad approach to evaluation which includes many different techniques and devices for finding out what progress the pupils are making.

Essay Tests in Evaluation

There are several different types of questions and items that may be used in tests and examinations. It is considered to be good testing practice to use several types of tests or test items over a period of time, employing each for the purpose for which it is most appropriate. The types of tests may include essay as well as the various new-type or objective tests. Suggestions for preparing, administering, and using the various types of tests may help you. Let us look for a moment at essay-type tests and test questions.

Student teachers frequently do not realize the care that must be taken in developing effective essay-type tests. Sometimes they prepare them hurriedly, not giving enough thought to the clarity with which they are stated, the extent to which they cover the significant aspects of the work, or the time that may be needed for pupils to answer them.

Consequently, the results they achieve with essay-type tests are not always satisfactory. The following suggestions may help you develop good essay tests:

1. Do not include too many questions for the time available. The time factor is especially important in planning essay-type tests because they often require much thought, organization, and writing by the pupils. If the pupils are writing the test under pressure, it may fail to give you an adequate basis for evaluating pupil progress.

2. Each question should contain only one idea. If there are two related ideas, indicate by (a) for the first part and (b) for the second.

3. Avoid questions that are too broad because it is difficult for pupils to answer them in a straightforward manner, especially if the time is limited. Questions that start with such words as "discuss," "explain," or "comment" usually are too broad.

4. Examine the questions carefully to be sure that they are not ambiguous. If more than one interpretation can be placed on a question, you should give full credit to pupils who place an interpretation on it different from the one you intended.

5. In reading the test papers, the teacher should have well in mind the nature of the answer that is acceptable. In fact, it would help if you were to write out the kind of answer that would be most acceptable.

6. Have the cooperating teacher and, if possible, the college supervisor go over the essay questions before you administer the test. It is also helpful for you to leave the test for a day or two, and then read it again carefully to check for clarity of meaning. You may also have another student teacher read the test and react to it.

7. Do not blame the pupils if they have difficulty understanding your test questions. Let them know that you will explain the meaning of any question if they have difficulty interpreting it. It is the teacher's responsibility

to make questions so clear that only one interpretation can be placed on them.

Objective Tests in Evaluation

For certain purposes, you will want to use the new-type or objective tests. These include such types of test items as true-false, yes-no, multiple choice, matching, and fill-in. If you have had a course in tests and measurements, it should not be difficult for you to prepare objective test items. If you have not had such a course, it may be helpful to read appropriate chapters in a book on tests and measurements for suggestions on preparing and using the various types of objective test items. Although a detailed discussion of objective-type tests is not possible here, some suggestions especially appropriate for the student teacher are as follows:

1. The test items should sample all the more important skills, attitudes, subject matter, and other learning outcomes that were included in the work covered by the test. Make a complete list of the important learning outcomes, and prepare the items for each so that they are well distributed.

2. Do not use too many different types of items in one test. If the test is a long one, include several types of items; if a short one, limit it to one or two types. During a unit, it is appropriate to use several types of items in different tests.

3. Since each type of test item may be more appropriate for some purposes than for others, select the type which is best suited to the subject and the learning outcomes being evaluated. For instance, for factual material one-word answer items, multiple-choice items, and matching items may be best. For testing attitudes and understandings, you may find essay questions more satisfactory.

4. Try to avoid ambiguous statements. Have another student teacher, the cooperating teacher, or the college

supervisor read the test critically, and read it yourself after having placed it aside for a day or two.

5. In objective-type tests, student teachers sometimes include petty items. Be sure that every item included in the test is developed from a learning outcome that is significant in terms of the objectives of the unit and the course.

6. Prepare instructions for each part of the test which explain such things as (1) the approach that should be used by the pupil in answering, (2) the number of questions or items in each part, (3) a suggested time allotment, and (4) how you intend to score test items or questions.

7. Check the length of the test in terms of the time available. This needs to vary for different grade levels and for groups within a grade. From previous experience with the group, the cooperating teacher may suggest the number of items of each type which the pupils can answer in a class period.

8. Develop a procedure for scoring the test which is simple and easily administered, yet conforms to good testing practice. The scoring procedure may influence the way in which the test should be set up and administered, so that the scoring may be done as efficiently as possible.

9. Objective-type tests may be duplicated or, if properly planned, read orally to the class.

10. Before administering the test, read it as a whole to be sure that in its entirety it is a well-constructed evaluation instrument.

11. Keep a record of significant information about each test, such as (1) the time taken by each pupil, (2) the items which were ambiguous, and (3) the reactions of pupils to the test. On the basis of this information, estimate the number of items you should include in future tests for each class, the way the instructions should be given, and how items might be stated more clearly.

Things for You To Do

You should gain as much experience as possible in evaluating pupil progress during your period of student teaching. There are some things you can do while you are observing the cooperating teacher at work with a class, while other activities must wait until you are in charge of a group yourself. The following activities may help you prepare for evaluating pupil progress:

1. While you are observing the cooperating teacher at work, ask him if you may evaluate such pupil activities as the following: (1) a bulletin board display, (2) oral reports, (3) a dramatization, and (4) written projects. Write out your evaluation briefly, indicating the strong qualities, the shortcomings, and the ways in which the activity might be improved. Have the teacher read your evaluations, and with his approval give them to the pupils.

2. Plan carefully the evaluation of a class activity by the group, using the discussion approach with yourself as the leader. Give attention to the following: (1) plan the significant things that should be brought out in the evaluation, (2) prepare suggestions to guide the class in its discussion, (3) plan to have as many pupils as possible participate, and (4) summarize the evaluation with constructive suggestions for improvement. You may lead such an evaluation for an activity sponsored by the cooperating teacher or for one when you are teaching the class.

3. For some individual activity, have each pupil prepare a brief written evaluation of his own work, summarizing it under these headings: (1) What have I done well? (2) What needs improvement? (3) What steps should I take to do better next time?

4. If you are student teaching at the end of the year, ask the cooperating teacher if you may work with him in developing a plan for having the class evaluate its progress

toward the objectives of the course for the entire year. Your plan for such a group evaluation needs to include: (1) the objectives for the course, (2) the units covered for the year, (3) the more important learning outcomes, such as attitudes, skills, understandings, subject matter, and personal qualities, and (4) ways of working with the group in the evaluation. If it is to be effective, such an evaluation needs to be developed cooperatively with the class.

5. For some unit of work, prepare an essay test for the entire unit as follows: (1) list the objectives of the unit, (2) list the significant learning outcomes, (3) develop an essay test that covers these learning outcomes as well as possible, (4) have someone read the test to offer suggestions for improvement, and (5) develop a definite procedure for scoring it.

6. For some unit of work, develop an objective-type test, giving consideration to steps such as those suggested under (5) above.

7. Examine several available books on tests and measurement, and prepare a statement of specific suggestions for preparing each of the following types of test items: (1) true-false, (2) yes-no, (3) multiple choice, (4) matching, and (5) fill-in.

Recording the Progress of Pupils

The Teacher's Record

Most teachers have some kind of a record book in which they place the results of tests and other evaluation devices. As a student teacher, you should keep a record of any formal evaluation that you may make of the progress of your pupils. You may obtain a copy of a teacher's record book for this purpose or organize a record plan of your own. In any case, be sure that you have an accurate and well-organized record of test scores, marks, and other evaluation results. Consult the cooperating teacher about this matter to find out whether the results of your tests and the marks you give should be placed in his records as well as in your own.

Most teachers develop a plan of their own for recording the evaluation results of their pupils. Sometimes they record these results as marks based on the marking system of the school, while in other cases they keep the raw scores earned on tests. If the raw scores are used, they are translated into marks at the close of a reporting period. The cooperating teacher may prefer to have you follow his plan for keeping a record of test results rather than your own.

The Pupil's Record

There is some value in having the pupil keep an individual record of his own progress, especially in the skill subjects, such as spelling, mathematics, and foreign languages. A record of progress kept by the pupil may provide him with considerable motivation for improving his work. If the co-operating teacher has the pupils keep such a record, you should follow the same plan. If that is not the usual policy in your classes, consult the cooperating teacher to obtain his approval before you suggest that pupils keep achievement records of their own.

Records in the Office

Pupil marks and standardized test scores are periodically placed on permanent records in the office. In some schools, this is done each reporting period, but in others only final marks at the close of the semester or the school year are placed on the permanent records. The permanent office records are usually referred to as cumulative records, because they are continued from grade to grade for each child.

The practice for placing marks on the permanent records varies from school to school. Usually, the classroom teacher has some responsibility for seeing to it that the marks he gives his pupils are ultimately placed on the permanent records. In some schools, he places the marks on the cumulative record cards himself, but in others he reports them to a records clerk in the central office. Inform yourself concerning the practice in your school, and participate in preparing the permanent records in so far as that is possible. It will help you in your first year of teaching if you have some idea of how these records are maintained.

There is usually an established routine for placing the results of standardized tests on the permanent records. In schools where many standardized tests are given, only the scores for the more important ones are recorded in the office. It is best to record test scores immediately after they are given. Find out the procedure for recording standardized test scores in your school, and share in this responsibility while you are in the school.

Reporting Pupil Progress

Once teachers have evaluated the progress which pupils have made in their subjects, they need to report the results to those who should be informed about them, namely, the pupils and their parents. For many years, this was done in the secondary school simply by issuing periodic report cards. In the past decade or two, there has been a considerable study of our methods of reporting pupil progress. This study has been concerned with finding ways of giving pupils and parents more information about the growth which the pupils are making in various aspects of the school's program. Therefore, what was once a simple device in the form of a report card has in many schools today become a complex and time-consuming procedure. In the next few pages, some suggestions will be given to help you, as a student teacher, participate in reporting pupil progress to the pupils and their parents in schools using the new approaches to reporting, as well as those with the more traditional ones.

Conferences With Pupils

One way of helping pupils keep informed about their progress in school is to have conferences with them. These conferences may be of an informal nature following a specific learning activity in which the pupil has participated, or they may be well-planned conferences in which the teacher summarizes rather fully with the pupil the work that he has been doing. Such conferences can be helpful in keeping the pupil informed concerning the progress he is making in your subject, pointing out to him his successes, his shortcomings, and things he should do to improve.

It is not intended that teacher-pupil conferences should take the place of the formal progress reports which are ordinarily given at the end of a reporting period. They should, rather, supplement the formal report. The conferences should also serve to keep the pupil informed from time to time concerning his progress so that the formal reports do not come as a surprise to him. The best practice is to have the pupil fully informed about how well he is doing at all stages of his learning experience.

A few schools have a time during the day when the home room teacher may have conferences with his pupils. This is more common in junior high schools and in schools with core-type classes than in other secondary schools. Most schools, however, have no time set aside for such conferences. This means that they have to take place informally during the class period, at a time when the pupils are engaged in supervised study. Conferences after school hours can also be arranged, but they should not interfere with after-school activities or with bus schedules.

Progress Reports to Parents

The report card, which is the device most often used for reporting pupil progress to parents, usually gives a summary evaluation of the pupil's work in each subject in the form of a letter or percentage mark. This type of marking and reporting system is essentially the same in all schools where it is used, although there may be differences in details. Usually, the chief difference is found in the meaning attached to the marking symbols. In some schools the marks are clearly defined, but in others the teachers have much freedom in deciding what the marking symbols mean.

A few secondary schools, particularly junior high schools, are employing pupil-progress report forms that are much more descriptive than the older forms of the child's progress in school. If new-type report forms are used in your school, you should study these forms carefully to find out (1) the point of view on which they are based, (2) what aspects of pupil growth are covered, (3) the meaning of any symbols which are used, (4) how the forms are to be filled in, and (5) the procedure for giving the forms to pupils and parents. The new-type reports have characteristics such as these:

1. They are frequently based on the potentialities of the individual child rather than on a uniform group standard. In effect, this means that the individual child rather than the group serves as the standard for evaluating the pupil's progress. In this plan, the teacher must know the achievement level of the child at the beginning of the work, his ability level, and the progress which he has made. With this information he prepares a report of the pupil's progress for the parents.

2. They give a more detailed analysis of the child's work by indicating progress on several objectives of the course rather than by giving only a summary mark.

3. They usually give information on the child's growth in areas other than subject matter, such as attitudes, study skills, personal and character qualities, and citizenship.

4. They encourage cooperation with the parents by requesting written comments, conferences with parents, and other contacts to discuss the pupil's work.

5. They are more concerned with the development of the individual as a total person than with a rating of achievement in subject matter.

Conferences with Parents

A recent development in reporting pupil progress is to have periodic conferences with the parents. In departmentalized schools, it is difficult for the teacher to have conferences with the parents of all the pupils. In those schools, home room teachers usually have the conferences with parents. This means that the home room teacher must be well informed concerning the child's progress in all subjects and in extraclass activities.

As a student teacher, you should participate in at least several such conferences. At the beginning you should merely be an observer, but gradually you may take an active part in them. As you gain experience, you may be able to conduct some parent conferences entirely on your own.

The following suggestions may help you observe or conduct parent-teacher conferences:

1. Be well informed concerning all aspects of the child's educational growth, not only in your classes but in other classes as well. Also have information about the child's participation in extraclass activities, his personality and character development, and his school citizenship.
2. Prepare for the conference by (1) summarizing the important information about the pupil, (2) listing the particular items that should be discussed, and (3) planning the procedure for the conference.
3. Try to take a positive approach in the conference, pointing out the good things that the child has done and offering suggestions as to how he might strengthen his shortcomings.
4. When discussing problem cases with parents, try to realize the parent's keen interest in his child and the emotional attachment he has for him. Be as patient and dip-

lomatic as you can in discussing a pupil's problems with his parents.

5. Immediately following the conference prepare a brief summary of the results to be placed in the pupil's folder.

Reporting to Counselors

In some schools, counselors are responsible for working with pupils on their individual problems. The counselor's effectiveness with his pupils depends largely upon the cooperation he receives from other teachers. He needs much information about the work and conduct of his counselees in their classes, in extraclass activities, and elsewhere in the school program. He must depend on other teachers for that information.

In some schools a procedure has been established for informing counselors concerning the progress, the activities, and the conduct of their pupils. Sometimes the pupil progress report goes to the counselor before it is sent home with the child. Information about the pupil's conduct, citizenship, and personal development may be sent to counselors on anecdotal forms designed for the purpose. Study the policy and procedure in your school for informing counselors about the progress and development of your pupils.

Things for You To Do

Some of the things which you can do to gain experience in recording and reporting pupil progress have been suggested in the preceding pages. These activities and others may be summarized as follows:

1. Obtain copies of the various record books and forms that are used in your cooperating school, including the teacher's records, the records for each reporting period, and the permanent records. Find out the purpose of each record, the relationship between them, and how they

are maintained. If you are permitted to retain the record forms, compare them with those which other student teachers obtain from their schools. This may be done at a conference with other student teachers after you return to the college campus.

2. Assist the cooperating teacher in recording marks and standardized test scores for your pupils during your student teaching period. If it can be arranged, take the responsibility yourself for one group.

3. Observe several teacher-pupil conferences that are concerned with reporting progress to the pupil. Note especially the following: (1) the information the teacher has available about the pupil's work, (2) the preparation the teacher makes for the conference, (3) the arrangements for the time and place of the conference, (4) the way in which it is conducted, (5) the part the pupil has in it, and (6) the summary evaluation which the pupil may take with him.

4. After you have observed a number of teacher-pupil conferences for reporting pupil progress, conduct several such conferences yourself, using the outline suggested in (3) above.

5. Observe several teacher-parent conferences that are concerned with reporting pupil progress. In your observation, follow the suggested outline in (3) above, substituting parent for pupil.

6. Obtain copies of the various progress report forms and study the way in which they are used. If you are permitted to retain them, compare them with report forms and procedures in other cooperating schools in a conference with other student teachers when you return to the college campus.

In Summary

In this chapter, suggestions have been given to help you discharge your responsibilities for evaluating, recording, and reporting the progress of your pupils. It should be emphasized again that arriving at a mark is not the major purpose of evaluation. Rather, you should think of evaluation as a means of analyzing the growth of your pupils toward the objectives of the unit and of the course. The results of any evaluation should serve as a basis for helping individual pupils improve. The records in the office are usually in terms of pupil marks, scores on standardized tests, and similar summary information. In reporting progress to the pupil and his parents, you should try to give information other than that contained in a subject matter mark. If it is in harmony with the policy of the school, you should have conferences with the pupils and participate in conferences with parents. A favorable attitude on the part of the pupil toward his work should be one of the outcomes of the evaluation of pupil progress.

Chapter 8

PROBLEMS OF MANAGEMENT
AND DISCIPLINE

Management of the Classroom

Management Influences Learning

Problems of classroom administration often are of more concern to the student teacher than any of his other responsibilities. There is a reason for this. Usually the student has made some study of methods of teaching in his courses in education. The details of classroom administration, however, are difficult to study except in the situation in which they apply. Consequently, your first contact with problems of classroom administration will probably come when you begin your student teaching.

Do not minimize the importance of the administrative details of the classroom, since they may have a direct bearing on the success of your teaching. A well-prepared teaching plan may fail to develop satisfactorily if you have neglected some of the details of classroom organization and management. For instance, the writer has seen a student teacher spoil the effectiveness of a class by distributing test papers in such a way that it created considerable disorder and confusion. Problems of seating, lighting, and the appearance of the room likewise are reflected in the success of the total learning situation.

In this chapter, there is not sufficient space to cover all the details of classroom organization and management. Furthermore, these differ so much from one school to another that definite suggestions are difficult to make. In any case, it may be helpful to give you an awareness of the type of management details that you may encounter, with the suggestion that you study them carefully in the situation where you are teaching.

Keeping an Orderly Room

Of first importance is the impression that is made upon pupils when they enter your classroom. The student teacher frequently has the room neat at the beginning of the day, but has difficulty keeping it that way as the day proceeds. You should realize, however, that each class throughout the day is impressed by the appearance of your room just as much as the first period class. Try to develop a routine so that at the close of each period the room will be neatly arranged. With the help of the pupils, this can be done in the last minute or two of the period.

You may assign pupils regularly to certain housekeeping responsibilities, or, if you prefer, different ones may assist you informally each period. Some of the things you may do to help the appearance of your room are as follows:

1. If there is movable furniture, have the chairs, tables, and other furniture arranged in order at the close of the period. They may be arranged in rows, in a semicircle around the teacher's desk, or in some other way consistent with your approach to teaching the class.
2. The materials on the teacher's desk should be neatly arranged. If papers have been turned in, work materials collected, or reference books used, they should be placed in folders or arranged neatly on the desk or in the cupboards.
3. In social studies, science, and other classrooms where reference materials are used, have a routine for returning the materials to the shelves, for arranging them neatly, and for checking them to be sure that all are returned.

4. Erase the blackboards at the end of each period, except for those materials that are to be used by all classes. Materials to be saved should be put on the side boards and written in a neat and attractive manner, keeping the center boards free for use each period.

5. It may be needless to add that, at the end of each period, the floor should be free of scraps of paper and other waste materials that may detract from a neat appearance.

Pupil Absence and Tardiness

You are responsible for checking attendance in your classes. This should take a minimum amount of time and should not detract from the learning situation. In classes where the desks are arranged by rows, a seating chart may be helpful for checking attendance rapidly. If furniture is arranged informally, it may be convenient to check attendance by groups of pupils. Another plan is to have a pupil assume the responsibility for checking attendance, so that you may proceed immediately with the learning activities.

Procedures for reporting the absence and tardiness of pupils vary from school to school. In some places, an absence list for the entire school is prepared in the office and is sent to all teachers. An attendance officer or someone designated for this work checks on pupils who are absent and determines the reasons for it. Usually teachers are requested to report absences to the attendance officer immediately, but in some schools the checking of reasons for pupil absences is left entirely to the individual teacher. Where the teacher has this responsibility, he must be sure that any pupil who is absent from his class has a good reason for it.

After a pupil has been absent, the usual practice is to have him present an admission slip from the principal, the attendance officer, or the home room teacher before he is readmitted to class. Such admission slips should be checked carefully at the beginning of the class period. If a pupil fails to present such a slip after being absent, he should be requested to obtain one immediately.

Practices for checking tardiness also vary. In some schools pupils tardy for a class are required to report to the office for an admission slip; in others, they are sent to the teacher of the preceding class for a slip; and in still others, such tardiness is left entirely to the judgment of the teacher. A good way of discouraging unnecessary tardiness is to begin your classes promptly. By the time the bell rings, the class should be under way with the learning activities for the period. The cooperating teacher may help you become informed about policies and practices concerning tardiness and absence from class.

Keeping the Room Comfortable

The learning situation in a classroom will be much more satisfactory if the air is fresh and the temperature is moderate. In most secondary schools today the temperature is controlled automatically by a thermostat in each classroom. A reasonable temperature in a school room is from 68 to 70 degrees Fahrenheit. Even though there is automatic heat control, observe the temperature occasionally to be sure that the thermostat is properly adjusted for your room.

Proper ventilation presents more of a problem than heat control because this usually depends entirely upon the teacher. When the climate is suitable, some of the windows should be open all the time to provide continuous ventilation. When the weather is too cold to keep windows open, a good plan is to have a complete change of air in your room between classes. This may be done by raising two or three windows while classes are passing, so that there may be a quick change of air. If you do this regularly every period, it should take care of your ventilation problem. Some schools have mechanical ventilating systems, which may make window ventilation unnecessary.

Do not rely too much upon your ability to tell whether the air is becoming stale. If you are in the room continuously, the air may be stale long before you are aware of it. Aside from danger to the health of the pupils, stale air results in sluggishness and loss of interest in learning activities.

Control of Light

Because very few schools provide for automatic light control, you need to take care of it through adjustment of window shades and the regulation of artificial light. There are usually two problems in light control: (1) the room may be too bright because of the position of the sun, or (2) it may be sufficiently dark so that artificial light is necessary. You should take care of these problems by having a routine for adjusting light regularly throughout the day.

A good plan for light control is to adjust window shades and lights either at the beginning or at the end of every period. When the sun is on your side of the building, the window shades should be partially drawn in the front of the room to break the glare of the sun for pupils facing that way. As the sun moves during the day, the shades should be adjusted accordingly. Much of the day, however, the light in the front of the room should be broken by having the shades partly drawn. Late in the day or when it is cloudy, do not hesitate to turn on the lights. From the first day of your teaching, develop the habit of adjusting the lights and shades regularly throughout the day.

Problems in Seating Pupils

Unless you do student teaching at the beginning of the year, seating pupils may not be a problem for you because the cooperating teacher may have taken care of it before you arrived. It might be helpful, however, if you understood some of the things that a teacher has in mind in seating the pupils. The older plan of assigning each pupil a seat which he takes every day is followed in most secondary schools. It is a fairly common practice, however, to permit pupils to select the seats they want to take. Even though pupils select their seats, the teacher may still find it necessary to make some suggestions concerning those choices. For instance, the taller pupils should take the larger seats and, if they are arranged in rows, those in the middle or rear of the room. Left-handed pupils should be placed near the window where there is ample light, or, if they are provided, in tablet-arm chairs especially for left-handed pupils.

The problem of pupil conduct sometimes is raised in connection with seat assignments, although our less formal approach to classroom discipline has reduced this emphasis. Many educators today believe that pupils do their best work if they are seated near their friends. Furthermore, the emphasis on group activities, pupil participation in planning, and the direction of learning activities by the pupils themselves makes it essential to have a desirable social situation in the classroom. The first requisite of such a situation is to have pupils seated where they are likely to be most relaxed and satisfied. Besides permitting pupils to sit where they wish, teachers frequently prepare sociograms to obtain information for suggesting seats to pupils. The teacher reserves the privilege, of course, of moving pupils if that is necessary to improve their conduct or the learning situation.

A few teachers assign pupils to seats alphabetically because it is more convenient for checking attendance, returning papers, and similar administrative matters. Although there are administrative advantages in this plan, it is difficult to defend it from an educational standpoint. Alphabetical seating ignores the size of the pupils in relation to the seats, the left-handedness of some pupils, and the preference of pupils to be seated near their friends. If the cooperating teacher uses this plan, observe it carefully to see how satisfactory it is.

Before definite seats are taken by pupils, the teacher should know the sight, hearing, and other physical deficiencies which they may have. Although you may ask pupils for such information about themselves, you cannot rely upon them for it. Frequently they are embarrassed to tell about their physical deficiencies, with the result that those who have sight, hearing, or other difficulties may select the least appropriate seats. The health records of the pupils are the only satisfactory way of becoming informed about physical deficiencies that have a bearing on seating plans.

Using Study Materials

When reference and other study materials are used in the classroom, there should be a well-organized routine for distributing and collecting them. The nature of that routine will depend, of course, upon the materials and upon the arrangement of the room. Whatever the plan may be for distributing or collecting such materials, it should be done with a minimum of time and confusion. One plan is to have certain pupils who regularly assist you in distributing study materials, and therefore know the routine. There should be enough pupil assistants so that the materials may be distributed or collected in a minute or two. At the end of the period, a pupil should arrange the materials neatly on the shelves and check them to be sure they are all returned.

In some classes such equipment and supplies as scissors, rulers, protractors, and construction paper are used. As with reference materials, plans should be made for distributing and collecting them in an efficient manner, for arranging them neatly in cupboards, and for checking to be sure that all are returned.

Collecting and Distributing Papers

A simple routine should be developed for collecting and distributing test papers, home work, and similar papers. If the seats are arranged in rows, the papers may be passed forward by rows and then collected from the front pupils. If a code number is placed on each paper to indicate the row and seat, they can be rearranged in proper order for rapid distribution by rows after you have read them. If pupils are seated in a circle or in some other informal way, this plan may be adapted to such a seating arrangement. Such a simple routine may help considerably to reduce the delay and disorder that sometimes attend the collection and distribution of tests and other papers.

It is also best to collect or distribute papers at a time in the period when it will cause the least interference. For instance, unless you plan to review them in the class, it may distract least from the day's work to return them at the end of the period.

Effective Relations Within the Class

Your Experience with Discipline

As a student teacher, you will be placed with a cooperating teacher of some experience and competence. It is likely, therefore, that he will have effective working relationships with his pupils, that classroom details will be well administered, and that the conditions for a satisfactory learning situation will pertain. In other words, the cooperating teacher is not likely to have serious discipline problems. Furthermore, unless you begin your work early in the year, he may have established effective disciplinary relationships before you arrive. Consequently, as a student teacher you may not have an opportunity to observe what teachers do to establish effective working relationships in their classes, nor to gain experience in establishing those relationships your-self.

You should have many discussions with the cooperating teacher concerning the approach that he uses to establish effective working relationships within the group. Find out, for instance, how he gets started with the pupils at the beginning of the year; how he encourages them to work quietly and effectively with each other; how he obtains mature, courteous, and cooperative pupil conduct; and what he does when pupil relationships do not function smoothly. The following discussion on working relationships within the group may help you in your observation and in your work as a student teacher.

A Good Approach to Group Discipline

The word "discipline" has a negative connotation. It suggests that pupils are going to do things that are wrong, and that the teacher must have some penalties ready for them. This is a negative rather than a positive approach to human relations in the classroom. But it is the approach which has been used in most secondary schools in the past, and which still pertains in many schools today.

More and more teachers today are taking a constructive attitude toward discipline problems, believing that the emphasis should be on developing wholesome, cooperative, and courteous pupil attitudes, rather than on rules, repres-sion, and punishment. The chief concern with this approach is the establishing of effective human relationships, relation-ships between teacher and pupil and among the pupils them-selves which are based on courtesy and consideration for others and the requisites of a wholesome and effective learning situation. If such relationships pertain in the class-room, problems of discipline in the traditional sense are not likely to arise. Furthermore, many teachers believe that such a positive approach to human relations and discipline is the only one that is in harmony with the needs of pupils in a democratic society.

Good human relationships in the classroom are both an end in themselves and a means to an end. In the sense that good human relationships are preparation for life in a democratic society, they are of course an end in themselves. But they are also a means to an end to the extent that they provide the basis for a desirable learning situation in the classroom. If pupils are considerate of each other, if they work well together, and if they have a friendly and understanding relationship with the teacher, the classroom is likely to have an atmosphere that is conducive to effective learning.

Teachers today recognize also that the classroom relationships will vary for different subjects and for different types of learning activities in the same subject. In mathematics, much of the time pupils may be confined closely to their seats; whereas in art, homemaking, and industrial arts, they may have much freedom to move about the room. Similarly, the classroom situation may differ with the activity. If a test is given in social studies, English, or science, the pupils will obviously remain in their seats and work individually with no contact with their fellows. If there are committee or other small group activities, the furniture needs to be rearranged and the pupils may be permitted to converse quietly with each other. When the class is engaged in some construction project where various types of equipment and materials are used, it may be necessary to have pupils move freely about the room as they do in art, industrial arts, and homemaking. Whatever the learning activity may be, the classroom relationships should be planned to achieve one purpose: namely, to establish that situation which is most appropriate for the learning activity in which the class is at the moment engaged.

Creating a Favorable Situation

As a basis for the relationships which have just been described, it is essential that you have a favorable atmosphere in your classroom. That is, pupils should have the feeling that they want to work together in a mature, friendly, and courteous manner. These are some things that you may do to create such an atmosphere:

1. Give careful attention to matters of classroom organization and administration so that confusion will not result from collecting and distributing papers, using reference books, checking attendance, and similar details.
2. Be so well prepared in the teaching methods, the subject matter, and the materials that are needed for a learning situation that the activities may proceed effectively and smoothly.
3. Establish a favorable atmosphere in so far as heat, light, ventilation, neatness, and the attractiveness of the room are concerned.
4. Emphasize that appropriate conduct should be based primarily on courtesy and consideration for others rather than on the authority of the teacher.
5. Establish with your pupils a sympathetic and friendly relationship, based on an understanding of their individual characteristics and an interest in their personal needs and problems.
6. Give pupils the impression that mature conduct is the usual thing in your classes and that you assume it may be expected of them.

These Things May Happen

In the preceding discussion, the emphasis has been placed on taking a preventive and constructive attitude toward the problem of discipline. In other words, if the working relationships among your pupils are as favorable as they should be, disciplinary situations as we usually think of them are not likely to occur. It might be well to recognize, however, that as a student or a beginning teacher you may not be so effective at establishing a satisfactory working situation in your classes as to avoid all unfavorable problems. You should know some of the early symptoms of unsatisfactory human relationships in the classroom, and what you might do to meet those situations. The following are some early signs of an unsatisfactory classroom situation:

1. Pupils may become careless about starting work on learning activities immediately at the beginning of the period. For instance, they may stand at the windows, remain around the teacher's desk, talk to other pupils unnecessarily after the period has begun, or dash into the room at the last minute.

2. Pupils may move around the room unnecessarily to sharpen pencils, go to the waste basket, come to you for help, or converse with other pupils. Such activities are not undesirable if they are done quietly and do not interfere with the learning situation. But if they are an expression of restlessness by the pupils, they may be a matter of concern.

3. Pupils may make comments in undertones to their neighbors, interfering with the discussion or other learning activities that are taking place.

4. Pupils may speak up frequently during a discussion or other learning activities without being properly recognized by the teacher or a pupil chairman.

5. Pupils may become careless about completing their work, failing to have it ready at the time agreed upon.

6. Pupils may stop working some time before the end of the period, or they may hurry out of the room in a discourteous or disorderly manner.

You should not assume that when any one of these conditions arises that you have a serious group disciplinary situation on your hands. That is not necessarily true. These things may, however, be a warning signal that the pupil relations within your classroom are not as satisfactory as they should be. As a student teacher, your first step should be to discuss such a problem with the cooperating teacher. With his experience, he may be able to suggest whether a disciplinary problem is developing, and what you might do to avoid it.

Meeting Discipline Problems

It is difficult to offer suggestions for meeting discipline problems because what you should do depends greatly upon the situation that develops. There are some suggestions, however, that may apply to almost any situation.

In any case, scoldings and punishment ordinarily should not be the first step. It is much better to begin with a positive and constructive approach. For instance, you might discuss the problem frankly with the pupils, pointing out that some of them are interfering with the learning situation in the room. Help them see that their cooperation in improving the situation should lead to more pleasant relationships among the pupils and result in better learning. Encourage them to assume the responsibility for improving the classroom relationships, not because the teacher requests it, but because they owe this cooperation to their classmates. If your relationship with the group has been basically satisfactory, your discussion with them of such a problem should lead to improvement.

But suppose that this positive approach on your part is not successful? What should you do next? You may then feel compelled to become more formal in your classroom situation, and deprive the pupils of some of the freedom which they have enjoyed. For instance, if pupils have been careless about getting to work promptly at the beginning of the period, make it a point to begin the learning activity as soon as the pupils are in the room, not giving them time to visit with their friends. For a while, plan learning activities that are more teacher-centered, with less group work by the pupils. Until the pupils are again ready to be responsible for their own conduct, you may even feel called upon to impose penalties for certain actions. But punishment should be a last resort and should be imposed by a student teacher only after consultation with the cooperating teacher.

Avoid These Things

Frequently the student teacher does things which actually encourage rather than prevent undesirable pupil relationships in the classroom. These things of course are not intentional, but they do nevertheless have an undesirable effect. It might be helpful for you to know what some of these things are. The following are some of them:

1. Do not try to impress the pupils with your experience as a teacher. Admit frankly that you are a student teacher, that this is your first teaching experience, and that you have much to learn. The pupils will certainly be aware of your lack of experience and should respect you more if you do not try to disguise it.

2. Do not talk down to pupils as if you were much older than they. In fact, they may appreciate you much more because of your youth. Work with them as if they, as well as you, were mature people on a somewhat equal plane, except for the fact that you are in a position of leadership and responsibility in the classroom.

3. Do not suggest to pupils that you are severe in discipline, since this may be a sign to them that you are worried about it. They know that the competent teacher does not need to threaten his pupils.

4. Avoid making specific threats unless you are definitely ready to carry them out. Even then it is better to wait with threats until definite action on your part is necessary.

5. Avoid giving pupils a list of rules and penalties. This, in itself, is an indication that you are worried about discipline. They are likely to accept it as a challenge and may respond in just the opposite manner from what you would like. Although you should avoid making rules as much as possible, once they are made you must enforce them rigidly.

6. Do not impose group penalties, such as keeping the entire class after school or having the entire class do additional work. Group penalties may cause you to lose the cooperation of those pupils whose attitude and conduct have been satisfactory.

7. Avoid scolding or correcting individuals before the entire group, because the sympathy of the group will usually be with the pupil. If such action is necessary, ask the pupil to see you after school when you may discuss his conduct with him privately.

It may seem from this discussion that there is little you can do if a group disciplinary problem should develop. Such problems are indeed difficult to handle. There is only one satisfactory approach to group disciplinary problems, and that is to establish such a classroom situation that they do not develop. Frequent consultation with the cooperating teacher should help you maintain a satisfactory relationship among the members of your group.

Suppose the Teacher Is Away

There may be times when the cooperating teacher will be away and you will be in complete charge of the room. Sometimes the teacher will be away for only a period, but at other times illness, professional activities, or a field trip may keep him away for a day or two.

When you are alone with the class, you are in the same position as a substitute teacher, except that you have the advantage of being familiar with the group and the work that is being done. Discuss with the cooperating teacher how best you might proceed under those circumstances. Pupils should of course understand that, when the teacher is away, you are in a position of leadership which should be respected by them. If pupils do not cooperate as they should, stop the class activities immediately and discuss with them their responsibility for maintaining a desirable learning situation. In most cases this will take care of the matter.

If you have further difficulties, you should proceed much as you will later when you are a beginning teacher. For instance, you may want to discuss your problem with an experienced teacher, with a counselor, or with the principal. The principal or other supervisor will appreciate having you come to him with your problems before they reach serious proportions. He should understand the pupils in your group and may be of considerable help to you.

Individual Pupil Problems

Individual Problems Vary

In the previous section of this chapter, attention has been given to relationships that you will have with the entire group. A satisfactory group relationship is the best way of reducing the number of individual discipline problems. If the group situation is a pleasant and favorable one, individual pupils may be reluctant to disturb it. Even so, you may encounter some individual pupil problems that need special attention. You should have some idea of how to proceed with such problems.

It has already been suggested that you should inform yourself concerning the characteristics, the interests, and the background of every pupil in your group. That information should help you work more effectively with the pupil who may become a conduct problem. You may learn, for instance, that certain pupils have an unstable emotional background, others have a health handicap, still others fail to find any interest in school, and some have a difficult home situation. Having such information early about your pupils may enable you to prevent some individual conduct problems from arising.

As you locate problem cases in your classes, you might do well to study each one carefully. Answer such questions as these:

1. What are the backgrounds of the pupil as revealed by school records?
2. What is the nature of the pupil's behavior?
3. What effect does his behavior have on that of other pupils?
4. Does his behavior interfere with the total learning situation?
5. Can you find any reasons for his unsatisfactory behavior?
6. What has the cooperating teacher done over a period of time to remove the causes of the child's unsatisfactory behavior?
7. What does the cooperating teacher do if the pupil's behavior interferes with the learning situation?
8. What suggestions do you have from your study of the pupil which may remove the causes of his unsatisfactory behavior and lead to improvement?

The Emotionally Unstable Pupil

It might be helpful to discuss briefly some of the types of problems that teachers most frequently have in their classes. In most secondary school groups, there may be a pupil or two who show signs of emotional instability. This may express itself in a number of ways. The pupil may be overly aggressive, he may be quick-tempered, he may appear to be nervous, he may be unusually shy, or he may show signs of withdrawing from the group. In working with an emotionally unstable pupil, it is particularly important that you be even-tempered, show no signs of irritation, be very calm in any conversations with him, and in other ways show a friendly and sympathetic attitude toward him. If the pupil should display any temper or an uncooperative attitude, do not be hasty in any action toward him. In any case, you need to wait until the pupil has relaxed before any action on your part may be effective.

Frequently, pupils who are nervous or emotionally unstable may relax if they move about the room, go for a drink, erase the blackboard, sharpen a pencil, or raise a window. Try to watch these pupils and take some appropriate step during the period to relax their tensions. You need not feel embarrassed before the rest of the group if an unfortunate situation develops with an emotionally unstable child. Usually the other pupils are aware of his instability, and may be sympathetic toward any problem that you have with him. It is, therefore, not necessary to take action just to "save face" before the rest of the class. In fact, the attitude of the class may be more favorable toward you if you display sympathetic understanding of the emotionally unstable child.

The Show-Off

The pupil who may be called a "show-off" is another type of problem frequently found in the secondary school. The "show-off" enjoys doing things that entertain the rest of the group, even though his actions disrupt the learning situation. The most effective approach with the "show-off" is to take away his audience. This may be done by placing him in the rear of the group where he is least likely to attract attention.

The "show-off" is not so likely to be a serious problem in a pupil-centered classroom. He wants the approval of his fellows and may refrain from doing things that interfere with the activities in which other pupils are interested. Furthermore, a pupil-centered activity frequently gives the "show-off" an opportunity to participate in a way that satisfies his desire for attention.

The Chronic Talker

Another problem is the chronic talker—the pupil who just cannot keep still. Whether he has prepared himself for the activity or not, this pupil always seems to have something to say. He tries to dominate every discussion, even to the point where some other pupils are unable to participate.

It is not easy to gain the cooperation of the chronic talker because sometimes he does not realize how much he impedes an effective discussion. He is likely to complain if the teacher or a pupil leader fails to call upon him whenever he wants to contribute. The teacher should try to help the chronic talker see himself as one member of the total group. One approach to this type of problem is to have a conference with the pupil in which you suggest to him that all pupils should have an opportunity to participate equally in any discussion. Another approach is to give pupils definite responsibilities in the class activities through oral reports, panel discussions, and other ways which make it difficult for one pupil to dominate. Still another possibility is for the teacher or a pupil to act as observer for a discussion, keeping a "flow chart" to show the participation of each member of the group. This information may be used to show the class as a whole how participation may be more equally distributed, encouraging the less aggressive pupils to contribute more, and restraining the chronic talker.

Sarcastic comments by the teacher, penalties, and other repressive measures are not particularly effective in restraining the chronic talker. Such action by the teacher may make him feel that he is being discriminated against. Furthermore, he may gain the sympathy of his classmates if it appears that you are picking on him. Try to find a positive approach to improve the behavior of the chronic talker.

The Pupil Who Withdraws from the Group

The pupil who withdraws from the group often presents the most serious problem for the student teacher because it is difficult to ascertain the reasons for his behavior and to find ways for improving it. His tendency to withdraw may be merely a matter of shyness, it may result from a feeling of inferiority based on a physical handicap, it may be an outgrowth of some unsatisfactory situation in the child's background, or it may be caused by some unfortunate experience he has had. In one instance, a particularly shy pupil was required to give an oral report under penalty of failure for the course if he did not do so. As a result, the pupil, who was beyond the compulsory attendance age, withdrew from school. Compulsion of any kind is seldom a satisfactory approach for improving the behavior of a pupil who has withdrawal tendencies.

In seeking ways of helping the pupil who withdraws from the group, a thorough study should be made of his background to see if the reasons for his withdrawal can be ascertained. The school counselor, the nurse, or the physician may be helpful in diagnosing such behavior, while in extreme cases the school psychologist or psychiatrist, if one is available, should be consulted. In planning for the participation of such a pupil in class activities, it should be recognized that usually he lacks confidence in himself in the presence of the group. Sometimes this pupil is more willing to participate in a group activity than to assume the responsibility for an oral presentation alone. The teacher should also try to locate special talents or interests of the pupil which may serve as the basis for a particular contribution that he can make to the group. One shy pupil in a junior high school class, for instance, knew more about horses than any other pupil because he worked at a riding stable after school and on week ends. Many of his classmates were envious of his opportunity to ride such beautiful horses and take care of them. His teacher of language arts encouraged him to prepare a discussion on horses and riding. This proved to be an exceptionally interesting discussion for the class, as well as a satisfying experience for the boy. One experience such as this is not sufficient to correct the child's unsatisfactory behavior, but it can be effective if it is the first of a series of experiences which are encouraged by an understanding and skillful teacher.

The Undependable Pupil

Pupils who are not dependable in completing their work may create a problem for you. Most often these pupils fail to prepare their home work, where that is required, but occasionally they fail to be ready with their part in a group activity developed by the class. The best way to approach this child is to find activities in which he has an interest. That is not always easy to do. For group activities, the pressure from other pupils may be effective. In chronic cases, the teacher may have to use some compulsion with such pupils. Such a negative approach should not be used, however, if a more constructive one can be found.

Things for You To Do

As has been suggested earlier in this chapter, the things you may do as a student teacher to gain experience in meeting management and discipline problems are somewhat limited. The following is a summary of some things that may be helpful in giving you background for such activities as a beginning teacher:

1. Develop a definite plan for keeping your classroom in order and neatly arranged throughout the day, including attention to the following: (1) keeping blackboards neat, (2) adjusting window shades, (3) keeping the teacher's

desk neat, (4) keeping books, equipment, and supplies neatly arranged in cupboards and on shelves, (5) arranging pupil chairs at the end of the period, and (6) checking the room at the end of the period.

2. Prepare a plan for collecting and distributing materials in an efficient and orderly manner, having the following types of materials in mind: (1) tests and other pupil papers, (2) reference books used in classes, (3) equipment, and (4) supplies used for projects.

3. Develop a definite plan for checking and recording attendance which is appropriate for your classes, keeping in mind that this needs to be done quickly and without interfering with the learning situation.

4. Develop a definite plan which is appropriate for your classroom for controlling light and ventilation throughout the day.

5. Have a conference with the cooperating teacher regarding his policy for seating pupils. On the basis of this conference and your observation while you are student teaching, develop a definite policy for seating pupils which you may use in your subject as a beginning teacher.

6. Have a conference with the cooperating teacher about the way he proceeds at the beginning of the year to develop effective pupil relationships within his classes and to prevent group discipline problems from developing. Observe how the cooperating teacher maintains a satisfactory relationship within the group throughout the year. With the information you gain from such conferences and observation, develop a definite statement of policy which you may use as a beginning teacher to develop and maintain an effective learning situation in your classes.

7. If an unsatisfactory group situation develops when the cooperating teacher is in charge of the class, note what he does to improve the situation.

8. Observe your classes carefully to locate all the pupils who seem to present individual behavior problems. Select several of these for careful study, giving attention to the

following: (1) information in the office records about the pupil, (2) records of previous problems with the pupil, (3) the precise nature of the pupil's present behavior problem, (4) the things done by the cooperating teacher to help the pupil, and (5) things that you need to do to work effectively with the pupil when you are student teaching.

In Summary

Because you have the advice and support of the cooperating teacher, problems of management and discipline should not concern you too much. Even so, you should try to get all the experience you can in developing effective pupil relationships in your classes and in working with problem pupils.

In this chapter it has been emphasized that you should take a positive approach to matters of discipline, emphasizing desirable human relationships in the classroom as the best step toward creating an effective learning situation. Good administrative organization of classroom details, satisfactory preparation of teaching plans, and an understanding of each individual pupil, will contribute greatly toward developing satisfactory working relationships within your classes.

PART III

At Work with Guidance and Extraclass Activities

Chapter 9

HELPING WITH GUIDANCE

Pupils Need Guidance

Emphasis on Guidance Today

Although guidance is by no means new in the secondary school, emphasis on it has increased greatly in recent years. There are a number of reasons for this. One is the fact that the school life of the child has become increasingly complex, making more choices and decisions necessary for him and creating more adjustment problems. A generation or two ago, the secondary school emphasized a college curriculum with only a few electives in its entire program. Today, there are usually several curricula with many elective courses leading to college admission, to vocational schools, or to employment in certain occupations without further formal education. The offering of many extraclass activities and numerous pupil services have further complicated the secondary school program. Then, too, the secondary school has, in many communities, become a large institution with many administrative officials, hundreds of pupils, and numerous rules and regulations.

Furthermore, the society in which the pupil lives has also become more complex, confronting him with problems that were unknown to the youth of yesterday. For example, consider the problems which a boy faces today if he takes a job during the summer months. He not only has the problem of finding the job, but he must become informed about the

173

labor laws, union regulations, social security practices, and federal income taxes. Problems in the home and in the community have likewise become more complex, frequently creating tensions and emotional maladjustments that are reflected in the pupil's behavior and achievement in school.

A better understanding of the techniques and methods of guidance has also served to direct more attention to guidance activities and services. Not only are home room and classroom teachers better prepared to recognize guidance problems and to help pupils with them, but there are today guidance specialists in almost every area of a child's personal, social, and educational development. Most schools have a guidance director, counselors, and a nurse, while many have access part time or on call to the services of a physician, dentist, psychologist, psychiatrist, home visitor, and social worker. With the help of these specialists, guidance services which were unheard of a generation ago are made available today to the pupils in our secondary schools.

Pupils Have These Problems

It may be helpful for you to have some idea of the types of guidance problems which face secondary school pupils. It is obviously impossible to present here a complete list of such problems, but the more common ones include the following:

1. Educational problems such as these:
   What subjects should I take in high school?
   How can I succeed in school?
   What extraclass activities are available?
   What high school courses are needed for college admission?
   What educational opportunities are available beyond high school?
   Should I attend college? If so, which college is best suited to my needs?

2. Vocational problems such as these:
   How can I obtain summer and after-school employment?
   For what vocation am I particularly suited?
   What educational preparation is needed for the vocations in which I am interested?
   Should I attend a post-secondary school to prepare for a vocation? If so, which one is best suited to my needs?
3. Social problems such as these:
   How can I get along well with other people?
   How can I make friends?
   How should I approach a girl for a date?
   What courtesies should I show a girl on a date?
   How should I dress for a school party?
4. Health problems such as these:
   How can I reduce my weight?
   How can I gain weight?
   What should I do for a bad complexion?
   How can I improve my posture?
5. Personal problems such as these:
   How may I be better understood by my parents?
   How can I get along with certain teachers?
   Am I making a wise choice of companions?
   What hours should a boy or girl of my age keep?
   Should I have more spending money?

As you work with secondary school pupils, they will raise many such questions, and perhaps some of a decidedly more personal nature. No matter how silly or unimportant their problems may seem to you, do not express any surprise. Such problems are exceedingly vital to those pupils whom they happen to concern. Do everything you can to gain an understanding of such problems and how you can help secondary school youth to meet them.

Your Part in Guidance

The teacher is the key person in the guidance program of the secondary school. It is the teacher who comes in contact most frequently with the pupils, and consequently he is in the best position to help them. He observes them daily in the classroom, he sees them in the home room, he works with them in extraclass activities, and he meets them in other ways both in school and out. These contacts give the teacher an understanding of the individual pupil which is essential as a basis for effective guidance.

As a student teacher, you will have many of the same contacts with the pupils as the cooperating teacher. You will work with them regularly in their classes, observe them in the home room, and meet them occasionally in extraclass activities. Then, too, the fact that you are a student teacher may be an advantage as you participate in guidance activities. Because you are nearer their age level than the cooperating teacher, the pupils may feel that you will understand their problems better, and therefore may confide more readily in you. Furthermore, the older pupils may be interested in admission to college, the cost of attending college, the curricula and courses available at your college, the problems that confront a college freshman, participation in extracurricular activities, joining a fraternity or a sorority, and other problems of college life. Since you are still a college student, you are in an excellent position to help pupils with such problems. Let the cooperating teacher and the pupils know that you would be happy to discuss college problems with the entire class or with individual pupils.

Suggestions That May Help

The problems of guidance are so complex and the skill required to meet them is so great that every teacher should have some preparation for helping pupils with guidance problems. If you have had a course or two in guidance, it should help you observe and work more effectively in this area. For the student teacher with little or no preparation in guidance, the following suggestions may be helpful:

1. Be as well informed as you can concerning the backgrounds of each pupil in your home room and classes, including his home background, out-of-school activities, achievement records, psychological background, and social and personal problems.

2. Show a serious and sympathetic interest in any problem that your pupils may present, regardless of how petty or ridiculous it may seem to you.

3. Give pupils the feeling that you will keep in complete confidence any problems they discuss with you, even to the point of not discussing these problems with the cooperating teacher except with their permission. It is a prime requisite of effective guidance not to violate a pupil's confidence.

4. Raise problems with the pupils if you feel that you can be of help on the basis of observations that you have made in your classes, in extraclass activities, or elsewhere.

5. Help pupils think through their problems, but do not tell them the answers. Rather, you should help them find the best answers for themselves.

6. Encourage pupils to come to you for a follow-up visit concerning a problem, but do not pursue a problem further unless the pupil seems interested in doing so.

7. Suggest to the pupil where he may go for additional help and information in finding solutions for his problems, including books he may read, other teachers he may see, places in the community he may visit, and local business and professional people he may interview.

Specialists Are Available

In most of the medium-sized and large secondary schools today, there are some specialists who can be of help with guidance problems, including a director of guidance, counselors, the nurse, a physician, and sometimes a psychologist and a psychiatrist. Some of these specialists may devote full time to your school, but others may be available only part time or on call because they serve the entire school system.

In small schools, the principal frequently serves as the director of guidance. Although he may not be a specialist in guidance, his professional background and experience often qualify him well for certain types of guidance activities. Even in small schools today, however, it is a common practice to have one person with some special training in guidance who devotes at least part time to this work.

Although the cooperating teacher may be the one to refer guidance problems to the specialists, the student teacher should know about the types of responsibilities which the various specialists assume. Usually the specialists serve two purposes in the guidance program. First, they provide leadership in developing such a program, and assist home room and classroom teachers to prepare for their responsibilities in that program. They provide such leadership through work with the faculty in developing the program, group conferences on guidance problems with the faculty, individual conferences with teachers, conferences with parents to explain guidance services, the preparation of bulletins on guidance activities and services, and the presentation of materials and information on guidance problems to the faculty, pupils, and parents. Second, the specialists assist with those guidance problems which demand more experience, preparation, and skill in guidance than are usually had by the home room and classroom teachers. They help teachers recognize the problems that need special attention, they suggest ways in which the teachers may work with such problems, and they give special clinical help when it is needed. You should discuss the work of the guidance specialists with the cooperating teacher, and find out what types of problems he refers to the specialists.

Guidance in the Home Room

Guidance Reaches the Pupil

Educators are pretty much in agreement that the key person in the guidance program must have frequent and intimate contact with the pupils. In most schools this person is the home room teacher. He sees the pupils in his group daily and has the opportunity to establish such rapport with them that effective guidance is possible.

If you, as a student teacher, observe and assist with the work of a home room, you have a splendid opportunity to gain experience in guidance activities. If the home room is not a part of your regular student-teaching assignment, it would be well for you to request this additional responsibility. Beginning teachers frequently encounter difficulty with the home room, usually because they have not had sufficient experience with it as student teachers.

The first requisite for success in home room guidance is an understanding of the individual pupils in your group. You should be well informed concerning their home and out-of-school backgrounds, their avocational interests, the school activities in which they engage, and their past achievement in school. You should also have information concerning their health, mental abilities, personality and character qualities, and adjustment problems. The types and sources of information about pupils have already been discussed at some length in an earlier chapter. At this point it should be sufficient to repeat that the home room teacher should get all the information he can about each pupil, he should establish rapport with each one as an individual, he should get to know the pupils well early in the year, and he should exercise the best of judgment, tact, and skill in using this information to help pupils with their guidance problems.

Responsibilities of the Home Room

It is no exaggeration to say that the responsibilities of the home room teacher for guidance extend into any and all problems which pupils may have. This is such a broad statement, however, that it may be of little help in identifying your responsibilities for guidance in the home room. For that reason, the following list of the more common guidance responsibilities of the home room teacher is presented:

1. Assistance to pupils in planning their program of elective curricula and courses, and help in choosing the extraclass activities in which they may participate.
2. Conferences with pupils concerning their achievement in school, particularly at the time that pupil progress reports are issued. The purpose of these conferences is to assist pupils in improving their achievement in school.
3. Responsibility for checking on the absence and tardiness of pupils, and for conferring with pupils who are unnecessarily absent or tardy.
4. Responsibility for discussing with pupils the conduct problems they may have in other classes and about the school.
5. Assistance to pupils in becoming oriented to the school program, particularly when they first enter the school.
6. Conferences with pupils about social and personal problems.
7. Responsibility for referring difficult guidance problems to the specialists in the school.
8. Conferences with pupils about educational and vocational interests, and about continuing their education beyond high school.
9. Keeping in touch with parents about the progress of their children in school, problems they are encountering, and their educational and vocational choices.

Time Is Needed

In order to do effective guidance in the home room, adequate time is needed for this purpose. In some schools, the only time the home room teacher has with his group is a few minutes in the morning, and perhaps at noon, when the group comes together to check attendance, to hear announcements, and for other administrative purposes. Obviously, this time is totally inadequate to carry on guidance activities. There needs to be sufficient time throughout the week for the home room teacher to conduct group discussions and to have periodic conferences with individual pupils.

In some schools, a period daily or several times weekly is provided when home room activities may be carried on. This period may extend from twenty or thirty minutes to a full class period in length. If you become responsible for such a home room period, give the same attention to planning the work for it as you do for any class. This means that you should have an objective in mind for each home room period, have necessary materials available, and be able to suggest activities which may help pupils reach the objective. If home room activities are to be effective, pupils should take a significant part in planning them and carrying them to completion. See an earlier chapter for suggestions on pupil participation in planning learning activities.

The Home Room in Core Programs

In schools which have core-type classes, the home room is frequently combined with the core classes. The most common plan is to have a group of pupils remain with the same teacher for two to three periods daily, and to cover in that time the content and activities ordinarily included in language arts, social studies, and the home room. Usually the home room activities are integrated with those of language arts and social studies, although practice varies much in this respect. Where the home room becomes part of a core-type class, a teacher may have two home room groups at different times in the day. The core-type classes which include the home room are found more frequently in junior high schools than in other types of secondary schools.

There are several advantages in having the home room become a part of the core class. It gives the home room teacher sufficient time with a group to become well acquainted with each pupil; it reduces the number of pupils which the home room teacher has during the day, making it easier to study each one as an individual; and it encourages the integration of home room activities with the curricular program. In schools that have combined the home room with core-type classes, administrators and teachers generally believe that more effective guidance has resulted.

Guidance Through Class and Extraclass Activities

The individual teacher can make a tremendous contribution to the guidance program of the school. This is true because the teacher meets the pupils regularly, comes to know much about them through class and extraclass contacts, and sees them in situations where guidance is appropriate. Much of the guidance activity of the teacher may center around the learning problems growing out of his particular subject, such as guidance on health problems in the physical education class, on social relationships in the homemaking class, on vocational interests in the industrial arts class, and on educational problems in the English and social studies classes. The classroom teacher also comes in contact with many of the personal, emotional, and social problems of the pupils. Then, too, he is able to accumulate much information about pupils which will be helpful elsewhere in the guidance program. These contributions to guidance of the individual teacher will be discussed in the next few pages.

Guidance Problems in the Classroom

There are certain pupil problems for which guidance is appropriate that may arise in the classroom or come to the attention of the classroom teacher. In many cases, the teacher can be exceedingly helpful to pupils in meeting these problems, though sometimes it may be advisable to refer them to a specialist. As a student teacher, you should be on the alert for guidance problems that arise in the classroom; you should observe the cooperating teacher as he helps pupils with them; and you should be available to offer your own assistance whenever that seems appropriate. The types of guidance problems you are most likely to see in the classroom include the following:

1. Problems of orientation and adjustment for pupils new in the school, such as becoming acquainted with the building, the bell schedule, rules for absence and tardiness, policy concerning books, equipment, and supplies, the use of the library, and making friends with other pupils.
2. Problems related to classroom policies and practices in your room and elsewhere in the school, such as home work, examinations, marks, pupil-progress reports, and discipline.
3. Problems related to success in your subject, such as standards of work, minimum essentials that may be required, skills necessary for success, types of activities included in the subject, sources of special help, sources of information bearing on the subject, prerequisites for taking the subject, and qualities one should possess to continue with advanced work in the subject.
4. Problems related to educational and vocational choices on which your subject has a bearing, such as the vocations for which it is a prerequisite, its relation to high

school graduation requirements, its bearing on admission
to college and other post-secondary schools, and its relation to various curricula in college.

5. Problems of human relations in the classroom, such as
consideration for others, cooperation in group activities,
courtesy, recognition of the authority of the teacher or a
pupil leader, tendency to withdraw from the group, and
unduly aggressive attitudes.

It is important to recognize problems such as these before
they reach serious proportions for any pupil. In some cases,
a problem will be obvious just from observing the behavior
of pupils in their relations with the teacher or their classmates. In others, they become apparent through periodic
conferences that the teacher should have with his pupils
concerning their progress in school. Sometimes the counselor, the home room teacher, or previous teachers may point
out guidance problems for pupils in your classes. The records of pupils in the office of the principal or the director of
guidance may also be helpful for this purpose. All too
often, however, the classroom teacher just stumbles on the
guidance problems which confront his pupils.

As a student teacher, keep in mind the types of guidance
problems which pupils face, and try to locate pupils in your
classes who need help with them. You may expect that
every pupil at one time or another may have such problems.
As you establish good rapport with individual pupils, they
may bring some of these problems to you voluntarily, hop-
ing that you may listen sympathetically and be of help.
Unless the pupil indicates that he is confiding particularly
in you, it may be best to consult the cooperating teacher or
encourage him to do so. Even though you are a student
teacher, pupils will soon learn that you are helpful and will
bring their guidance problems to you.

Information for Counselors

The guidance specialists and home room teachers need much information about individual pupils as a basis for effective guidance. An excellent source for such information is the classroom teacher. In fact, accumulating information about pupils is one of the best contributions which the classroom teacher can make to the guidance program. In some schools, a regular administrative routine has been set up for the classroom teacher to send information about pupils to the home room advisor and the guidance specialists. Often anecdotal records are the basis for such a procedure. In many schools, however, information about individual pupils is transmitted by the classroom teacher entirely on an informal basis.

As a student teacher you can be helpful in obtaining data about pupils in your classes which may be used for guidance purposes. In fact, because of your position as a student teacher, pupils may confide in you and, in other ways, information about pupils may come to your attention more readily than to the cooperating teacher. With the approval of the cooperating teacher, transmit such information to the appropriate guidance workers. Information about pupils for guidance which can be readily obtained by the classroom teacher includes the following:

1. The achievement of pupils in your subject, including their marks, learning difficulties, and strong qualities.
2. The adjustment problems of pupils in your classes, including their relationships with the teacher and other pupils, their interest in the work of your class, and their adjustment to school regulations and routine.
3. Information about the health of pupils, including both mental and physical health, such as emotional upsets, nervousness, poor posture, and similar problems.
4. The results of various types of tests administered by the

classroom teacher, including achievement, diagnostic, mental, and aptitude tests.

5. The personal problems which pupils may have as revealed by conferences with the classroom teacher, by incidental comments, or by observation, including home and family, financial, boy-girl, employment, recreational, and similar problems.

6. The school citizenship and conduct problems of pupils in your classes, including violation of school regulations, lack of cooperation, discourtesy, and improper use of school property.

Providing Background for Guidance

One of the contributions the classroom teacher can make to the guidance program is to provide pupils with background information which will help them make more intelligent educational and vocational choices. For instance, the teacher of English may have pupils engage in oral and written activities which center around such topics as going to college, noncollege educational opportunities beyond high school, preparation needed for various vocations, opportunities in different vocations, and similar topics of interest to high school pupils. The study which pupils make for such activities in the English class gives an opportunity to acquire a background of information which will help them make educational and vocational plans.

The types of activities in which pupils engage are also valuable for educational and vocational guidance. For instance, the competence of pupils in the basic skills of such subjects as the language arts, mathematics, and science may indicate whether or not they should attend college, what college curricula are most appropriate for them, and in which vocations they are likely to find success. The interest and skill of pupils in written activities are related to journalism; in oral activities, to teaching, law, and the ministry; in detailed laboratory work, to nursing, medicine, pharmacy, and science; and in skill with tools, to carpentry, electrical work, auto mechanics, and plumbing. These are only a few examples of the relationship between certain types of activities which pupils have in various subjects and their educational and vocational plans.

In order to provide such backgrounds for guidance in the various subjects, teachers need to be aware of the relations between their subjects and the guidance problems of secondary school youth. Furthermore, they must display much imagination and resourcefulness in developing learning activities that have implications for guidance. It is much easier to develop such activities when pupils participate extensively in developing the plans for units of study. As you develop the teaching plans for your classes, keep in mind the opportunities that present themselves for helping pupils acquire backgrounds for meeting guidance problems.

Guidance Through Extraclass Activities

There are many opportunities for guidance in the extraclass activities of the school. The various activities frequently have a direct bearing on the work of certain vocations, such as the relation between the school newspaper and journalism, speech activities and the practice of law, and science clubs and the study of medicine. Of even greater value to guidance, however, is the close rapport that often develops between pupils and teachers in extraclass activities. Perhaps the best example is the great confidence boys often place in the advice and judgment of the coach for the athletic teams, although a similar relationship may develop between teachers and pupils in other activities as well. In this situation, teachers are able to discuss personal, educational, and vocational problems with pupils in an atmosphere that may be never achieved in the classroom. As you assist with extraclass activities, be aware of the guidance problems which those activities present.

Things for You To Do

You as a student teacher can do a number of things to prepare for a teacher's responsibilities for guidance. The following activities are suggested:

1. Make a list of all the guidance specialists in the co-operating school and ascertain the responsibilities for guidance which each one assumes. Find out, if you can, under what conditions and for what purposes home room and classroom teachers may call upon each one for help with guidance problems.

2. Prepare a chart or diagram which shows the organization of the entire professional staff as it bears on the guidance program. This diagram should include the principal, assistant principal, supervisors, teachers, librarian, and other staff members, as well as those who are clearly designated as being responsible for specific guidance duties.

3. Find out what professional materials on guidance are available for teachers and other staff members in the professional library of the school or the guidance offices. Examine these materials and prepare a bibliography of those which may be especially helpful to you as a beginning teacher.

4. Find out what materials on guidance problems are available for pupils in the school, such as books and pamphlets on occupations, college catalogs, catalogs for noncollege post-secondary schools, an occupations file, and similar materials. Examine these materials and make a record of those which may be especially helpful to pupils in your subject.

5. Obtain copies of bulletins on the guidance program which have been prepared by the guidance specialists in the cooperating school. Study these bulletins to get a better understanding of the guidance services of the school and to obtain ideas concerning the teacher's

responsibilities for guidance. If you can obtain permission to do so, retain any copies of bulletins that may help you as a beginning teacher.

6. Have the cooperating teacher assign to you five or six pupils from his home room for whom you will assume guidance responsibility. These pupils should include a cross section of all types in the home room, not only problem pupils. Confer with them from time to time on the various guidance problems which arise, such as (1) pupil progress reports, (2) school conduct and citizenship, (3) choice of curricula and courses, (4) choice of extraclass activities, (5) difficulties in certain subjects, (6) adjustment problems, (7) relations with teachers, (8) relations with other pupils, and (9) personal problems. Keep closely in touch with the cooperating teacher concerning any unusual problems that may arise and the help you give the pupils.

7. Take the responsibility for planning and carrying on a series of group discussions and other activities in the home room on some guidance problem. Examples of such problems are: (1) orientation to the school for a group of entering pupils, (2) choice of elective curricula and courses for the following year, (3) the social graces in preparation for a school party, and (4) problems growing out of pupil progress reports. These plans should be made with the help of the cooperating teacher.

8. Make a detailed list of all the implications for guidance which are found in the subject you teach, including such things as the following: (1) the vocations on which your subject has a bearing, (2) the relation between your subject and graduation from high school, (3) the relation between your subject and admission to college and other post-secondary schools, (4) the activities in your subject that are related to the work of certain vocations, and (5) the reference materials in your subject that may help pupils with various types of guidance problems.

9. Plan one unit of work in your subject in which you emphasize especially the guidance implications of the unit.
10. Develop a procedure for regularly recording anecdotal information about the pupils in your classes. This procedure should include a form for recording the information, a regular time when you will prepare such records, and a plan for filing them.

In Summary

Because of the emphasis on guidance in the secondary school today, your experience as a student teacher should give considerable attention to the responsibilities that teachers assume in this area. A few suggestions have been given in this chapter to assist you in gaining such experiences. While you are working in the cooperating school, many opportunities will present themselves for studying the guidance program which have not been suggested here. You are urged to capitalize on every opportunity for studying the guidance program of the school, conferring with guidance specialists on their responsibilities for guidance, observing the guidance activities in the home room and the classroom, and working with pupils on guidance problems.

Chapter 10

EXTRACLASS ACTIVITIES

Nature of the Program

Participating in Extraclass Activities

In most secondary schools, responsibility for extraclass activities constitutes an important part of the teacher's work. This responsibility presents a particular problem for the beginning teacher because all too often he has had little preparation for it. In his college courses in education, attention has probably been concentrated on classroom activities, while the extraclass program has been neglected.

Likewise, in student teaching, there is usually so much emphasis on classroom teaching that there is little time to observe and participate in the extraclass program. Then, too, the extraclass activities frequently come at a time of the day when the student teacher is not available. The importance of these activities in the in-service teacher's work makes it essential, however, that the student have some experiences in planning, carrying on, and supervising them. You are urged, therefore, to obtain as much experience as possible in the extraclass program of the cooperating school. In preparing the over-all plan for your student teaching, include in it opportunities to observe many types of extraclass activities, and provide for actual participation in planning and supervising those in which you have a particular interest.

Purposes of Activities

Student teachers frequently do not realize that extraclass activities have important educational objectives similar to the classroom program. In fact, the inclusion of these activities in the program of the school can be justified only in terms of the objectives which they are to achieve. The more important objectives in the program of extraclass activities are as follows:

1. To give pupils significant experiences in democratic living.
2. To give pupils opportunities to gain experience and skill in leadership.
3. To give pupils opportunities to participate in developing the life of the school as a whole.
4. To provide opportunities for pupils to use the skills and backgrounds acquired in the classroom program.
5. To provide exploratory opportunities for pupils as a basis for educational and vocational decisions.
6. To provide opportunities for pupils to develop avocational interests and skills.

Some schools have a formulated statement of objectives for the program of extraclass activities. This statement may be found in the teachers' handbook, the pupils' handbook, or a bulletin which describes the extraclass program. If your cooperating school has such a statement of objectives, you should obtain a copy of it and become thoroughly familiar with it. Keep these objectives in mind as you observe and participate in the extraclass activities of your school.

Types of Activities

For some years, there has been a trend toward incorporating the extraclass activities into the curriculum of the secondary school. Although this trend has gone farthest in the junior high school, there is also much evidence of it in senior high school. Because of this trend, many activities that are sometimes referred to as extraclass are, in some schools, an integral part of the curricular program. For instance, in many schools such music organizations as the glee clubs, band, and orchestra are now on a regular class basis and carry credit toward graduation, much like English, mathematics, and social studies. Similarly, in some schools the publications, such as the newspaper, the magazine, and the yearbook are part of the regular program, with the participants placed in special classes for this purpose. Some activities have a place in the school schedule, but they do not meet as regular classes nor count as credit for graduation. These activities most often include clubs, the student council, and assemblies.

There are, of course, many pupil activities which continue to be offered on a basis different from that of the usual classes, although they are often closely integrated with the curricular aspects of the school program. These activities include athletics, dramatics, debate, other speech activities, school service organizations, and social functions. In this discussion of the student teacher's relationship to the extraclass program, all types of activities will be included, but particular attention will be given to those which continue to be conducted primarily on an extraclass basis.

Planning Your Participation

It has already been suggested that you should plan your participation in extraclass activities. Failure to do so is likely to mean that these activities will be neglected in your student-teaching experience. The nature of your participation should depend largely on the skills and interests which you developed in high school and college. For instance, if you have been active in college journalism, you may assist with the school newspaper, the magazine, or the yearbook; if you have been a member of a student government organization, the student council may interest you; if you participated in college dramatics or other speech activities, then the senior play, the drama club, or the debate team may be appropriate activities; or, if you have an unusual hobby interest or skill, you may associate yourself with one of the hobby clubs. You are almost certain to have some interest which has a bearing on one of the activities in your cooperating school.

As a student teacher, you may be so busy with classroom responsibilities that it will not be possible for you to assist with many extraclass activities. It may seem best to participate actively in only one or two types of activities, but to observe as many others as you can. Thus you can gain some experience in supervising activities, as well as obtain an overview of the program as a whole. Your plan for participating in extraclass activities should be based on a study of the entire program, and should meet with the approval of your cooperating teacher and college supervisor.

Helping with Clubs

Kinds of Clubs

In most junior and senior high schools today, there is a considerable offering of club activities. In some schools, there is an activities period daily or several times weekly when the clubs meet; while in other schools, club meetings take place either before school, during the noon hour, or after school. Occasionally, the meetings are held in the evening, although this is not particularly common.

In secondary schools, there are a number of different kinds of clubs. They may be grouped as follows:

1. School service clubs, such as cheer leaders, safety patrol, library helpers, and cafeteria assistants.
2. Subject area clubs, such as art, foreign language, history, astronomy, homemaking, electricity, and auto mechanics.

3. Civic-social-moral clubs, such as Boy Scouts, Girl Scouts, Junior Red Cross, social service, student government, and citizenship.
4. Hobby clubs, such as photography, model airplane building, leather craft, fishing, hunting, and knitting.
5. Sports and physical education clubs, such as folk dancing, riding, riflery, swimming, and first aid.

In some schools, club activities have been integrated with the regular class program. Sometimes this is done by having the club become part of the class activities, such as a Latin club, a history club, and a homemaking club. Where this is the practice, certain days are set aside when the class is conducted as a club activity. In a few schools, certain clubs meet daily or several times weekly and have a planned program similar to that of the classes in any subject. For example, one school with clubs scheduled in this way has such groups as photography, library service, and journalism, which meet daily for a full class period. Whatever the practice in your school, plan to observe and participate in some club activity.

Planning Club Activities

The success of a club, like that of any class, depends largely upon the thought and imagination that goes into planning the club activities. If you are to assist with a school club, you should know how to organize and carry on the activities in which the club may engage. The following suggestions may help you as you work with pupils in planning club activities:

1. There should be definitely stated club objectives for the year which have been developed by the club members.
2. There should be an over-all plan of activities for the entire year, which includes projects, educational programs, entertainment programs, social activities, and business meetings.

3. Definite plans for meetings should be made several weeks ahead so that those who are responsible for the meetings will be prepared.
4. The leadership in planning the activities should come from the pupil officers and committees, but with some participation by all the members of the club.
5. Some attention should be given to a study of ways in which pupils may work effectively together in carrying on club meetings and in planning club activities.
6. The faculty sponsor should exert leadership in a diplomatic manner, giving help and suggestions whenever needed, but encouraging pupil leadership and participation to express itself as much as possible.
7. It is helpful to type or mimeograph the club program for the entire year, indicating the objectives, meetings, and other activities. Copies should be given to all club members.

Planning Club Meetings

The effectiveness of a club depends to a large extent upon the way in which the meetings are conducted. If they are well planned, if the pupil leaders understand their responsibilities, and if the members participate in a businesslike way, the meetings may be productive of worth-while results. Failure to plan and conduct the meetings efficiently may be disastrous for the club. As a student teacher, you should participate in planning and carrying on several club meetings. The following suggestions may be helpful:

1. It is usually best to have one major activity or objective for a club meeting, such as an educational activity, entertainment, work on a project, or a business session. If the time is divided among several objectives, it may be that none will be achieved.
2. It is not necessary nor, for that matter, desirable to have a business session as a part of every club meeting. The

business session is likely to consume so much time that other objectives for the meeting may not be realized.

3. The faculty advisor should meet with the pupils responsible for a given club meeting well ahead of the time of that meeting so that adequate plans and preparation may be made for it.

4. Be sure that the pupils in charge arrange for such details as informing visitors of the time of the meeting, escorting visitors to the meeting, providing necessary materials and equipment for the meeting, arranging the furniture, and similar details.

5. Help the pupil chairman plan his part as master of ceremonies so that he will know how to introduce the activities and carry them on efficiently.

6. During the club meeting, the faculty sponsor should remain in the background as much as possible, participating only as a member of the group. If the meeting appears to be getting out of hand, he should gain recognition from the presiding officer and tactfully suggest ways for improvement.

7. The activities of the club should always be carried on in a quiet, orderly, and efficient manner. It is the responsibility of the faculty sponsor to see that that is done.

Things for You To Do

There are several things you can do as a student teacher to gain experience in working with club activities. The following are possibilities:

1. Study the entire club program for the school, giving attention to the following: (1) the different kinds of clubs in the school, (2) the schedule for club meetings, (3) how faculty sponsors are selected, (4) how pupils select a club, (5) how clubs are financed, (6) the policy concerning dues, pins, etc., (7) what types of activities the clubs engage in, (8) how many clubs a pupil may participate in, (9) the policy concerning evening and

Saturday meetings, and (10) the policy concerning field trips. Summarize and record this information, and compare it with information obtained by other student teachers for their cooperating schools.

2. Make an intensive study of one club in the school, preferably one with which you are assisting, to gain such information as the following: (1) the objectives of the club, (2) what officers it has and their duties, (3) the standing committees, (4) the nature of its constitution, (5) the program for the year, (6) what help officers are given to learn their duties, (7) the activities in which the pupils engage, (8) educational activities, (9) entertainment, (10) how meetings are planned, (11) how frequently officers and committees meet, and (12) how the faculty advisor helps pupils plan club activities.

3. Associate yourself with a club that interests you, and serve as cosponsor for it during your student-teaching period. This means that you should share in the responsibilities for assisting the club, including such activities as these: (1) meet with club officers, (2) meet with committees, (3) help club officers with their responsibilities, (4) check with committees on plans for meetings, (5) attend all meetings, (6) be sure committees entertain guests, (7) help pupils with club projects, and (8) help committees and officers evaluate meetings and other club activities.

4. Assume full responsibility as the sponsor for one or more club meetings. This should include meeting with the pupil committee, helping it develop plans for the meeting, being sure that the details have been arranged, and assisting pupils to prepare for their responsibilities at the meeting.

5. Assume the responsibility for advising one of the permanent committees of the club. For instance, if there is a committee on entertainment, you may serve as the advisor for this committee, meeting with it and assisting it in making plans for the entertainment activities.

6. You may serve as the speaker, entertainer, or other key person for the meeting of one of the clubs in the school.
7. You may go from one club to another, visiting them in order that you may observe their activities and how they are being carried on. This activity would mean that you could not associate yourself closely with one club as a cosponsor.

Helping with Assemblies

Purposes of Assemblies

In many secondary schools, it is the practice to have frequent assembly programs. In some schools, they appear on a regular schedule, such as weekly or twice monthly; while in others, assemblies are held only when there is a special reason for them.

Properly planned and carried on, assemblies can make a significant contribution to the educational program of the school. The particular purposes which assemblies should achieve include the following:

1. To develop good school spirit and morale.
2. To provide opportunities for pupils to acquire poise and ease before an audience.
3. To give pupils an opportunity to use the skills in English, dramatics, music, and other subjects which have been acquired in the various classes.
4. To give pupils experience in participating in a large audience situation.
5. To provide cultural opportunities through lectures, musical concerts, dramatic presentations, and entertainment programs.
6. To give pupils experience in leadership through participation in planning, directing, and presenting assembly programs.

Sources of Programs

There are many sources of programs for assemblies in junior and senior high schools. For the junior high schools, certain organizations in the senior high school, such as the glee club, band, and dramatics club, may provide assembly programs. For both junior and senior high schools, there are often individuals and organizations in the community outside the school who may present programs for school assemblies. For instance, in every community there are lecturers, musicians, music organizations, and entertainers whose services may be available. Then, too, in most schools some faculty members may have talents that are appropriate for assembly programs.

Most educators believe, however, that the chief source of assembly programs should be the pupils themselves. If the pupils plan, direct, and present the assembly programs, they are likely to receive greater educational benefits from them. The music organizations, the clubs, the sports groups, home rooms, classes in the various subjects, and individual pupils are sources of programs within the school. In many schools, a schedule for assemblies is developed early in the year so that the clubs, classes, and other pupil groups who are to participate may be informed about it. Although this schedule may include some programs by outside groups, the great majority of them should be pupil assemblies.

Planning an Assembly Program

It would be a valuable experience for you to work with one of the teachers and a group of pupils in planning and presenting an assembly program. The following suggestions may be helpful if you assist with such an activity:

1. Begin planning for an assembly program far in advance of the time when it is to be presented to be sure that

the pupils will be ready for it. This will give pupils more opportunity to participate in planning and directing the program.

2. Use pupils as much as possible in planning the program, in locating and preparing the stage settings, and in directing the program itself. You may have individual pupils or pupil committees assigned to various responsibilities, such as (1) planning the program as a whole, (2) obtaining stage settings, (3) handling the lights, (4) inviting guests and serving as hosts, (5) preparing programs, and (6) serving as ushers.

3. Have a number of rehearsals in the room in which the program is to be presented, regardless of whether it includes only a few pupils or a large group. The pupils will feel more at ease if they have had such rehearsals.

4. Organize carefully the stage settings for the program. This should be done both for dramatic presentations and other types of programs. For instance, the chairs, lights, lectern, and drapes need to be arranged for a speaking program as well as for a dramatic presentation.

5. Help the pupil who is to serve as chairman or master of ceremonies plan every detail for his part in presenting the program, from the introduction at the beginning to the dismissal at the end. He should have an opportunity to practice several times in the assembly room.

6. Provide advanced publicity for the program through bulletin boards, the school newspaper, the home rooms, and other avenues.

7. Help the pupils in charge of the program return stage properties and equipment that were used.

8. Be sure that the pupils extend appreciation in an appropriate manner to those who assisted in planning and presenting the program.

Things for You To Do

When you prepare your over-all plan for student teaching, try to include some provision for participation in assembly programs. You should, of course, like other teachers in the school, attend all the assemblies. But in addition to attending assembly programs, you should gain experience in planning and presenting them. The following are some things that you might do to gain such experience:

1. Obtain a copy of the schedule of assemblies for the current year and, if they are available, those for several preceding years. Study these schedules to find out the sources and the types of programs which have been presented. Notice especially those programs which are related to your curricular and extracurricular interests.
2. Observe carefully how one of the teachers works with a group of pupils to plan and present an assembly program, giving attention to the following: (1) how pupils participate in planning the program as a whole, (2) how pupils participate in directing the rehearsals for the program, (3) provision for lights, scenery, and other stage effects, (4) training the master of ceremonies, (5) invitations to guests, and (6) arrangements for ushers.
3. Have one of your classes prepare an assembly program as a culminating activity for a unit. For instance, one student teacher had a class prepare a Pan-American Day assembly program as an outgrowth of a unit on the relations between the United States and Latin America. The decision to prepare such a program should be made early in the unit, so that much of the work may be directed toward it. Pupils should participate in deciding that such a program should be presented and they should have much of the responsibility for planning and directing it.
4. Take charge of one part of an assembly program which is being prepared under the supervision of the cooperating teacher. For instance, you may work with the pupils

who are responsible for the stage, with the publicity committee, with the pupil who is to be master of ceremonies, or some other group.

5. If it can be arranged, meet with a student-faculty committee that has charge of planning the entire schedule of assembly programs for the year. This will be possible only if it is the practice in your school to plan assembly programs in this way. Observe the following: (1) how the committee is appointed, (2) the relative responsibility assumed by faculty and by student members, (3) the sources of programs, (4) how they contact pupil groups to have them prepare programs, (5) whether the faculty, the student council, or some other group needs to approve the schedule, and (6) what publicity is given the schedule once it is ready.

6. You may present an assembly program yourself if you have some special talent that might be of interest to the pupils. This may be for one of the grades only or for the entire student body. For instance, you may give a talk on attending college to a senior class assembly.

7. You may serve as cosponsor for a pupil committee that is planning an assembly program. This is especially appropriate if the home room or a club which you are observing has the responsibility for such a program. The cooperating teacher may serve as the chief advisor for the pupil group, with your assistance in any way that seems appropriate.

Helping with Social Functions

Purposes of Social Functions

Frequently, the beginning teacher thinks of social functions primarily as entertainment for the pupils. If these activities are properly planned, however, they can make a really significant contribution to the educational growth of the child. In fact, the time and expense of social functions can be justified only in terms of worth-while educational outcomes. Some of the purposes which social functions should achieve are the following:

1. To improve the interest, spirit, and morale of the pupils in the total program of the school.
2. To provide experiences which develop confidence, poise, and ease in social situations.
3. To help pupils develop skills in good social usage and practice.
4. To provide pupils with opportunities to employ skills that have been gained in such classes as English, dramatics, art, music, and other subjects, as well as avocational skills gained either in school or through out-of-school activities.

In order to achieve these purposes, it is essential to give much time and attention to the preparation for and the planning of social functions. For instance, pupils need to learn how to participate effectively in social functions. Such preparation can be provided in certain subjects, in the home rooms, and in some clubs. Social dancing, for example, may be taught in physical education; certain aspects of etiquette may be included in homemaking; and the writing of invitations, the introduction of guests, and the preparation of thank-you notes are appropriate topics for study in English. Other skills and backgrounds for participation in social functions may be included elsewhere in the school program.

In addition to the backgrounds which pupils should acquire, there must be thorough planning and preparation for each social function. Much of this should be done by pupil committees, such as decorating the room, planning the program, preparing refreshments, inviting the guests, and cleaning up after the party. As with any other learning activity, the effectiveness of pupil participation in planning social functions depends primarily upon the inspiration, the encouragement, and the help provided by the teachers. Consequently, there needs to be competent faculty assistance for all pupil committees engaged in planning these activities.

If the objectives are to be achieved, there should be many social activities during the year. A few of these should be major functions, but most of them will be minor activities during the home room period, in the club meetings, and immediately after school hours. For instance, a club should plan several meetings of a social nature during the year, providing for appropriate entertainment, games, and refreshments. Both major and minor social functions should be so planned that they may achieve worth-while objectives.

It is particularly important that all pupils participate in the social functions of the school. So often it happens that the very pupils who need this experience most are the ones who fail to attend. You should be sufficiently familiar with the background of each pupil to know which ones need encouragement to come. Your major responsibility in this respect is for the pupils in your home room, but you should not neglect an opportunity to encourage other pupils with whom you may have contact. Sometimes pupils do not come because they do not have appropriate clothes, because they are reluctant to ask a girl for a date, or because they are not confident of their social skills. If you have the confidence of your pupils, you can do much to assist them in such matters. In any case, you and the cooperating teacher should make it your concern to encourage the participation of all your pupils in the social functions of the school.

Planning Social Activities

The practice with respect to planning social activities varies greatly among secondary schools. In some schools, the student council plays a significant part in arranging for such functions, while in others they are under the charge of pupil committees which represent the organization or pupil group concerned. Whatever the plan for arranging these activities, a faculty member or group usually works with the pupils. It is with this faculty group that you, as a student teacher, may have an opportunity to participate. The following committees may be needed to plan major social functions:

1. An over-all steering committee to see that arrangements for the social function are planned, that they are co-ordinated, and that they are completed.
2. A publicity committee to advertise the function and to encourage all eligible pupils to attend.
3. A program committee to plan entertainment, such as readings, dramatic presentations, music, and similar activities.
4. A refreshments committee, which plans the refreshments, prepares or purchases them, and makes plans for serving them.
5. An invitations committee which takes care of inviting faculty members, chaperons, and guests.
6. A decorations committee to provide for a suitable atmosphere in the room or rooms that are used.
7. A clean-up committee to see that the rooms which have been used are left in proper condition.

It was suggested in a previous section of this chapter that pupils should prepare for participation in social functions by developing certain social skills, understandings, and attitudes. For each social function, attention should be given to helping pupils gain such backgrounds—if it is a dancing party, there should be adequate instruction some time in advance for those pupils who desire it; if it is a dating party, this should receive some attention; and if pupils are to serve as hosts, to invite guests, and to serve refreshments, appropriate study should be made of these matters. In other words, a social function should provide the motivation and opportunity for teaching pupils those skills, attitudes, and understandings which are needed for effective participation.

Things for You To Do

As a student teacher, there are some things that you may be able to do to gain experience in assisting pupils with planning and carrying on social activities. The following are some suggestions:

1. Make a thorough analysis of the way in which a major social function is planned, prepared, and conducted, giving attention to the following: (1) the pupil committees, (2) the assistance given by faculty members, (3) how far in advance the preparations are begun, (4) how it is financed, (5) publicity for it, (6) arrangements that are made for rooms to be used, janitor service, furniture, and other equipment, (7) provision for chaperons and faculty supervision, (8) invitations to and arrangements for guests, (9) plans for refreshments, (10) the program, games, and entertainment, (11) preparation given pupils for the social function in home rooms, classes, and elsewhere, (12) hours for the function, and (13) arrangements for cleaning up.

2. Take the responsibility for advising one of the pupil committees preparing some part of a social function, such as the committee on publicity, on entertainment, on invitations, or on refreshments.

3. Serve as one of the faculty members on the steering committee which has the responsibility for supervising the arrangements for the social activity as a whole. It may be that you can serve only as an observer, but you may assume some definite responsibility.

4. Assist some pupil or group of pupils who are providing the entertainment, preparing invitations, preparing the refreshments, decorating the rooms, or doing some other work to prepare for the social function. Help with their plans, with obtaining supplies and equipment, and with the actual work of decoration itself.

5. Assist a home room group, an English class, or some

other group to plan a series of discussions on good social usage and etiquette at a social function.

6. Attend as many of the social functions in your cooperating school as you possibly can. Observe the various aspects of the function with the thought that some day you may have the responsibility for assisting pupils with such an activity.

Helping with Publications

Purposes of Publications

It has already been suggested that, in some schools, the pupil publications are now carried on as classroom activities. In many schools, however, the newspaper, the magazine, the yearbook, and other publications continue to be extra-class activities. In some instances, they are closely correlated with classroom work, but in others they are completely divorced from it. It is desirable, of course, to have these activities closely integrated with the pupils' classroom experiences.

Pupil publications, like other extraclass activities, should have definite educational objectives. Those which are most commonly recognized are as follows:

1. To give pupils an opportunity to apply skills in written expression which they have acquired in their various classes.
2. To contribute to the improvement of school spirit, citizenship, and morale.
3. To contribute to the more efficient administration of the school by serving as channels for school publicity.
4. To give pupils an opportunity to explore vocational interests and talents in the field of journalism.

Kinds of Publications

The most common publications in the secondary school are those to which reference has already been made, namely,

the newspaper, the magazine, and the yearbook. The practices with respect to these publications vary considerably
from school to school. For instance, the newspaper may
appear weekly, twice monthly, monthly, or at irregular
intervals. Similarly, the school magazine may be issued at
various intervals. Practices also vary with respect to the
manner in which the editorial staffs are selected. They may
be elected by the entire student body; they may be appointed
by a faculty committee or sponsor; or they may be rotated
from a class or club sponsoring the publication. If you have
an interest in school journalism, you should make a thorough
study of the administrative arrangements for the publications in your cooperating school.

The pupils' handbook, in some schools, is prepared by a
pupil staff or organization, such as the student council, a
citizenship club, or an English class. The handbook is issued, of course, only once a year, though in some schools
it is rewritten only once in several years. In many schools,
however, the handbook is not a pupil publication, since it
is prepared by the faculty or the administration.

Working with Pupils on Publications

There are several questions that arise in working with
pupils on school publications. One of these is the amount
of freedom that pupils should have in expressing their own
points of view. From an educational standpoint, it seems
best to give pupils a great deal of freedom in self-expression.
If pupils are restricted too closely in writing what they
think, it ceases to be a pupil publication. At the same time,
the faculty sponsor does have a definite responsibility to the
editorial staff, to the student body, and to the community
as a whole. Surely, any pupil publication should contribute
to developing a better school community and desirable
relations with the community outside the school. The
faculty advisor should help the editorial staff of any school

publication achieve that goal. He should devote much time to helping pupils understand the type of publication that is in good taste for a secondary school and that may contribute to developing the best type of school community. His relations with the pupils should be such that they respect his judgment concerning the type of materials that are appropriate for such a publication.

Another question which frequently concerns the advisors of school publications is how much they should edit the material from the standpoint of English usage and form. As with the question of freedom of expression, this is not easy to decide. If the advisor edits too freely, it ceases to be the work of the pupils. Still, one must remember that the pupils are most likely to improve if their work is thoroughly studied and criticized by the advisor. Furthermore, these publications are taken outside the school and are read by parents and other citizens. In most instances, the advisor should criticize the materials, but the pupils should make their own changes. In any case, the advisor should not permit materials that are glaringly incorrect or in bad form to go into print. He should read the entire publication before it goes to press since, in the eyes of the administration, the parents, and the community, he is responsible for the content, the point of view, and the editorial form.

Keep in mind that a pupil publication should be a learning activity. This means that as many pupils as possible should have the experience of participating. Furthermore, the pupils working on the publication should have a variety of experiences. For instance, it may not be best to have the same editor-in-chief for an entire school year. The responsibilities of the pupils should be changed occasionally so that they may have a variety of experiences and more pupils can participate.

Things for You To Do

In deciding upon things that you, as a student teacher, may do to gain experience with school publications, you should know that these are a tremendous responsibility and take a great deal of time. If you have a real interest in secondary school journalism, you should consider this a major part of your student-teaching assignment and allow adequate time for it in your over-all student-teaching plan. The following are some things that you can do to gain experience in supervising pupil publications:

1. Get an overview of all the pupil publications in the school, including the newspaper, the magazine, the yearbook, the handbook, and others, by obtaining copies of each and studying them carefully. Give attention to the following: (1) the editorial staff, including how it is composed, how it is appointed, and the term of office, (2) the faculty help that is given, (3) how it is financed, (4) freedom of expression, (5) frequency of publication, (6) schedule for pupils to work on the publication, (7) policy concerning advertising, and (8) arrangements for printing.

2. Asked that you be assigned as cosponsor to one of the school publications, assisting the regular sponsor in any way that seems desirable. This assignment may be for the school paper, the magazine, the yearbook, or some other publication. Arrange with the faculty advisor to assume certain responsibilities for working with the pupil staff.

3. Assume the responsibility for supervising a specific part of a pupil publication. For instance, if you are working with the newspaper staff, you may assist the pupils preparing the sports section, the advertising, or the editorial page. On the yearbook, you may supervise the art work, the advertising, the photography, the section on activities, or the material for one of the classes.

4. If you have had sufficient experience in journalism, you may assume the responsibility for supervising the preparation of one entire issue of the newspaper or magazine.
5. In cooperation with a faculty sponsor, you may assist the student council, an English class, or a citizenship club in the preparation of a pupils' handbook.

Helping with Pupil Participation in Administration

Purposes of Pupil Participation

In most secondary schools today, pupils participate in one way or another in the administration of certain school affairs. Although the student council is the organization which provides much of the opportunity for such participation, there are also other pupil organizations for this purpose. As with other extraclass activities, the student council and similar organizations should achieve certain educational objectives. The more important objectives include the following:

1. To give pupils significant experiences in democratic citizenship activities.
2. To develop a better working relationship between the administration and faculty on the one hand and the pupils on the other.
3. To give pupils an opportunity to develop attitudes and skills in self-responsibility and in the self-direction of their own affairs.
4. To provide experiences for pupils in democratic leadership, as preparation for similar responsibilities in adult life.
5. To give pupils opportunity to employ skills in English, citizenship, and other fundamentals gained in the various subject areas.
6. To develop a school community in which pupils may live and work happily and effectively together.

Ways for Pupils to Participate

It has already been suggested that the student council is the most common organization through which pupils participate in the administration of school affairs. The way the council is organized, its duties and responsibilities, and the plan for its meetings, however, differ widely from school to school. In some schools, it is highly organized, meets for a full period daily like any class, and has tremendous influence in shaping the total life of the school; while in other schools, its meetings are less frequent and its responsibilities are limited. It is almost always an elected group, usually chosen by home rooms, and is in turn responsible to its constituents. In schools with core-type programs, the council often represents core groups.

The other organizations through which pupils participate in administering school affairs are sometimes under the direction of the council, but often they are entirely independent. These groups include safety patrols for pupils going to and from school, corridor monitors, cafeteria assistants, library assistants, office assistants, and officials for sports events. These activities may be carried on informally under a faculty advisor, or they may function through organized pupil groups that meet regularly to study problems, to take official action, and to discuss ways of effectively discharging their responsibilities. In some schools, such groups do little more than enforce faculty regulations; in others, they implement policies and regulations passed by the student council; and in still others, they have legislative as well as administrative powers. The student council and other pupil administrative organizations ordinarily have a faculty committee or advisor to assist them in their work.

Some of the pupil administrative activities are closely correlated with the work in certain subjects. For instance, in some schools, pupils in the business courses are responsible for selling cafeteria tickets and doing the bookkeeping for the cafeteria; the library assistants may be the members of an English class; and the sports officials may be selected from a physical education class. Whether they are correlated with class work or not, they should be regarded as significant educational activities which entail much preparation and study on the part of the faculty advisors and the pupils. There should be a planned program to prepare pupils for such responsibilities, there should be regular meetings of these groups, and there should be frequent evaluation of their effectiveness in terms of the purposes they are to achieve.

Things for You To Do

Every teacher should have at least one interest in the extraclass program of the school. If you do not have special talents which qualify you for assisting with a hobby club, with school journalism, music activities, or the sports program, the student council or some other service organization may be an appropriate activity for you. In any case, you should be familiar with such activities and know how they contribute to the program of the school as a whole. The following are some things that you might do, as a student teacher, to gain an understanding of pupil administrative and service activities:

1. Make a list of all the ways in which pupils participate in the administration of school affairs in your cooperating school. Give attention to the following: (1) the pupil organizations concerned, (2) how these groups are organized, (3) the responsibilities of each, (4) the faculty help they receive, (5) administrative or faculty limitations on their authority, (6) meetings for the group, (7) how members are chosen, and (8) the help pupils are given to prepare for their responsibilities. Sources of such information are the pupils' handbook, the constitu-

tion for the student council and other organizations, the pupil officers, and the faculty advisors.

2. Visit the meetings of as many of the different pupil groups as you can to observe the activities in which they engage, how they are organized, how meetings are conducted, and what help they are given by the faculty advisor.

3. Associate yourself with one of these pupil groups, serving as a cosponsor with the faculty advisor for part or all the time that you are in this school.

4. Visit with various pupils in school regarding the work of these pupil groups to ascertain pupil attitudes toward the student council and similar pupil groups.

5. Have a conference with the officers of the student council or some other administrative group to get suggestions from them concerning the ways in which a faculty advisor can be most helpful. Try to obtain the pupils' point of view to help you both as a student teacher and, later, as a beginning teacher, serve more effectively as the advisor to such a group. Plan for this conference by listing specific questions that you want to ask, basing them on the results of your observation of such a pupil group.

In Summary

In this chapter on extraclass activities, no reference has been made to athletics and music. There is a reason for this. There is a definite tendency in many secondary schools today to have the music activities be a part of the class program much like English, social studies, mathematics, and science. Where that is the policy, these activities are in charge of regular teachers who have particular preparation for that work. If you are a music teacher, your student-teaching schedule should include participation in such activities as band, orchestra, chorus, and glee club. If you are a teacher of another subject, but would like experience with music organizations, that can probably be arranged.

The situation with respect to athletics is similar to that for music. The sports activities of the secondary school are now supervised largely by specialists appointed for that purpose. These specialists are usually, though not always, members of the physical education staff. If you are interested in athletics, consult the cooperating principal and your college supervisor to see if some participation in such activities can be provided.

In this chapter, we have tried to emphasize the importance of obtaining experience in supervising extraclass activities. It is almost certain that you will have some responsibility for them in your first teaching position. It becomes highly desirable, therefore, for you to include some contact with these activities in your student-teaching program. This will take much time, but your student-teaching experience is not complete without it. Give the same enthusiasm and attention to preparing for these activities as for your class work so that worth-while educational objectives may be achieved.

PART IV

At Work in School and Community

Chapter 11

ADMINISTRATIVE AND PROFESSIONAL RESPONSIBILITIES

The Teacher's Part in Administration

The Teacher as Administrator

No member of the professional staff is more important to the administration of the school than the teacher. Those who have administrative titles provide administrative leadership, but much of the detail of administration must be done by the teachers themselves. For the beginning teacher, administrative details frequently cause more concern than problems of classroom teaching. This is true because, in many instances, the beginning teacher has had little contact with the administrative responsibilities of a teacher in his student-teaching program. If your student-teaching experience is to cover all the responsibilities of a teacher, it should include much opportunity to observe and participate in the teacher's administrative duties. In this chapter, the administrative responsibilities of the teacher are discussed, and suggestions are given for including such activities in your student-teaching program.

Preparing Records and Reports

In a previous chapter, some reference has been made to the teacher's responsibility for preparing certain records and reports. Some of these records and reports are closely related to the teacher's work in the classroom. Consequently, you may have much direct contact with them. For instance, the teacher is usually the key person in the preparation, the issuing, and the return of pupil progress reports or report cards. Usually, the home room teacher assumes the responsibility for the progress reports for his group, but the classroom teacher records the marks for his pupils on the progress report forms. You should inform yourself regarding the administrative routine that is followed to place the marks on the progress report forms, the manner in which these reports are issued to pupils, and the responsibility of the home room or classroom teacher for seeing to it that they are returned. In some schools, this procedure is explained in a teachers' handbook or bulletin, but in others you may obtain this information through a conference with the principal, the assistant principal, or the cooperating teacher.

The permanent or cumulative records are usually kept in the central office, although in some schools they are in the hands of the home room teacher. These records usually go with the child from school to school within the system, and are retained permanently in a central office after he graduates. Because of the importance of the cumulative records for college admissions, for employment, and for other purposes, it is essential that they be absolutely accurate. Frequently, errors in pupil records are made when the teacher places marks and other information on the cumulative forms. Early in your student teaching, obtain a copy of the cumulative record form from someone in the central office, and study carefully the routine for placing information about pupils on these records.

In some states, the attendance records are exceedingly important because they are used in computing state aid to local school systems. Usually, either the average daily membership or the average daily attendance of pupils is the basis on which the state provides such financial aid. In order that these records may be uniform throughout the state, the form in which they are kept may be specified either by state law or by regulations of the state department of education. In some states there is a state school register, the form of which is prescribed by the state department of education. You should consult the college supervisor about the school register before you begin your student teaching to find out whether or not one is prescribed in your state. If so, obtain a copy of it and study carefully the way in which this record is kept. As a student teacher, assist the cooperating teacher in keeping the records of attendance for your home room group and classes.

Responsibility for Materials and Equipment

In a few large schools, textbooks are issued direct to the pupils by a textbook clerk or a teacher assigned to this task. In these schools, the issuing of textbooks is of no particular concern to the individual teacher. In many secondary schools, however, the classroom teacher obtains the books from the textbook clerk, the principal, or some other person, and in turn issues them to the pupils in his classes. Where this practice pertains, the teacher is responsible for keeping a record of books issued to his pupils, and for seeing to it that they are returned in good condition.

In some schools, a record form is provided for this purpose, but in others the nature of the textbook records is left entirely to the individual teacher. If such a record form is not provided, the teacher should keep in good form a record of every book issued to pupils, the number of the book, the age of the book, and its condition when it was issued. When the books are returned, they should be checked by the teacher to be sure that they are in as good condition as when they were issued, subject to reasonable wear. If books are issued to pupils during your student-teaching period, assist the cooperating teacher in issuing them and in preparing the necessary records.

In the modern classroom, the teacher frequently has a variety of reference books, pamphlets, and other materials. That is particularly true in science, social studies, English, homemaking, and industrial arts. The teacher is responsible for checking these materials to avoid loss or unnecessary wear. Sometimes these materials are issued to teachers in the same way as textbooks, but in other cases they are assigned indefinitely to a classroom as part of its permanent equipment. Whether the reference materials are definitely charged to the teacher or not, it is essential that he keep a detailed record of them. Furthermore, he should have a definite plan for checking them so that they will not be misused or lost. As a student teacher, you should be informed about the records of reference materials and the procedure for checking them.

In some subjects, such as science, industrial arts, home economics, and business, much equipment is assigned to teachers. Some of this is fragile, and it may be expensive. There should be a definite routine for checking this equipment periodically, both to be sure that it is not lost and to safeguard it against unnecessary abuse. Most teachers of these subjects have developed such a procedure. Since you will be responsible for this equipment when you are teaching, you should know this procedure and do everything you can to follow it.

In most school systems, an inventory is kept of the equipment and materials that are assigned to classrooms. This inventory includes, in addition to the instructional materials and equipment, the furniture that is assigned there. The usual practice is to take such an inventory once a year, and to check it against previous inventories to ascertain possible loss. In some school systems, teachers are held responsible for materials, equipment, or furniture that is missing. Ask the cooperating teacher about the classroom inventory, and help in the preparation of it, if this is done while you are student teaching.

Responsibility for Discipline

In a previous chapter, your responsibility for the conduct of pupils in your classes, the home room, and extraclass activities under your supervision, has been discussed. In most schools, teachers are expected to assume some responsibility for pupil conduct in the school as a whole, such as the following:

1. Supervision of pupils in the cafeteria, on such matters as crowding at the serving tables, proper disposal of waste, leaving tables clean, being courteously quiet, returning dishes and trays, and observing good manners.
2. Supervision of pupils in corridors and on the school grounds, on such matters as unnecessary noise, pushing and running, observing corridor regulations, and cleanliness.
3. Supervision of pupils in assemblies, on such matters as orderly entrance and exit and courteous attention to the program.
4. Supervision of pupils on buses and bus loading stations, on such matters as reasonable orderliness and quiet, waiting courteously for one's turn, and cooperation with the bus driver.

The policies for such supervision vary greatly. Sometimes a teacher is assigned such a responsibility as part of his regular load; in other cases, the responsibility is rotated throughout the year from one teacher to another; and, in still others, all teachers are asked to concern themselves with such matters as they think best. It is not unusual to have the student council or some other pupil organization be responsible for supervising pupil conduct in the corridors, cafeteria, and elsewhere. Where that is the practice, the pupil group formulates certain regulations and establishes a plan for enforcement. Even so, the teachers have some responsibility for pupil conduct, though it may be more in the nature of support for the pupil organization and its policies.

Study the teachers' handbook or have a conference with your cooperating teacher concerning the teacher's responsibility for pupil conduct in corridors, on the grounds, and elsewhere. Because pupils who are not in your classes or home room may not be aware of your place as a student teacher on the school staff, you must be tactful in sharing responsibility for pupil conduct. The cooperating teacher may have some suggestions concerning your participation in supervising pupil conduct throughout the school.

Attending Pupil Functions

Teachers usually have some part in supervising pupils at various after-school and evening functions, such as concerts, social activities, athletic contests, and dramatic presentations. But the practice concerning such supervision varies greatly from school to school. In some schools, all teachers are asked to attend the pupil functions in so far as they are able, but with no definite assignment being made; in other schools, teachers have a definite responsibility for supervision at these functions. Usually one or more teachers are designated as chaperons or sponsors, with major responsibility for pupil conduct at the activity. The student council may also share in supervising after-school and evening activities, although such participation is not as common as for activities during the school day.

As a student teacher, you should attend as many of these functions as possible, giving particular attention to the responsibility teachers have for supervising pupils. Notice the pupil problems that arise, and the things that teachers do to meet them. You may actually share in supervising these activities, especially when they concern pupils with whom you have contact in your home room and classes.

Administrative Faculty Committees

Teachers frequently participate in the administration of the school by serving on certain faculty committees with administrative responsibilities. These committees may be assigned such activities as assemblies, athletics, clubs, pupil discipline, or social functions. Sometimes these committees serve merely in an advisory capacity to the administrative officials, while in others they assume full responsibility for the matters that are assigned to them. For instance, a faculty committee on assemblies frequently works with pupils in deciding on the nature of assemblies for the year, scheduling them, and making the necessary arrangements. A committee on discipline may make recommendations to the faculty or to the principal on policies concerning pupil discipline throughout the school. Other committees likewise may assume much of the leadership in determining policy for certain problems in school administration. In some schools, faculty committees work closely with such pupil groups as the student council on various administrative matters. As a student teacher, try to keep in touch with the activities of such faculty committees, observing their meetings and the manner in which they discharge their responsibilities.

Things for You To Do

Some of the things which you can do to gain experience and background for assuming the teacher's responsibility in the administration of the school have been suggested in the preceding discussion. The following list summarizes the above suggestions and several others that may be helpful:

1. Prepare a complete statement of all of the administrative responsibilities which teachers are asked to assume in your cooperating school. This statement should include

such information as the following: (1) a list of the administrative responsibilities, (2) how these responsibilities are divided among the teachers, (3) what responsibilities are assumed by all teachers, (4) what faculty committees there are and the responsibilities of each, (5) how such pupil groups as the student council work with faculty members on administrative matters, and (6) how the administrative officials of the school check to see that these responsibilities are discharged. This information may be obtained from the teachers' handbook, the principal or assistant principal, or the cooperating teacher. Summarize and record this information so that you can compare it with that of other student teachers for their cooperating schools.

2. Assume the responsibility for keeping the state register or other attendance record for your home room group. Study carefully how the records are kept, the periodic reports that may be sent to the principal, and other uses made of these records. Ask the cooperating teacher or someone in the principal's office whether these records are transmitted to the office of a county or a state school official and, if so, what use is made of them. As you keep these records and prepare the reports, check frequently with the cooperating teacher to be sure that they are correct.

3. Prepare the teacher's record of all books that are issued to the pupils during your student-teaching period. Find out the following about these records: (1) the information required about the condition of the books, (2) what is expected of pupils who misuse books, (3) what reports concerning the books are sent to the central office, (4) where the books are obtained by the teacher, and (5) the responsibility of the teacher for books that are lost.

4. If books are issued to pupils from a book room by a clerk or a teacher designated for that work, have a conference with that clerk or teacher concerning (1) the way in which the books are issued, (2) the records that are kept, (3) the responsibility of pupils for lost or mis-

used books, and (4) what responsibility the teacher may have for the issuing of books.

5. During your student-teaching period, assume the responsibility for checking the reference materials and equipment in your classroom to see that none is lost or misused. Find out from the cooperating teacher what procedure he employs to accomplish this purpose.

6. Obtain a copy of the classroom inventory and study it to see what materials and equipment it covers, how frequently it is checked, and in what form it is kept. Find out what is done if equipment or materials are lost. The classroom inventory may be kept in the office of the principal, the business manager, or the superintendent, and probably cannot be taken from that office.

7. For a week or two, assist a teacher who has the responsibility for supervising the cafeteria, the loading of buses, or the school grounds. From that teacher, find out: (1) what hours he is on duty, (2) what regulations he enforces, (3) who makes the regulations, (4) what is done with uncooperative pupils, and (5) how this responsibility is included in his faculty load.

8. During your student-teaching period, associate yourself with one of the faculty committees which has administrative responsibilities. The principal or cooperating teacher can make the arrangements for you. As you meet with the committee, find out: (1) how it is appointed, (2) to whom it is responsible, (3) what its responsibilities are, (4) how it cooperates with the administrative officials, the faculty, and pupil organizations, (5) how frequently it meets, and (6) whether its actions are advisory or final.

Improving the Instructional Program

There was a time when the instructional program of secondary schools was shaped largely by the principals and supervisors. Subject to the approval of the superintendent and the board of education, they decided what curricula should be offered, what courses should be taught, what the extraclass activities should be, the nature of the daily schedule, the marking system, and all other policies and practices for the instructional program. Sometimes they even developed the courses of study, or had this work done under their direction by outside specialists. In other words, any changes in the instructional program were made by the administrators and supervisors.

Recent years have seen a great change in the approach to improving the instructional program. Although administrators and supervisors still provide much of the leadership for this purpose, the teachers themselves participate actively in studying the program of the school and making improvements. There are various ways for doing this, but the most common ones are through faculty meetings, curriculum committees, faculty study groups, and workshops.

Attend Faculty Meetings

Perhaps the oldest method of faculty participation in improving the program of the school is through faculty meetings. There are many different kinds of faculty meetings and they serve different purposes. Some faculty meetings are devoted largely to administrative matters, others provide inspiration or information on professional matters, and still others are directed toward improving certain aspects of the school program. As a student teacher, you may profit by attending the faculty meetings. It might be best to ask the principal or the cooperating teacher about attending such meetings, but there is little doubt that they would be happy to have you.

Some secondary schools are organized in subject departments, with a department head who is responsible for providing leadership for his group. Where there is such an organization, it is common to have departmental meetings.

These meetings are ordinarily concerned with purely departmental matters, such as the instructional materials to be used, changes in the course of study, adoption of textbooks, correlation with the work of other departments, and professional study that bears on the work of the department. It would be well for you to attend meetings of the department in which you are teaching. Again, it is best to consult first the department head or the cooperating teacher.

Although much of the discussion at faculty meetings may deal with administrative or professional matters that will interest no one outside the faculty group, you are urged not to repeat or discuss these matters with anyone. This applies to members of your own family and close friends as well as others. Problems raised at faculty meetings are confidential professional matters, and it is highly unethical to mention them to persons not on the school staff. Furthermore, an innocent comment by you may be considerably changed if it is repeated, and may cause you or members of the faculty some embarrassment. The only ethical policy to follow is not to discuss school matters with anyone outside the school staff.

Faculty Study Groups

Faculty study groups and workshops are becoming more and more common in the secondary schools, although they differ widely in the way they are administered. In some school systems, they are held before school opens in the fall or after it closes in the spring; in others, the study group meets at regular intervals after school hours or on Saturday morning; in still other schools, these study sessions are held on days when teachers are released for this purpose or on vacation days during the school year. Regardless of the plan for the study groups, their purpose is much the same, namely, to give teachers an opportunity to study professional problems that have a bearing on the program of the school.

In some study groups, broad professional discussions are conducted, but in others the attention is directed toward a practical problem in the program of the school. For example, the faculty may be engaged in developing new pupil-progress reports, improving procedures for evaluating pupil progress, or developing a program to improve instruction in reading.

Faculty study groups and workshops are contributing a great deal to the improvement of the instructional program in the secondary schools. By giving teachers a larger part in developing the school program, workshops and study groups also tend to improve morale. Furthermore, study groups and workshops provide a splendid opportunity for individual teachers to grow professionally. As a student teacher, you may not have the time to devote to a workshop or study group like the other teachers, but avail yourself of the opportunity to see the work that is done there and participate as much as you can.

Things for You To Do

You can do a number of things to observe and participate in the various teacher activities for improving the instructional program. Some of these things are as follows:

1. Attend all general faculty and department meetings, if that meets with the approval of the principal, the department head, or other person responsible for the group. Observe (1) the way in which the meetings are planned for the year, (2) how meetings are conducted, (3) who serves as chairman, (4) what topics are discussed, (5) how much time is devoted to routine matters, (6) what time is given to professional improvement, (7) whether teachers are required to attend, (8) how much teachers participate, and (9) how decisions are reached.

2. Attend and participate in a faculty workshop or study

group, if one is held during your student-teaching period. Observe especially (1) how the study group was initiated, (2) whether teachers participate voluntarily, (3) what part teachers have in organizing and conducting it, (4) the nature of the problem under study, (5) what professional materials are available, (6) consultant service that is available, (7) whether key teachers are given time for this work, (8) whether participation counts as in-service credit, and (9) in what form the results are prepared.

3. Serve on a faculty committee for your department which is engaged in such an activity as developing a new course of study, preparing curriculum guides, locating new reference and study materials, or preparing tests and other evaluation instruments.

4. Attend the social functions of the teachers, if that is permissible. Ask the principal or the cooperating teacher about it before you attend.

The Teacher and His Profession

Teachers Belong to Organizations

There are many professional organizations at the local, state, and national levels to which teachers belong and in which they participate. Most school systems have a local teachers' association which embraces all teachers, both elementary and secondary. Frequently, the local organization is affiliated with a state association, sending delegates to the state meetings and in other ways participating in the activities of the state group. At the national level, there is the National Education Association to which teachers may belong regardless of the grade level or the subject area in which they are teaching. The teachers' unions are similar in many respects to the professional organizations. Their purpose is primarily to improve the salaries and status of the teachers. The unions have local organizations and may be affiliated with such national labor groups as the CIO and the AFL.

There are also many professional organizations for teachers in various subject areas. On the national level, these include the National Council for the Social Studies, National Council of Teachers of English, National Council of Teachers of Mathematics, and National Science Teachers Association, as well as others in almost every subject field. There are also state and local organizations in many of the subject areas.

In another chapter, some suggestions are given concerning the part teachers should take in these organizations. At this point, we merely want to suggest that teachers belong to such organizations. In some systems, the schools are closed when certain organizations meet; while in others, teachers who wish to attend are released from their duties. Certainly, if the officers approve, you should attend the meetings of one of the local professional groups. You should also attend the meetings of state and national organizations, if these are sufficiently accessible. In some schools, the student teacher is asked to take the classes of the cooperating teacher on days when he attends meetings of professional organizations. In fact, frequently this is the only way that a teacher can attend without personally employing a substitute. Although this may keep you from attending, obviously when the cooperating teacher is away your first responsibility is to your classes.

Teachers Provide Professional Leadership

The professional leadership in any community comes from the superintendent of schools, the principal, other administrative and supervisory staff members, and the teachers. Of course, most of the leadership comes from the administrative and supervisory personnel, but the teachers can exert a desirable influence if they wish. Much of the teacher's leadership is exerted through informal activities, such as membership in various community organizations, talks before community groups, and serving on educational committees of such organizations as the YWCA, YMCA, and AAUW.

Some professional leadership activities in the community, however, are carried on when there is a campaign for more school funds, for a new school building, and for support for modifications in the school program. These activities usually are concentrated in a short period of time and are carried on in a highly organized manner. They include speaking engagements before local groups, the preparation of advertising materials, the writing of stories for the local newspapers, and other public relations activities. Teachers frequently participate in various ways in such professional activities in the community. You should discuss with the cooperating teacher or some other staff member the public relations activities of the school, especially those in which the teachers participate.

Visiting Days for Parents

It is now almost a universal practice in American schools to have certain days or evenings when parents are urged to visit the schools. American Education Week, sponsored by the National Education Association, is the best example of this type of activity. Frequently there are for American Education Week special activities of interest to parents, though much of the school program continues as usual. In some schools, there is a well-planned visiting night during American Education Week or at some other time, when parents may observe various aspects of the school program in action.

Some schools do not have special days for visits, but urge parents to come to school frequently throughout the year. They are invited especially for special events, such as school assemblies, teas, and social functions, but they are also urged to visit classes at any time. Some parents take advantage of such an invitation to visit the schools frequently.

Parent visits are mentioned here because the teachers have a significant part in planning for them and in serving as hosts when the visitors come. The success of parent visits, therefore, depends primarily on the understanding and support received from the teachers. As a student teacher, you should be informed about the policy for parent visiting and support it in any way that seems appropriate.

Teachers Do Professional Study

Professional study on the part of teachers is now a common practice in most schools. Such study is done through extension classes, summer school attendance, travel, individual reading, and study in a professional library provided in the school. As a student teacher, you are no doubt so busy with your own studies that you have little interest in the professional study of the cooperating teachers. At the same time, you should know that teachers engage in such study as a means of professional improvement. Discuss with the cooperating teacher the professional study in which he has engaged, and find out which has been especially helpful. Try to formulate a plan for professional study which may be appropriate for yourself as a beginning teacher.

Things for You To Do

It is not easy to suggest specific things which will help you participate effectively in the professional activities of a teacher. These activities usually extend over a much longer period of time than your student-teaching period. However, you can observe some of these activities and gain a few ideas about them to help you as a beginning teacher. The following activities are suggested:

1. If it is permissible, attend the meetings of the local teachers' association during the time that you are doing student teaching. Observe such things as these: (1) how many teachers belong, (2) whether it is affiliated with a state or national organization, (3) whether there is more than one local organization, (4) what the dues are, (5) whether administrators and supervisors belong, (6) how frequently the local association meets, (7) how much of the time is devoted to teacher-welfare problems, and (8) the nature of professional improvement activities. A conference with the president or another officer of the association will help you answer these questions.

2. Some state and national organizations have student memberships at nominal dues. Consult your cooperating teacher and college supervisor about these organizations, and join some of them. As a student member, you will probably receive the monthly publications, be able to attend meetings, and have the privilege of purchasing bulletins and pamphlets at members' rates.

3. Attend meetings of the state organizations that may be of interest to you. If you are not a student member, you can probably go as a guest of one of the teachers.

4. If a building publicity program or some other publicity campaign is being carried on by the schools, study all the literature that has been prepared for that purpose, attend some of the citizens' meetings when this program is discussed, and in other ways inform yourself concerning the manner in which such a program of publicity is carried on and the part that teachers have in it.

5. If the teachers have a professional library in the school, visit it and examine the materials that are available there. Consult the librarian to obtain information as follows: (1) where funds are obtained to purchase professional library materials, (2) what contribution teachers make to it, (3) how materials are circulated, (4) how extensively the library is used by teachers, and (5) what materials are available in your field.

6. Through discussions with various teachers in the school, get all the ideas that you can concerning professional improvement through in-service study as a basis for preparing an in-service improvement plan of your own. Get their ideas concerning the professional value of (1) extension and summer courses, (2) workshops and study groups, (3) travel, and (4) attendance at professional meetings.

7. Ask your cooperating teacher about special activities to encourage parent visits, particularly for American Education Week, a parents' night, or some other activity. Find out such things as the following: (1) the over-all plans for this activity, (2) how parents are invited, (3) how many parents come, (4) what is done to help parents understand the program of the school, and (5) the responsibility the individual teacher has for entertaining the parents.

In Summary

In this chapter, a brief overview has been given of the administrative and professional responsibilities of teachers. How many of these activities you may observe and participate in as a student teacher will depend largely upon the length of time that you spend in the cooperating school. In any case, observe as many of these activities as possible, and gain as much experience as you can through actual participation. Be sure to make ample provision for such activities in your over-all student-teaching plan.

Chapter 12

KNOW THE COMMUNITY

Education in a Community Setting

In recent years, educators have emphasized the importance of developing an educational program in terms of the setting of the community. Even a moment's reflection substantiates the desirability of that approach. For instance, the school is not alone in providing educational experiences for the child. It is assisted by many community agencies through which the child has a variety of worth-while and significant experiences. It is important, therefore, that you should be informed about the community and the cultural, educational, and recreational opportunities which it provides for secondary school youth.

We should also remember that the citizens of the community support the schools, and that it is their children who attend. Therefore, it is the parents and citizens who ultimately decide the type of schools that the community should have. This means that it is important for the administration and the teachers to keep closely in touch with the thinking of the citizens in the community. In most communities, the administration takes the leadership in establishing the school-community contacts; but because the teacher is the key person in the instructional program, he should also be informed concerning the thinking and attitudes of parents and citizens on matters of education.

Living in the Community

If the teacher is to have an adequate understanding of the community, he should make his residence there. In other professions, this suggestion would hardly have to be made. But there has been a tendency for teachers to make their permanent homes in one community while they teach in another. This has been encouraged by the fact that teachers have a long vacation when they may return to their home community and live with parents or other relatives. Teachers, therefore, have the reputation in some communities of being a transient professional group. In some small communities, this situation has become sufficiently serious so that the boards of education have made regulations requiring teachers to remain in the community on week ends a certain number of times during the month. Obviously, such regulations are a reflection on the good taste and judgment of members of the teaching profession. We should do everything in our power to see that they are not necessary.

Furthermore, it seems only reasonable to believe that any person who is enthusiastic about helping the boys and girls in a community should be sufficiently interested to live there. He should transfer his membership in community organizations such as churches, service clubs, lodges, and similar groups. Whether he is there for one year or for twenty, he should enter enthusiastically into the civic, religious, cultural, and professional life of the community. The teacher will be happier and more successful if the community in which he teaches becomes his home.

Schools Contribute to Community Life

Not only should the teacher as an individual contribute to the life of his community, but the activities of the school as a whole should also make such a contribution. For instance, such school organizations as the band, the orchestra, the glee clubs and chorus groups, the dramatics club, and other pupil groups should make their services available to such community organizations as the service clubs, churches, and women's clubs. Then, too, school organizations may participate in special community events, such as fairs, parades, and holiday activities. Such participation provides splendid educational experiences for the pupils, at the same time that it contributes to the cultural and recreational life of the community.

The activities of the school frequently are a center of cultural and recreational activities for the community. For instance, the athletic contests, music concerts, speech programs, and dramatics productions provide splendid cultural and recreational opportunities. Certain physical facilities of the school, such as the auditorium, the athletic fields, art rooms, shops, and homemaking laboratories may be used by community groups. In ways such as these, the school may serve as a recreational and cultural center for both youth and adult groups in the community.

Youth-Serving Agencies

Whereas the school makes a contribution to the life of the community, there are certain agencies in the community which make a contribution to the program of the school. Usually, these contributions are made on a cooperative basis with the school authorities and representatives of the agencies planning activities together. The youth-serving agencies which most often cooperate with the school are the Boy and Girl Scouts, the YMCA and YWCA, the 4-H Clubs, and recreational activities sponsored by the local government or by a civic group. Then, too, some churches have youth-serving organizations which contribute to the educational as well as the spiritual growth of their members.

Sometimes the sponsors of these groups prefer to work co-operatively with the schools.

The cooperation between the schools and these agencies takes various forms. Faculty members may be requested to serve on the committees for such groups, as the group leaders or as advisors. Then, too, these agencies sometimes use school facilities for their meetings and other activities. Occasionally, some organizations become a part of the extra-class program of the school. That is sometimes true of 4-H Clubs, Boy Scouts, Girl Scouts, Hi-Y, and Girl Reserves. Whatever the form this cooperation may take, it is important that teachers recognize the educational and cultural advantages which these organizations provide for secondary school youth. Teachers should use the interest of youth in these organizations as a basis for oral and written activities in school; they should be considerate of the out-of-school time which pupils spend with these groups; and they should help the leaders of these groups locate pupils who may profit from participation. As a student teacher, you should become familiar with the youth-serving organizations in your community and with the cooperation that exists between the school and these groups.

Making a Community Survey

In some schools, teachers and administrators have made a survey to gain a better understanding of those aspects of the history and life of the community which may have a bearing on the program of the school. Such a survey serves several purposes: (1) it gives teachers background for developing learning activities that are related to the life of the community, (2) it serves as a basis for developing a curriculum designed to meet community needs, and (3) it gives teachers, especially those who come from elsewhere, a better appreciation of the community in which they work. Where community surveys have been made, they usually cover information such as the following:

1. History: When the community was settled; significant events in its development; and how its development contributed to that of the State and the Nation.
2. People: Its population; past growth and prospects for future growth; cultural, nationality, and racial origins; and present educational and cultural levels.
3. Education: Public school facilities; private school facilities; opportunities for vocational education; and opportunities for higher education.
4. Business and Industry: Predominant industries; shopping facilities; wage and salary levels; and opportunities for employment of youth, both while they are attending school and after leaving school.
5. Government: Type of local government; how local government developed; political parties which predominate; and names of government leaders.
6. Health and Hospital Facilities: Hospital and medical services available; health problems.
7. Churches and Religious Agencies: Denominations which have churches; and youth organizations affiliated with churches.
8. Youth-Serving Agencies: What organizations are available; facilities provided by various agencies; and numbers of youth participating.
9. Recreation: Recreational opportunities for adults; and recreational opportunities for youth.
10. Cultural Opportunities: Libraries and museums; music organizations; lecture and concert series; and miscellaneous cultural opportunities.
11. Civic and Service Organizations: Service clubs; fraternal organizations; and civic and service agencies.

The procedures employed in a community survey are determined largely by the thoroughness with which it is to be made and the availability of information from various agencies. Obviously, the more complete the information, the more valuable such a survey can be for developing a school program. Sometimes civic and service groups in the city are sufficiently interested in a community survey to assist with it. Their support, if not their active participation, is essential to its success.

A comprehensive community survey is such a tremendous undertaking that you, as a student teacher, could not engage in it alone. If a survey is made by the school system while you are there, you are urged to participate in it. This should give you a better appreciation of your cooperating community, as well as valuable experience in the procedure of making such a survey.

In any case, you should make some study of the community where you are student teaching. If there are several student teachers from your college, you may work together as a group on a community survey. If you are alone, such a survey must be very limited. It is suggested that you prepare an outline of information about the community, similar to that presented above, and that you consult the superintendent's office, the library, the city officials, the Chamber of Commerce, and similar agencies for that information. Make your community study as thorough and extensive as your time and the available facilities permit.

Educational Resources of the Community

Types of Community Resources

In an earlier chapter, it was suggested that every community has certain resources which may be used by teachers of social studies, English, science, industrial arts, homemaking, and other subjects. These resources include industrial firms, historical and cultural agencies, business firms, health institutions, libraries, museums, and government groups. Teachers of social studies, for instance, may use such agencies as the police and fire departments, the local courts, historical groups, and certain industrial and labor organizations. Some of these agencies have pamphlets, film strips, movies, and other materials which are of value to the social studies program. Then, too, they provide opportunities for field trips and visits by class groups or pupil committees which are seeking information and ideas for units being studied. Similar examples may be found for science, industrial arts, and homemaking. In fact, for every subject in the curriculum there are likely to be some resources in the community which may be used for teaching purposes.

Then, too, in most communities there are people with special talents and backgrounds who can make a contribution to the instructional program of the school. These include government officials, professional people, labor and industrial leaders, business representatives, lecturers, musicians, travelers, and a host of others. Teachers and pupils frequently invite such persons to lecture to class groups, to address assemblies, or to be available for interviews by pupils who are seeking information on problems which they are studying. In this chapter some suggestions will be given for locating human and material resources in the community which may be useful for teaching purposes.

Locating Community Resources

In some school systems, so much importance is attached to the use of community resources for instructional purposes that a detailed classified list of such resources has been prepared. This list is usually the result of a survey which has been made by the faculty or other persons employed for that purpose. This type of survey is different from the community survey discussed earlier in this chapter, though the two may well be carried on together. Whereas the community survey previously mentioned is designed primarily to gain information as a basis for developing a more effective curriculum, the survey discussed in this section is made to locate specific agencies, persons, and materials that may be used as teaching aids in the various subjects.

If a list of community resources has already been prepared for your subject, you should of course make use of it in planning and carrying on your learning activities. In most schools such a list is not likely to be available. In so far as time permits, you should prepare such a list of resources for your subject, classified according to the units or topics which your subject covers. The following are suggested sources of help in preparing a list of persons, agencies, and materials available in your community:

1. Persons in the cooperating school, such as the librarian, the teachers, the principal, and the director of audio-visual aids.
2. The telephone directory, especially the classified section.
3. The business directory, if one is available for your community.
4. The Chamber of Commerce or a similar organization representing business and industrial interests.
5. Municipal officials or their assistants.

A Survey of Community Resources

Making a comprehensive survey of resources in the community which may contribute to the instructional program is such a tremendous task that you could hardly undertake it alone. It would need the cooperation of the principal, the teachers, and various agencies in the community. It is entirely possible, however, that you may take an active part in such a survey, if one is made while you are student teaching. In fact, if there are several student teachers from your college in your cooperating school, as a group you could make a large contribution to such a survey. The following are suggestions for making a survey of the human and material resources in your community which may be used in school:

1. The survey should be made by subject areas, because the resources may be different for each subject. Since there are community agencies which may contribute to several subjects, there is some advantage in having teachers from related subjects cooperate in such a survey.

2. The cooperation of various members of the staff should be obtained to plan and carry on the survey, including the principal, the librarian, the director of audio-visual aids, the director of guidance, and the nurse.

3. A plan for classifying the resources needs to be determined, such as the subjects to be covered and the topics within subjects to be included in the list.

4. A list needs to be prepared of the business and industrial firms, the civic agencies, the educational institutions, and the persons to be contacted in the community. Business directories, telephone directories, municipal officials, and others may be helpful in preparing that list.

5. The procedure for gathering the information should be developed, including (1) questionnaires to be sent out, (2) correspondence to be carried on, and (3) personal calls to be made.

6. The cooperation of the community needs to be solicited through the newspapers, service organizations, and personal contact.

It becomes obvious that such a survey, thoroughly done, demands much time and may incur considerable expense. For that reason it should preferably be developed and carried on by the faculty of the school. A group of student teachers working together, however, could be of much help in organizing and making such a survey. Its value to you may well justify the time you may devote to it.

Things for You To Do

Since you are likely to remain in the cooperating community for only a short time, it may not be possible for you to make a thorough community survey or a detailed list of resources available for teaching purposes. It is more important that you learn some of the procedures which teachers use to become acquainted with their community, how they participate in the life of the community, and ways of locating community resources for teaching purposes. The following activities are suggested with those purposes in mind:

1. Attend one or more meetings of a service club and other adult groups in the community with one of the cooperating teachers.
2. Attend regularly the church of your choice during the time that you are doing student teaching.
3. If your church has a Sunday school, work with one of the Sunday school classes or some other church youth group as a cosponsor during your student-teaching period.
4. Make a list of all the youth-serving agencies in the community, such as the Boy Scouts, the Girl Scouts, the YMCA, and the YWCA, summarizing such information as the following for each: (1) the purpose of the organization, (2) the youth group which the organization serves, (3) the number of youth served by the organization, (4) the type of activities in which it engages, and (5) how the school and the organization cooperate in serving youth.
5. Serve as an assistant leader for a Girl Scout troop, a Boy Scout troop, or some other youth organization in the community for the time that you are doing student teaching. If you do student teaching in your college community, this participation might well be carried on for a longer period of time.
6. Through conferences with the cooperating teacher and other members of the staff, find out to what extent and in what way they use various human and material resources for instructional purposes.
7. Make a list of all the industrial, business, civic, and other agencies in the community that might make a contribution to the subject you are planning to teach. Classify this list according to the units or topics included in the

courses you teach, or in some other appropriate way. For each agency, find out whether pamphlets, films, film strips, recordings, or other materials of educational value are available.

8. Try to find out the policy of the school with respect to the use of community resources in the instructional program of the school. For instance, inform yourself about (1) the policy concerning field trips, (2) expenses of speakers who are invited to the school, (3) how arrangements should be made with community agencies for field trips, films, and pamphlets, and (4) arrangements for sending pupils to study various agencies or to interview individuals on problems being studied in school.

9. As a part of a unit you are teaching, use some community resources as a basis for the learning activities. This should be done with the approval and help of the cooperating teacher.

In Summary

Educators today believe that the instructional program of the school should extend into the community which the school serves. Furthermore, they are aware that the development of an effective school program demands the participation and support of parents and other citizens. It is, therefore, important that you as a teacher do everything you can to strengthen the program of the school by developing a close relationship with various community agencies. As a student teacher, you should gain experience in a cooperative school-community approach to the education of secondary school youth.

Chapter 13

YOUR PROFESSIONAL
RELATIONSHIPS

Relations with Faculty and Staff

You Are a Teacher

A teacher's effectiveness in a school and a community depends in large part upon his relationships with other staff members, with pupils, and with citizens. If he works well with other teachers, is sympathetic towards his pupils, and is tactful with parents and citizens, he will be more effective in his professional activities both in the school and the community. As a student teacher, you will have many contacts with teachers and pupils, and you may occasionally meet parents and citizens. You should give some thought to your relationships with these persons, so that those relationships may be appropriate, effective, and in good taste.

Because they are college students, student teachers sometimes find it difficult to think of themselves as mature, professional individuals. As a result, their attitudes and conduct may not be those which are appropriate for teachers. It is important that you consider yourself not a student, but a teacher, one who is mature, professional, and tactful in his relations with others and in his conduct in the school and the community.

The Principal Is Head of the School

The student teacher should recognize that the principal is the official head of the school. It is he who represents the superintendent and the board of education in conducting the educational program in the school so that it is in harmony with the policies and regulations which they have adopted. He is also responsible for the work of student teachers in his school. He is usually the one who makes the arrangements for student teachers with members of his staff, supervises the preparation of schedules for student teachers, and advises cooperating teachers concerning their work with student teachers. He also keeps in touch with the superintendent concerning the student teaching program and implements the policies of the board of education as they affect student teachers. Consequently, he may show a keen interest in your activities as a student teacher.

When you first come to the cooperating school, it is appropriate that you report to the principal. This is advisable even though you know your schedule and who your cooperating teachers are to be. In effect, your position is similar to that of any new teacher who is placed on the staff. In this initial visit with the principal, you should clarify your relations with him for your student teaching period. Find out whether he would like to have you report to him occasionally for conferences or suggestions. Furthermore, let him know that you appreciate the opportunity to serve as a member of his staff and to gain experience in his school.

When you complete your student teaching work, you should again visit with the principal before you leave. Ask him to evaluate your work in classes and about the school, in so far as he has been able to observe it. Let him know that you appreciate the courtesies that have been extended to you by members of the staff while you were in school.

The Superintendent and Board of Education

In some school systems, student teachers are asked to report to the superintendent's office. That may be true especially in small school systems, because there the superintendent may take a more direct interest in your work as a student teacher. In large school systems, he usually delegates this responsibility to an assistant superintendent or to the principal. You should realize that the superintendent is responsible to the board of education for every activity in the school system, including the work of student teachers. He may, therefore, show a keen interest in your activities and success as a student teacher.

In some schools, the superintendent or the principal has meetings with student teachers to discuss their responsibilities, their relation to the program of the school, and other matters that bear on their success. You should welcome the opportunity to attend such meetings. Furthermore, such meetings should be accepted as part of your professional responsibilities, much like the meetings which faculty members are requested to attend. Remember that the superintendent or the principal is giving his time to help you improve professionally through these meetings. Be prompt, show a sincere interest in the discussions, and do your best to follow any suggestions that are given.

It is not likely that you will have direct contact with members of the board of education. You should know, however, that, if student teaching is being done in the schools, the board of education must have considered the matter and given its approval. They are likely to continue such approval only so long as their experience with student teachers is a satisfactory one. Conscientious work and cooperation on your part should contribute to such a satisfactory situation.

In some communities, the board of education has developed a careful statement of policies and regulations for student teachers. These are usually based on experiences with student teaching activities in the past. Although some of the regulations and policies may be inconvenient for you, you should recognize that they have been formulated in the best interests of the pupils and the student teaching program. Observe them as carefully as you can.

Observe Personnel Policies

Every school system has a statement of personnel policies which are to be observed by teachers and other staff members. As a student teacher, some of these personnel policies will apply to you. Inform yourself about them by studying the teachers' handbook and through conferences with the cooperating principal and teacher.

Since teacher personnel policies cover a wide variety of matters, it is impossible to mention all of them here. The following are a few questions you should raise about personnel policies and regulations that may affect you:

1. What hours is a teacher expected to be in school?
2. How should a teacher report to the principal, assistant principal, or office secretary in case of absence?
3. How should the teacher report if he is taken ill during the school day and finds it necessary to go home?
4. What is the policy concerning smoking by teachers in the school building and on the school grounds?
5. What is the policy with respect to keeping pupils after school for extra work or punishment?
6. What arrangements may teachers make to work in the building in the evening, on Saturdays, or on holidays?
7. What are the regulations with respect to parking cars by teachers around the school building and on the school grounds?

In small school systems, personnel policies and regulations may not be in printed or mimeographed form. In large school systems, however, they are usually in such form that you may obtain a copy. Request such a copy from the superintendent, the principal, or the cooperating teacher.

School Matters Are Confidential

In earlier chapters, it has already been suggested that problems discussed in faculty meetings and information about individual pupils should not be mentioned away from school, especially in the presence of persons not on the school staff. This suggestion applies also to other school affairs that concern your class work, student activities, or individual teachers. Particularly in a small community, citizens may be interested in any detail regarding the activities of the school. It is best not to discuss outside the school any matters or problems concerned with the program of the school.

Respecting a Teacher's Confidence

It is best not to discuss with any other teacher the conversations that you have with your cooperating teacher, the methods that the cooperating teacher uses, or anything else that transpires in your room when the cooperating teacher has charge. There is the danger that you may discuss some of the unusual things that happen in your classes, such as a problem with a pupil, an unusual approach to teaching, or some classroom incident. Because of your close working relations with him, the cooperating teacher may discuss confidential matters with you. The cooperating teacher should have every reason to assume that you will not discuss elsewhere your observation of his classes or your conversations with him.

Teachers Are Human

Since teachers are human, you may expect some frictions and disagreements among them. There may be petty jealousies, disagreement about departmental and school policy, and friction over the use of classrooms or equipment. Then, too, occasionally factions develop among teachers in some schools. For instance, one student teacher under the supervision of the writer did her work in a school where the faculty was divided into two factions, and those in one group did not sit with the others in the faculty lunchroom. This student teacher soon realized that if she had lunch with one group, she would not be accepted by the other.

Where personal disagreements between teachers exist or where there are factions in a school, it demands all the tact you can muster to avoid becoming involved. Do your best to be friendly with all teachers, without attaching yourself to any one group. If you do this, your stay in the school will be more pleasant and your work more effective.

Your Relations with Custodians

It is to the advantage of every teacher to have the friendship and cooperation of the custodian. This is not always easy to achieve. In order to do so, you should do everything you can to show him consideration in your requests for help and to take care of your room and equipment so that it will not cause him unnecessary work. The teacher who is a good housekeeper in his classroom is most likely to get along well with the custodian.

In some schools there is a definite policy concerning the way in which requests and orders may be given to the custodian. Usually, it is the principal, the assistant principal, or some other administrative person who supervises the school building as a whole, and consequently makes the contacts for the professional staff with the custodians. Where that is the policy, teachers may be expected to send to that person any requests for help from the custodian. For instance, the teacher of physical education may want the custodian to lay out a soccer field for a certain day; the teacher of English may want furniture for a skit or dramatization; or the teacher of homemaking may need chairs for a mothers' tea. Since such requests may take a considerable amount of the custodian's time, they should be made in sufficient time so he can plan his other work accordingly. Study the policy of the school on relations of the professional staff to the custodians, and observe that policy carefully.

Things for You To Do

The following are some things which you can do to inform yourself concerning the best way of establishing satisfactory relationships with the faculty and other members of the staff:

1. Study any mimeographed or printed statement of personnel policies which may be available in the principal's office or from the cooperating teacher, giving particular attention to those which concern you as a student teacher. If a copy is available, retain it as a basis for conferences with other student teachers.

2. Have a conference with the principal, the assistant principal, or some other administrative or supervisory person, concerning the relationships between the professional staff and the custodians, secretaries, clerks, and other persons with whom you may have contact. Have them suggest some of the problems that they have encountered in teacher-staff relationships. Make a summary of the suggestions and retain them for use as a beginning teacher.

3. Have a conference with the cooperating teacher concerning staff relationships, asking him for suggestions about relationships with the custodian, the cafeteria staff, the clerical and stenographic staff in the office, and members of the professional staff.

4. Have a visit with one of the custodians, asking him to tell you how he would like to have a beginning teacher cooperate in taking care of his classroom, equipment and

supplies, and other matters that concern the custodian's work.

5. Find out what the policy is with respect to issuing building and room keys to teachers, what teachers are expected to do about locking rooms, and where the teacher should keep her purse and other valuables.

Relations with Pupils

Be Friendly, Not Chummy

You need to make some definite decisions concerning your relationships with pupils early in your student teaching experience. Because they know you are a college student, they may be inclined to treat you as one of their own group. You should welcome a friendly relationship with pupils, but do not let them become too chummy. In the early stages, an attitude that is too familiar may express itself in several ways. For instance, some pupils may want you to eat with them regularly in the cafeteria; they may go out of their way to walk down the corridor with you; or they may wait for you after school to walk home. If this happens only once or twice, you need not be concerned about it. But if the same pupils wait for you day after day, it might be well for you to find some way of discouraging it. If they wait for you after school, make it a point to leave the building with one of the teachers. Similarly, find an excuse to have lunch with other teachers rather than with pupils. Be careful not to offend the pupils, but let them know that you are associating yourself primarily with members of the teaching staff.

Be Careful in Your Conversation

In visiting with pupils, exercise every care to avoid discussing inappropriate matters. They may want to discuss their teachers, other pupils, school policies, or school affairs. For instance, one student teacher found that several pupils went out of their way to tell her how much they preferred her to the cooperating teacher. In another case, the pupils were exceedingly critical to the student teacher of the teaching methods used by the cooperating teacher. Let them know immediately that it would be best not to discuss such matters with you.

Then, too, there is the danger that you may unintentionally discuss the work or problems of one pupil with another. For instance, you may drop a remark about difficulty that some pupil is having with his work; you may betray the mark that another pupil has received; or you may let some pupils see the papers of other members of the group. Sometimes beginning teachers have pupils help correct papers, with the result that they know the marks other pupils have received. You should regard the marks and the school problems of any individual pupil as a confidential matter to be discussed with no one except the pupil or his parents. Do not leave test papers, pupil projects, and pupil records where they might be examined by someone other than the owner. You may not do these things intentionally, but they may easily happen through an oversight on your part.

Observe Good Taste

Some student teachers and beginning teachers fail to show good taste in their conduct around pupils, particularly after school hours and away from the school building. Although some of the suggestions that are given here may seem a bit extreme, they are all based on errors of judgment that have been made by student teachers under the supervision of the author. The following are some things that you should avoid:

1. Avoid using language that is inappropriate in the presence of secondary school pupils.
2. In general, avoid smoking in the presence of pupils.

3. Try to avoid pupil "hang-outs," such as sports centers, drug stores, and other places, where your pupils gather outside school hours.
4. Perhaps it is needless to say that you should not "date" high school pupils.
5. Discourage pupils from calling on you at your home or the place where you are staying. If they do call, find some way of excusing yourself after they have made a brief visit. The author is reminded of one case where an attractive young woman student teacher had three of her high school pupils call on her one Saturday evening at her home. Fortunately, she had an engagement with another friend, and so after a short visit with the boys, excused herself. If incidents like this are diplomatically handled, you need not offend the pupils and at the same time may discourage further visits.

Things for You To Do

The following things may help you get a better understanding of the relationships that you may have with pupils:

1. Discuss with your college supervisor some of the problems that arise between the student teacher and his pupils, based on his experience with student teachers. This may be the subject for a group conference between the supervisor and student teachers.
2. Discuss with the cooperating teacher, the school counselor or some other professional staff member, some of the problems which they believe you may encounter as you establish appropriate relationships with the pupils.

The Place Where You Live

In an earlier chapter, it was suggested that the choice of a place to live has a direct bearing on your happiness and success in student teaching. It is also an influence on the friends you make and on your relations with parents and other citizens. Your landlady can be exceedingly helpful, for instance, in helping you meet desirable young people as well as parents. In a small community, choose a home where the people are respected and have good relations with their neighbors. In a large city, find a room in a desirable section.

Be careful about discussing school matters with your landlord or your landlady. You will find that your out-of-school time will be spent much more pleasantly if you try to get away entirely from discussing school problems. Furthermore, the landlady, who is your best friend today, may not be that tomorrow. It may be unfortunate if you should take her too much into your confidence. Once you start doing so, it is almost impossible to stop. From the very beginning, therefore, make it your policy not to discuss school matters at all with the people where you stay.

Choose Friends Carefully

Even though you live in a community only during the period of your student teaching, you will want to make some friends. Exercise care so that you may not form friendships too hastily. You may find some good friends among members of the teaching staff. Outside the school, you may also meet splendid young people through your church or a youth organization. Avoid associating yourself with any particular group until you are sufficiently well acquainted to know that these contacts are desirable.

It may seem that we are belaboring too much the importance of avoiding the discussion of school affairs with people in the community. This is such a serious matter, however, that it cannot be overemphasized. If you are doing student teaching in your home community, for instance, there is always the danger that some friend of your family or a neighbor will question you about teachers, pupils other than his own children, and school policies and affairs. If you mention school matters even to members of your own family, they may inadvertently discuss them with friends and neighbors. It is doubtful that any student teacher ever intentionally gossips about school matters in the community, but whether it is unintentional or not, the damage to the program of the school and to your position in it is the same.

In Summary

It may be that certain parts of this chapter have sounded a bit like sermonizing. That was not the intention. The suggestions given here are based on the experiences which the author has had with student teachers over a period of years. Your relations with the faculty, other staff members, pupils, and citizens have a decided bearing on your effectiveness as a student teacher. You should exercise care and good judgment in establishing these relationships.

PART V

After Student Teaching

Chapter 14

HOW WELL DID YOU DO?

Self-Evaluation of Your Work

Evaluation Leads to Growth

In order to grow professionally as a teacher, it is important that you continually ask yourself questions such as these: How well have I done? In what respects has my work been particularly good? What weaknesses are there in my work? What might I do to improve? Through such a continuous analysis of your work, you may be able to improve the effectiveness of your professional activities.

Some evaluation of your work should be made by others, such as the cooperating teacher and the college supervisor. But much of it needs to be done by you, yourself. It is important that you get into the habit of doing continuous self-evaluation because that is the way that you will make much of your growth as a teacher later on.

Evaluate Day by Day

If you are to make continuous growth in your professional activities, you should evaluate the success of every learning situation for which you have any responsibility. This should include every daily lesson in the classroom, every activity in the home room, in clubs, assemblies, and elsewhere, and any other teaching or professional responsibility you may have as a student teacher. In other words, you should evaluate your professional activities day by day if you are to make continuous improvement.

It is impossible to suggest one plan for evaluating your work which will be applicable to the classroom, the home room, and extraclass activities alike. Your evaluation will be more effective if you have a procedure suited to each activity in which you engage. For each activity, it is suggested that you develop a statement which may serve as a guide for your self-evaluation. For instance, you should have a guide for evaluating the effectiveness of your daily class activities, home room activities, club meetings, and other similar teaching responsibilities.

As an example of such an evaluation guide, the following questions are suggested for evaluating a learning situation in your subject at the close of a class period:

1. Were there clear-cut objectives for the learning activities during the period?
2. Were the objectives understood and accepted by the pupils?
3. Were the activities the most appropriate ones for achieving the objectives?
4. Did the learning activities grow out of work that had previously been covered?
5. Was there enthusiastic participation by pupils in planning and carrying on the learning activities?
6. Were study aids and materials effectively used?
7. Were study aids and materials available to meet the interests, needs, and abilities of all the pupils?
8. Were all pupils able to understand and participate in the learning activities without undue difficulty?
9. Was participation distributed reasonably well among all pupils?
10. Were the needs of all individual pupils apparently met satisfactorily?
11. Was the time devoted to the learning activities used in the most efficient manner?

12. Were the objectives apparently achieved by all pupils?
13. Were the learning activities effectively summarized at the end in terms of the objectives?
14. Was there a clear relationship between these learning activities and those that are to follow?
15. Was there a satisfactory working relationship among pupils and between pupils and teacher?
16. Were matters of routine effectively administered—such as ventilation, light, the neatness of the room, the checking of attendance, the arrangement of furniture, and the distribution and collection of study materials?
17. What was the strongest aspect of the learning activities?
18. What aspect of the learning activities was most in need of improvement?
19. What suggestions would you have for engaging in similar learning activities more effectively in the future?

Evaluate Every Unit

The previous paragraph gave suggestions for the evaluation of learning activities on a day-by-day basis. In many subjects, you will use the unit approach to planning and teaching. It should be helpful to make some systematic evaluation of your work at the close of a unit. The questions you may ask yourself resemble those suggested above for more specific learning activities, but there may also be other questions that you should raise concerning the effectiveness of unit teaching:

1. Were you adequately prepared when the unit was first presented to the class, on such aspects of the unit as subject matter, learning materials, possible activities, and the general approach?
2. Was the unit initially introduced to pupils so as to encourage their interest and cooperation?
3. Was there sufficient participation by pupils in developing the plan for the unit?
4. Was there a clear relationship between the objectives

of the unit and the learning activities carried on during the unit?

5. Was there a sufficient variety of references and learning materials to meet the needs, interests, and abilities of all pupils?

6. Was there a sufficient variety of activities to satisfy the interests, needs, and abilities of all pupils?

7. Were the activities in the unit apparently related to the life experiences and needs of the pupils?

8. Were the activities and the subject matter of the unit sufficiently broad to extend into or be correlated with other subject areas?

9. Was there sufficient pupil participation in planning the various activities throughout the unit?

10. Were the pupils sufficiently prominent in directing and carrying on the various learning activities of the unit?

11. Were the skills and subject matter included in the unit developed in such a way that they became functional for the pupils?

12. Was sufficient use made of human and material resources available in the community on the subject and problems covered in the unit?

13. Was pupil interest apparently maintained at a high level throughout the unit?

14. Was effective use made of display boards, blackboards, tables, and similar classroom facilities throughout the unit?

15. Was there a sufficient number of cooperative group activities involving small numbers of pupils as well as the entire class?

16. Was sufficient attention given to spelling, vocabulary, and similar skills growing out of the unit?

17. Was there an effective culminating or summarizing activity for the entire unit?

18. Were tests and other evaluation instruments developed in terms of the unit objectives and were they used effectively throughout the unit?

19. Were the objectives of the unit apparently achieved by all the pupils?
20. What was the strongest aspect of the unit as it developed?
21. What aspect of the unit was most in need of improvement?
22. What specific suggestions would you have for planning and teaching a similar unit more effectively in the future?

Evaluation at the End of Student Teaching

It is important that you make a thorough and comprehensive evaluation of your total student teaching experiences at the end of the student teaching period. It is suggested that you make your own evaluation before you receive a summary evaluation from the cooperating teacher or the college supervisor. If your college has an evaluation form for this purpose, it is best for you to use that form. If such a form is not provided, the one presented here may be helpful.

The evaluation form on the next page may serve as a guide in the self-evaluation of your total student teaching experience. You may answer the questions in general terms or, if you wish, indicate a more precise estimate of your work on the rating scale. In using the evaluation form, recognize that the analysis of your work is of more importance than the accuracy of the rating which you indicate on the scale. This self-evaluation may serve as a basis for discussions with your cooperating teacher and college supervisor concerning the effectiveness of your work.

Evaluation by Others

Evaluation by Pupils

One of the most revealing ways of evaluating your effectiveness as a student teacher is to obtain the reaction of pupils concerning your work. They should have a point of view which is entirely different from that of the college supervisor or the cooperating teacher. Furthermore, since the effectiveness of your work with pupils is one measure of your success, it seems important that you obtain an evaluation from them.

Self-Evaluation of Your Student Teaching

DIRECTIONS: Place a check at the appropriate place on the scale. A check at the extreme left should indicate that your work was as effective as could reasonably be expected of a student teacher.

1. **Professional Relationships:** How effective were you in your relationships with the cooperating principal, teacher, and other staff members?

HIGHLY EFFECTIVE   FAIRLY EFFECTIVE   NOT EFFECTIVE

2. **Planning for Instruction:** How effective were you in preparing instructional plans and in developing plans cooperatively with pupils as a basis for learning activities in your subject?

HIGHLY EFFECTIVE   FAIRLY EFFECTIVE   NOT EFFECTIVE

3. **Learning Activities:** How effective were you in developing and carrying on class, small group, and individual learning activities to achieve the recognized learning objectives for your subject?

HIGHLY EFFECTIVE   FAIRLY EFFECTIVE   NOT EFFECTIVE

4. **Materials of Instruction:** How effective were you in locating and using textbooks, library materials, pamphlets, audio-visual materials, community resources, and other materials as an aid to the learning of pupils?

HIGHLY EFFECTIVE   FAIRLY EFFECTIVE   NOT EFFECTIVE

5. **Meeting Pupil Needs:** How effective were you in becoming acquainted with the characteristics of individual pupils, and in meeting their needs, abilities, and interests in your classes, the home room, and elsewhere in the school program?

HIGHLY EFFECTIVE   FAIRLY EFFECTIVE   NOT EFFECTIVE

6. **Evaluation of Pupil Progress:** How effective were you in evaluating the progress of your pupils toward recognized objectives, in assisting pupils with self-evaluation of their own progress, and in reporting pupil progress to the pupils and their parents?

HIGHLY EFFECTIVE   FAIRLY EFFECTIVE   NOT EFFECTIVE

7. **Administration of Classes and Home Room:** How effective were you in discharging administrative responsibilities, such as keeping records, preparing reports, caring for materials and equipment, and regulating heat, light and ventilation in your classes and home room?

HIGHLY EFFECTIVE   FAIRLY EFFECTIVE   NOT EFFECTIVE

8. **Responsibilities for Home Room and Extraclass Activities:** How effective were you in working with pupils in the home room, clubs, assemblies, and other extraclass activities?

HIGHLY EFFECTIVE   FAIRLY EFFECTIVE   NOT EFFECTIVE

9. **Relationships With Pupils:** How effective were you in developing friendly, understanding, and sympathetic relationships with your pupils in the home room, classes, and extraclass activities?

HIGHLY EFFECTIVE   FAIRLY EFFECTIVE   NOT EFFECTIVE

10. **Leadership in Home Room and Classes:** How effective were you in maintaining a sufficiently strong position of leadership in your home room and classes to maintain cooperation, courtesy, and order among pupils?

HIGHLY EFFECTIVE   FAIRLY EFFECTIVE   NOT EFFECTIVE

11. **Guidance of Pupils:** How effective were you in assisting pupils with decisions and adjustments in personal, educational, vocational, and citizenship problems?

HIGHLY EFFECTIVE   FAIRLY EFFECTIVE   NOT EFFECTIVE

12. **School-Home Relationships:** How effective were you in assisting with the PTA, conferences with parents, and other school-home relationships?

HIGHLY EFFECTIVE   FAIRLY EFFECTIVE   NOT EFFECTIVE

13. **School-Community Relationships:** How effective were you in attending and participating in adult organizations, in assisting with youth groups, and in becoming a part of the community?

HIGHLY EFFECTIVE   FAIRLY EFFECTIVE   NOT EFFECTIVE

14. **Professional Improvement:** How effective were you in participating in faculty meetings, study groups, teachers' organizations, and other activities to help teachers grow in their professional vision and skill?

HIGHLY EFFECTIVE   FAIRLY EFFECTIVE   NOT EFFECTIVE

The evaluation from pupils might be obtained in several ways. One way is to have individual conferences with three or four pupils near the close of your student teaching period. These pupils should be chosen in terms of the discrimination with which they may analyze your success as a student teacher. Such a conference should be private and under conditions that will encourage a frank discussion. You should inform the pupil concerning the reason for the conference, and suggest to him that his comments may be helpful in your future work as a teacher. In the conference, you should emphasize things that will help you improve your effectiveness as a teacher.

As a basis for such a conference, have certain questions in mind that you want to raise. These questions might be similar to those suggested previously in this chapter for self-evaluation of your work. For instance, you might raise such questions as the following with the pupils:

1. Were the purposes of the work from day to day sufficiently clear so that the pupils understood the reasons for the learning activities in which they engaged?
2. Was the work sufficiently well organized so that it was readily understood and easily followed by the pupils?
3. Was the work sufficiently interesting so that the pupils were enthusiastic about it?
4. Was sufficient help given pupils by the student teacher with the work that might have given them some difficulty?
5. Was sufficient help given pupils in locating reference and study materials for the various activities?
6. Were pupils given as much of an opportunity to participate in planning and carrying on the learning activities as they would like?
7. Were the learning activities interesting, meaningful, and of apparent value to the pupils?
8. Were the examinations and tests reasonable in terms of

the purposes which the learning activities should have achieved?

9. Was the student teacher as effective in his working relations with pupils and in his class control as he might have been?

10. Was there a feeling of confidence on the part of the pupils in the student teacher in so far as their educational and personal problems were concerned?

11. Was the student teacher sufficiently concerned about the problems and difficulties of individual pupils?

12. What suggestions may the pupil have for improving your effectiveness as a teacher?

It is suggested that you prepare a list of questions such as these before you meet with pupils, and that you have them sufficiently well in mind so that you need not use notes. After the conference, it may be helpful to make a record of the suggestions you received.

You may also wish to have pupils evaluate your work from time to time during your student teaching period, as well as at the end. One approach to such periodic evaluation is to have pupils give their reaction concerning the effectiveness of any learning activity in which they had a prominent part. This may be done with the work of one or more class periods, or for a specific learning activity. For instance, pupils who prepared a skit, a dramatization, or a debate, or who participated in a field trip under your supervision, may be asked to suggest how your planning of the activity could be improved. In conferences with individual pupils, you may raise questions such as these concerning the activity:

1. Was the objective for this learning activity clear to the pupils?

·2. Was the learning activity sufficiently well organized?

3. Were pupils given as much of a part in planning and carrying on the learning activity as they would like?

4. Was the learning activity clearly worth while to the pupils in terms of what they would like to get out of the course?
5. Was the teacher sufficiently helpful in all aspects of the learning activity?
6. Were sufficient study and reference materials provided or was sufficient help given you in locating such materials?
7. Were the objectives of the learning activity achieved by the pupils?
8. Were tests and examinations reasonable and clear in terms of the objectives of the activity?

Evaluation by the Cooperating Teacher

You should have your work evaluated by the cooperating teacher almost daily when you are teaching. Some evaluations may be done informally in brief conferences at the close of a class period, during the noon hour, or after school. Others should be of a formal nature with the teacher making a more careful analysis of your work over a period of several days. Usually, the cooperating teacher understands his responsibility for making such periodic evaluations of your work. If he neglects to do so, it might be well to suggest that you would like to visit with him occasionally about the success of your teaching activities. The previous section on self-evaluation may suggest questions that you should raise with the cooperating teacher.

In addition to these periodic evaluations, the cooperating teacher should prepare a detailed, comprehensive analysis of your work at the close of your student teaching period. In many teacher education institutions, an evaluation form is provided for this purpose. The practices concerning the summary evaluation by the cooperating teacher differ widely. In some schools it is prepared by the cooperating teacher and then discussed with the student teacher; in others, it is submitted to the college supervisor without being discussed with the student teacher.

Whatever the practice may be concerning the formal evaluation by the cooperating teacher, you should have a conference with him about the effectiveness of your work. If he neglects to suggest such a conference, it might be well for you to do so a week or more before your student teaching period comes to an end. This should allow him sufficient time to prepare an analysis of your work as a basis for the conference. You should also get ready for such a conference by preparing questions to ask the cooperating teacher.

Do not be sensitive about the comments that the cooperating teacher may make concerning your work. No matter how satisfactory your work as a student teacher may be, there should be much opportunity to improve yourself in one way or another. Try to give the cooperating teacher the feeling that you welcome any comments and criticisms that he may wish to give. Even though you do not agree with him, do not debate the point nor take a defensive attitude. After all, his suggestions are based on experience that is more extensive than yours. You should give careful attention to any suggestions he may give, make a record of them, and use them as seems appropriate.

It is usually best for the person who prepares an evaluation to discuss it himself with the student teacher, rather than have some one else do so. The college supervisor may, therefore, be reluctant to discuss with you any evaluation he has received from the cooperating teacher, lest that evaluation be misunderstood. Matters such as these should not be handled second hand. You are urged, therefore, to discuss your work at some length with the cooperating teacher, rather than to obtain his comments from the college supervisor.

In summary, then, it is suggested that you request from the cooperating teacher evaluations as follows: (1) at the close of each day or each learning activity, (2) periodically during your student teaching period, preferably at the close of every unit, and (3) a summary evaluation of your total student teaching work at the close of the student teaching period.

Evaluation by Other Faculty Members

It may prove helpful to have all faculty members in the cooperating school with whom you have had some contact give you their evaluation of your work. For instance, the principal could evaluate your effectiveness in the school program as a whole, your relationship with the faculty, and your participation in all-school professional responsibilities. The school nurse, the director of guidance, the curriculum coordinator, the librarian, the director of audio-visual materials, and other administrative and supervisory persons may likewise give you their estimate of your effectiveness in so far as their area of responsibility is concerned.

You should make appointments for conferences with these persons, preferably a week or two before the end of your student teaching period to be sure that time may be available for it. Before the conference, prepare the questions that you want to raise. It would be well to make a record of the significant points mentioned in the conference, particularly those that will help you as a beginning teacher.

Evaluation by the College Supervisor

In most teacher education institutions there is a definite procedure for the evaluation of the student teacher's work by the college supervisor. Usually there is an evaluation form for this purpose, as well as conferences with the supervisor, either with the student teaching group as a whole or with each student individually. In cases where there is such a policy, you will of course follow the usual practice.

If the college supervisor does not suggest a conference for a summary evaluation of your work, it might be well for you to request one. The self-evaluation form suggested earlier in this chapter may serve as a basis for such a conference if the college does not provide one of its own. As with other conferences, you should make some preparation for the evaluation conference with the college supervisor so that the questions you may have about the improvement of your work will be answered.

In Summary

In evaluating the effectiveness of your professional work as a student teacher, keep in mind that the purpose of evaluation is improvement. That can best be accomplished if evaluation is continuous and is made by every qualified person who has had contact with your work. More specifically, the following suggestions have been made:

1. As a student teacher, you should evaluate your own effectiveness:
    a) At the end of each class period or learning activity.
    b) Following each responsibility you have had for the home room, a club, assembly, or other extraclass activity.
    c) At the end of a unit of study in your classes.
    d) At the close of your student teaching work, through a summary evaluation of all the activities in which you engaged.
2. The cooperating teacher should evaluate your work:
    a) After each class period or learning activity for which you had some major responsibility.
    b) Periodically during your teaching period, covering a unit of work.
    c) At the close of your student teaching work, through a summary evaluation of all the professional responsibilities you have assumed.
3. Selected pupils in your classes, home room, and extraclass activities may be asked to evaluate your work

through conferences in which you solicit their suggestions for improving your effectiveness as a teacher.

4. The principal and other staff members, either periodically or at the end of your student teaching period, may give you an evaluation of those of your activities which they have observed.

5. The college supervisor should continuously evaluate your growth as a student teacher:

   a) After any learning activity for which you were responsible that he was able to observe.

   b) Periodically, during your student teaching period, covering several weeks of work.

   c) At the end of your student teaching period, as a summary evaluation of all your professional activities and contacts.

Chapter 15

YOU WANT A POSITION

You Need a Certificate

Certificates Have a Purpose

For many years, it has been the practice in most of the states to require certificates of those who teach in the public schools. Usually, the certificates are issued by the state department of education. An official or a bureau within the state department is generally designated to examine the credentials of applicants and to grant certificates to those who qualify.

Certificates issued by the state are required so that the children and their parents may be assured of teachers who meet at least certain minimum professional standards. Certificates granted by the state are not peculiar to the teaching profession. State licenses are generally required of physicians, lawyers, engineers, dentists, and other professional workers. The requirement of a certificate is an indication that the public recognizes the importance of teaching and the desirability of assuring parents and children of competent teachers.

The Common Requirements

The requirements for a teaching certificate vary greatly from one state to another. Furthermore, they differ widely from subject to subject, and from one grade level to another within a state. For instance, some states issue one certificate which covers the entire secondary school, from the seventh through the twelfth grade, while others have separate certificates for the junior and the senior high school. Similarly, some states issue certificates covering all or a group of subjects for a given grade level, whereas others grant them only for those subjects in which the applicant has a specified amount of preparation.

Although the specific requirements differ widely, in most states they include certain items that are thought to have a bearing on teaching success. Items such as these are sometimes included in the certification requirements:

1. Citizenship in the United States of America.
2. A minimum age requirement.
3. Evidence of good health.
4. Evidence of good moral character.
5. A minimum number of years of work at a university, college, or teachers college.
6. Course requirements in professional education.
7. A minimum amount of work in the subjects to be taught.

Because the requirements may differ from one subject to another, you should examine carefully those for the subjects you plan to teach. Furthermore, you should study them for the state in which you expect to be located. For the older subjects, such as English, mathematics, history, and science, the subject matter requirements are often stated in general terms; but in such subjects as art, speech, home economics, industrial arts, business, and physical education, both subject and professional courses are sometimes specifically stated. Early in your preparation for teaching, you should study the requirements for a certificate in the subjects that you would like to teach. The state department of education in your state is the official source for that information. Your college counselor may also be of help.

The practice concerning the renewal of teaching certificates varies among the states. Usually, one must teach for several years on a provisional or probationary certificate, after which a permanent or life certificate is granted. In some states, the permanent certificate remains in effect for life whether the holder teaches or not, unless it is revoked for a specific reason; but in other states, the permanent certificate is retained only under certain conditions, such as continuing to teach or periodically completing professional courses at a teacher education institution. When you begin to teach, inform yourself concerning the conditions for renewing a certificate, and prepare yourself to meet those conditions.

The Responsibility Is Yours

No doubt you have been given considerable help by your college counselors in finding out what the certification requirements are and in planning your program to meet them. It is important for you to recognize, however, that it is your responsibility to see that you meet certification requirements in your state. That is especially true if you are attending an institution in a state other than the one where you plan to teach. You may wish to qualify for teaching in more than one state. Be sure to inform your college counselor concerning your interest in teaching in other states, so that he may help you meet the teaching requirements there.

It is also your responsibility to make proper application for a teaching certificate, although your college counselor may be willing to assist you. Ordinarily, it is best to apply for a certificate shortly before the completion of your teacher education program. This should give you time to obtain such materials as a statement of citizenship, a certificate of health, letters of recommendation, or other materials and information which may be required. You should also have the college registrar send a transcript of your college work to the appropriate person in the state department of education as soon as the records for your work are complete. Be sure to attend to such matters before leaving college at the completion of your program.

You should know that, in some states, a board of education cannot legally pay you for services until you actually have a certificate. Consequently, you are required in some schools to place your certificate on file with the superintendent before you begin to teach. It is imperative, therefore, that you attend to the details of certification as soon as you are qualified.

Things for You To Do

There are, therefore, some things that you should do to satisfy the requirements for a certificate in the state where you expect to teach. The following are suggested:

1. Early in your teacher education program, inform yourself concerning the requirements for a certificate in the state where you plan to teach, giving attention to the subjects and the grade level in which you are interested. Write to the appropriate person in the state department of education for these requirements or consult your college counselor.

2. Before the completion of your college program, obtain an application blank for a certificate and gather the materials and information required in your state. Submit your application and the necessary materials sufficiently early so that the certificate may be issued soon after the completion of your teacher education program. Request the registrar to send a transcript of your college work as soon as your records are complete.

3. Inform yourself concerning provisions for renewing certificates and the conditions pertaining to permanent certificates in the state where you plan to teach. Prepare

to satisfy such requirements during your first years of teaching.

Finding a Position

Your College May Help

Most colleges have placement services which assist their students in obtaining a teaching position. Because it takes quite a bit of time to prepare your placement papers, you should fill in the necessary forms for the placement office some time before you complete your college work. For instance, if you plan to complete your work in June, it is advisable for you to place your name on file and complete the necessary forms in the placement office by the preceding January 1. Some positions for the fall are reported by employing superintendents as early as January or February, and even earlier in those subjects or grades where a shortage of teachers exists.

It may be advisable to add supplementary references to your placement file later in the year. For instance, you may not complete your student teaching until well along in the spring semester. Those who supervise your work will be better prepared to give a statement concerning your probable success as a teacher after having observed your student teaching. Do not delay the preparation of your placement papers until you complete your student teaching. It is a simple matter to add letters of recommendation to your original file at any time.

It is not possible to suggest here how your placement papers should be prepared. Undoubtedly, your placement office will have suggestions for you. In any case, be frank with the placement office, giving them a complete statement of your qualifications, your experience background, and your preferences for the type of school and the locality in which you wish to teach. One suggestion might be helpful concerning the persons you give as references. They should be qualified to give a statement concerning your probable success as a teacher. Select them carefully with that in mind. Furthermore, consult them before you give them as references. This is a courtesy that you should not neglect. It is not wise, however, to limit yourself too much concerning the locality, the type of community, and the kind of school in which you prefer to teach. The kind of position or the locality you prefer may not develop. It seems best, therefore, to suggest your preferences to the placement authorities, but not to limit yourself to the position of your first choice.

Commercial Placement Agencies

There are commercial agencies which help qualified persons obtain teaching positions. You may wish to use one or more of these agencies, as well as your college placement service. The commercial agency may be especially helpful if you wish to teach in a state or region other than where your college is located. Your college supervisor or placement officer may give you suggestions concerning good commercial agencies in your state and elsewhere.

You should know, however, that your contract with a commercial agency requires payment for its services, if you obtain a teaching position with its help. Inform yourself concerning the conditions under which the commercial agency provides its services to you.

Writing to Superintendents

You may wish to write letters to superintendents of schools informing them that you are available for a teaching position. It is best not to write letters indiscriminately to all the superintendents in a given region or state. Preferably, you should correspond only with superintendents in communities where a vacancy exists or is likely to occur. Some prospective teachers, however, have a particular interest in teaching in a certain community. It is certainly appropriate for you to write to the superintendent there to inform him that you are looking for a teaching position, that you are particularly interested in his school system, and that you would appreciate having your name placed in his file for reference in case a vacancy should occur.

If you write such a letter without previous knowledge of a vacancy, do not request the placement office to send your papers. Rather, you should inform the superintendent that your placement papers are on file either in your college placement office or in a commercial agency. The superintendent will write for your papers should a vacancy occur and he is interested in your application.

Keeping Placement Officers Informed

You have no idea how many prospective teachers fail to obtain a position they desire because they cannot be reached quickly when a vacancy occurs. That is particularly true with vacancies that occur during the summer months. At that time of the year, the employing superintendent may be anxious to locate a teacher in a hurry. During the summer months, however, people may go away on a vacation and cannot be reached. It is exceedingly important, therefore, that you keep the placement office informed of your whereabouts. The placement office will, of course, have your home address. If you are to be away from home, even for a few days, be sure to inform the placement office how you may be reached by letter, telegram, or telephone. That is especially important if your entire family is on vacation, and there is no one at your home address.

Then, too, it is important to keep the placement office informed concerning any change in your plans for teaching. Sometimes a prospective teacher has informed the placement office of his desire to teach only in a limited region, but when such a position fails to develop, he decides that he is sufficiently anxious to obtain a position to consider other locations. You cannot expect the placement office to inform you of positions outside the locality you have designated. Then, too, you should inform the placement office if you have decided not to accept a teaching position. The time lost to inform you of a position which you do not take may result in having no one from your college placed there.

It is also important to inform the placement office immediately if you have accepted a teaching position. This means that your name will be removed from the active files, and more attention can be given to others who have not been placed. Likewise, if you are an applicant for a position in several school systems, it is a courtesy to the superintendents with whom you have placed applications to inform them when you have accepted another position. If it is late in the summer, it might be well to call or wire superintendents who have indicated a particular interest in your application.

After your first year of teaching, your college placement office and the commercial agencies will be of help to you in locating a more desirable position. This does not mean that you should look for another position during your first year. It is best to remain in one location for at least two or three years to gain experience which you need. However, when the time comes that you are interested in a position elsewhere, inform the college placement office and any commercial agencies that you have been using and bring them up to date on your experience background.

How To Apply for a Position

Contact the Superintendent

In most communities, the superintendent of schools is the person to whom you should apply for a teaching position.

In a few school systems, candidates for positions in secondary schools may make application direct to the principal. Sometimes this is also the practice with elementary school positions, but less frequently so. In any case, the superintendent is the person who places your name before the board of education, although he may do so only after consultation with the principal of the school where the vacancy exists. The application should be made in the form of a letter in which you indicate briefly your preparation and the position in which you are interested.

It is not considered ethical for you to apply to a member of the board of education. It is true that this is sometimes done by applicants for positions, particularly if they are personally acquainted with a member of the board. Even so, it is not considered good professional practice. Some boards of education have a teachers' committee which interviews candidates for positions. After you submit your application to the superintendent, he will inform you if you are to meet a committee of the board of education. Be sure to work through the superintendent in any contact that you may have with members of the board of education.

The Letter of Application

The letter of application should be brief and to the point. It need not contain detailed information about your background because that is provided in the papers from the placement office. The letter of application may include information such as the following:

1. Your professional education, including the subjects in which you can be certified.
2. Any unusual experiences or background that may have a bearing on your preparation for the position in which a vacancy exists.
3. The position in which you are particularly interested.

4. The placement office or agency from which your placement papers may be obtained.
5. The name of a person, such as your college supervisor, who may be particularly qualified to give additional information concerning your background.
6. An indication that you would be willing to come for an interview, with a suggestion as to a time that might be convenient.

If you are applying for a position where a vacancy definitely exists, request the placement officer to send your confidential papers immediately to the employing superintendent. In that case, indicate in your letter of application that you have taken this step so that the superintendent will not duplicate the request. It is not necessary to give references in your letter of application. The placement papers will provide these.

It is suggested that you show your letter of application to the college supervisor or some other person who has had experience in placement. The letter of application is your first contact with the superintendent. Whether you are called for an interview depends largely upon the impression made by your letter of application. Be sure that this first contact is as favorable as you can make it.

Some suggestions concerning the form in which the letter of application is written may be helpful. It should be on business rather than social stationery, neatly written, and well spaced. A typewritten letter is preferred, although some superintendents request that it be in longhand. Use ink of a conservative color, such as blue or black. If you have any doubt about your grammar or spelling, have someone read your letter. It is not likely that an applicant will be asked to come for an interview if his letter is in poor form.

Arranging for an Interview

You should come for an interview only after making a definite appointment. The interview should be suggested in your letter of application, although you may call the superintendent or his secretary for an appointment. Arrange the time of the interview primarily at the convenience of the superintendent.

You should make definite preparation for an interview by informing yourself about matters that the superintendent may discuss with you. The following suggestions may help you:

1. Be sure that you know your certification status, including all the subjects and grade levels that you are permitted to teach.

2. Have in mind the type of position which you prefer, including subjects, grade level, and the school.

3. Have well in mind your specific preparation for teaching, including (1) the college courses you had in your teaching fields, (2) the extracurricular activities in which you engaged in high school and college, (3) your professional courses, and (4) out-of-school experiences, such as travel, work experience, camping, and work with youth groups. Preparing a summary of this background may be helpful.

4. Find out, if you can, the curriculum which is offered in your subject, including (1) course offerings, (2) grades where courses are offered, (3) required and elective courses, and (4) unusual features in the curriculum.

5. If you can obtain a salary schedule for this community, examine it carefully to find out (1) the salary at which you might begin, (2) the annual increments, and (3) salary provisions for further professional preparation.

6. Know the names and location of the schools where you may be placed. For instance, a secondary school teacher should be concerned with names of the junior and senior high schools.

7. Be sure that you know how to pronounce and spell the name of the superintendent. If there is a position in a specific school, you should also know the name of the principal.

A word should be said about the clothes that are appropriate for an interview. Recently, a young man came for an interview with a committee of the board of education wearing a sport shirt with the collar open. Needless to say, another applicant was appointed. Women likewise may show poor taste in their dress for an interview. For both men and women, it is suggested that business clothes be worn. For a man, this should mean a suit, tie, and hat, all of them reasonably conservative. For a woman, a suit, hat, and gloves appropriate for the season are recommended. One's attire should be neat, attractive, and conservative, and should not draw undue attention. Plan your dress carefully as part of the preparation you make for the interview.

Having An Interview

It is important that you be relaxed during the interview. For that reason you should have plenty of time to reach the superintendent's office without being hurried. If you drive, you should allow for traffic and parking difficulties. Consequently, do not plan a close schedule, but arrive an hour early rather than five minutes late. Not only does a late arrival make a bad impression, but if the superintendent has other appointments he may not be able to see you or may give you too little time.

When you have an interview, do not bring a member of your family or a friend with you. This is especially unwise for a beginning teacher since it may give the impression of lack of self-confidence. When you enter the office, give the secretary your name and state that you have an appointment with the superintendent. She will then inform you when he is free.

It is difficult to suggest how the interview may proceed since it varies so much with the superintendent. He is likely to visit for a minute or two to get acquainted before discussing the position with you. He may raise questions such as the following:

1. What is your college preparation both in your subject and professional courses?
2. What extracurricular activities did you engage in?
3. What hobbies and special talents do you have?
4. What out-of-school experiences have you had that may bear on your teaching success?
5. What is your point of view concerning certain aspects of the subjects you teach?
6. Why are you interested in teaching in this community?

The superintendent may also give you an opportunity to raise questions concerning the position for which you are an applicant. These may be appropriate questions for you to ask:

1. What is the nature of this position, particularly the courses and grade levels?
2. What is the nature of the neighborhood in which the school is located?
3. What is the salary situation?
4. What are the prospects of finding a desirable place to live?
5. When is an appointment likely to be made?

Do not remain too long for an interview. The superintendent may close the interview by indicating that he has no further questions or comment. Ask him if he would be good enough to let you know when a definite decision is made so that you may look elsewhere if not selected by him. Assure him that you have an interest in the position, thank him for the interview, and leave.

Salary Schedules

Many communities today have salary schedules which they follow in employing teachers. These are adopted by the board of education and are usually available in printed or mimeographed form. The salary schedule often has these features:

1. It is based on the number of years of college preparation, with different schedules for four, five, or six years of preparation. Sometimes there is a schedule for teachers with less than four years of college, and a few systems have a schedule for those with the Doctor's degree.
2. It is based on the number of years of experience, usually with a definite increment for each year of satisfactory teaching.
3. It may be based on the grade level at which you teach, with a different schedule for the elementary school, the junior high school, and the senior high school. This is becoming less common, as more communities adopt a single schedule for all grade levels.
4. It provides a maximum salary, which is reached after a stated number of years. In a few communities, teachers may exceed the maximum by special action of the board of education for unusual professional service.
5. A few schedules provide for extra increments before the maximum salary is reached for teachers who have made an unusual contribution to the school or the community.
6. Some communities have different schedules for men and women, though this is becoming the exception in recent years.
7. Some schedules provide special consideration for teachers with dependents, veterans of the armed services, and teachers with unusual backgrounds.

You should examine several different salary schedules, so that you may discuss salary problems intelligently with an employing superintendent. Obtain a salary schedule for the school system where you are student teaching. If other student teachers do likewise, you may exchange them when you return to the campus or you may have a group conference in which salary schedules are discussed.

Signing a Contract

Most schools give teachers a written contract which states the conditions of their employment, such as the salary, the months when they are on duty, and the conditions under which the contract may be canceled. You should realize that a contract is binding upon both the teacher and the board of education, once it has been signed. Study the contract carefully so that you are familiar with it.

Before signing a contract, you should satisfy yourself that you would like to teach in this community. The following may help you decide:

1. You should visit the school to which you may be assigned, become acquainted with the program, meet the principal, meet other members of the faculty, and see the neighborhood. You should know, however, that in most school systems the superintendent has the authority to transfer teachers to any school, grade, or subject for which they are certified.
2. Examine the housing situation to be sure you can obtain a suitable place to live at a rental that you can afford. Also examine other living costs in the community.
3. Find out whether you need an automobile to reach the school or whether public transportation is available.
4. Examine the salary schedule, both the salary at which you will begin and the provisions for salary increases.
5. If you are single and would like to go home occasionally, find out about transportation to your home community.

You should return the contract soon after receiving it, either signed or unsigned. If you wish to have time to think about it, write the superintendent indicating how soon you will give him a reply. Except by arrangement with him, this should not take more than a few days. Late in the summer, you must inform him of your decision at once.

Occasionally, a superintendent may offer a teacher a position, but not send the contract until sometime later. If you are made a definite offer and accept it, that constitutes an oral contract and you should consider it binding on both yourself and the board of education. The superintendent will not make such an offer without authority from the board. You should not accept the position unless you expect to keep your agreement. The written contract which arrives later merely formalizes a previous agreement. In other words, you should not break an oral agreement any more than a written one.

Resigning from a Position

If you resign from a position at the expiration of a contract, there is no particular problem. So that he may have ample opportunity to locate your successor, you should inform the superintendent in writing that you do not expect to return another year as soon as you have made such a decision.

It is another matter if you wish to resign before the expiration of your contract. You should recognize, of course, that the contract is binding on you as well as on the board of education. Many contracts state that a teacher may resign at certain times of the year or after proper notice has been given. You should abide rigidly by the provisions of your contract just as you expect the board of education to do.

Emergencies may arise which make an immediate resignation seem necessary, such as personal illness, illness in the family, or an unusual professional opportunity elsewhere. In that case, make an appointment with the superintendent to discuss the matter frankly. You will usually find him considerate of your situation, if it is a reasonable one. The two of you may then work out a plan for your release which will protect both your interests and those of the board of education. On the basis of your conversation with the superintendent, write him a letter requesting a release from your contract at a date upon which you have agreed. This is the professional way to obtain a release from a contract.

Things for You To Do

1. File the required forms in the placement office sufficiently early so that the placement papers can be ready when vacancies are reported. This should ordinarily be a semester before you complete your work, though your placement office may suggest another time. Consult the persons whose names you are giving as references to obtain their consent.

2. If you know a superintendent or principal personally, ask him if you may come for a practice interview to gain experience. The superintendent or principal in your cooperating school or in your home community may be willing to do this. Plan and conduct this interview just as you would expect to do if you were applying for a position, including the following: (1) write a letter of application, (2) make an appointment, (3) plan for the interview as suggested above, (4) prepare questions that you would like to ask, (5) dress appropriately, and (6) conduct yourself well in the interview. After the interview, have the superintendent or principal evaluate what you did.

3. Obtain copies of several salary schedules from the cooperating school, your home community, and several other school systems. If other student teachers do this, each of you may obtain one and exchange them. Examine these schedules, with attention to the following: (1) the salary at which one with your experience and education would begin, (2) the annual increment, (3) the maximum salary for one with your education, (4) the number of

years to reach the maximum, (5) the schedules for those with more education, (6) differences by grade level, and (7) provisions for veterans and teachers with dependents.

4. Obtain a sample copy of the teachers' contract form from your cooperating school and several other systems. If other student teachers do this, each may obtain one and exchange them. Examine these forms, with particular reference to the following: (1) the time of year when you are subject to duty, (2) provisions for sick leave, (3) number of days of teaching, (4) conditions under which you may resign, and (5) conditions under which the board of education may cancel the contract.

5. Write a letter of application and submit it for criticism to several people who have had experience with such letters, such as the placement officer, the college supervisor, a principal, or a superintendent of schools.

6. A group of student teachers may arrange a conference with a superintendent of schools to discuss with him the procedure in applying for and obtaining a position. Raise questions with him concerning (1) letters of application, (2) appointments for interviews, (3) how the candidate may best conduct himself, (4) the questions he would ask, and (5) questions he might expect the candidate to ask. This conference should be arranged with the help of the placement officer or the director of student teaching.

In Summary

There are, therefore, a number of things that it is advisable to do in making plans for obtaining a teaching position, such as the following: (1) making early application for a teaching certificate, (2) making the necessary arrangements early with a placement service, (3) learning how to make an application, and (4) planning carefully how to proceed with an interview. Give much thought to a position which you are offered before accepting; but once you have accepted, recognize your legal and professional obligation to fulfill your agreement in every way. Placement services may assist you in obtaining your first position, and in moving to better ones. Keep in touch with your college supervisor and with the placement services.

SUGGESTED READINGS

SUGGESTED READINGS

The following readings have been selected because they bear on your responsibilities as a student teacher. You will not be able to read all of them. Select those which may be helpful on the problems that concern you most.

SCHOOL-COMMUNITY RELATIONS

DOUGLASS, HARL R. *Secondary Education for Life Adjustment of American Youth.* New York: The Ronald Press Co., 1952, chap. xxiii.

DOUGLASS, HARL R., and HUBERT H. MILLS. *Teaching in High School.* New York: The Ronald Press Co., 1948, chap. xviii.

HYMES, JAMES L., JR. *Effective Home-School Relations.* New York: Prentice-Hall, Inc., 1953.

METROPOLITAN SCHOOL STUDY COUNCIL, Committee on Human Resources. *Fifty Teachers to a Classroom.* New York: The Macmillan Co., 1950.

NATIONAL EDUCATION ASSOCIATION. *It Starts in the Classroom.* Washington, D.C.: The Association, 1951.

————. Department of Elementary School Principals. *How to Know and Use Your Community.* Washington, D.C.: The Association, 1942.

OLSEN, EDWARD G., and others. *School and Community.* New York: Prentice-Hall, Inc., 1945.

YEAGER, WILLIAM A. *School-Community Relations.* New York: The Dryden Press, 1951, chap. xvii.

ZERAN, FRANKLIN R. (ed.). *The High School Teacher and His Job.* New York: Chartwell House, Inc., 1953, chap. vii.

EVALUATING AND REPORTING PUPIL PROGRESS

BERGER, DONALD. "When a Class Evaluates," *Educational Leadership,* VI (March, 1949), 395-99.

BROWN, EDWIN J. *Managing the Classroom.* New York: The Ronald Press Co., 1952, chaps. x, xv.

FAUNCE, ROLAND C., and NELSON L. BOSSING. *Developing the Core Curriculum.* New York: Prentice-Hall, Inc., 1951, chap. xiv.

GRUHN, WILLIAM T., and HARL R. DOUGLASS. *The Modern Junior High School.* New York: The Ronald Press Co., 1947, chap. xiv.

STRANG, RUTH. *Reporting to Parents.* New York: Bureau of Publications, Teachers College, Columbia University, 1947.

WILES, KIMBALL. *Teaching for Better Schools.* New York: Prentice-Hall, Inc., 1952, chaps. ix-x.

WRINKLE, WILLIAM L. *Improving Marking and Reporting Practices in Elementary and Secondary Schools.* New York: Rinehart & Co., Inc., 1947.

EXTRACLASS ACTIVITIES AND GUIDANCE

ANDERSON, VERNON E., PAUL R. GRIM, and WILLIAM T. GRUHN. *Principles and Practices of Secondary Education.* New York: The Ronald Press Co., 1951, chaps. x, xiii, xiv.

ARBUCKLE, D. S. *Teacher Counseling.* Cambridge, Mass.: Addison-Wesley Press, Inc., 1950.

DUNSMOOR, C. C., and LEONARD M. MILLER. *Principles and Methods of Guidance for Teachers.* Scranton, Pa.: International Textbook Co., 1949.

FEDDER, RUTH. *Guiding Home Room and Club Activities.* New York: McGraw-Hill Book Co., Inc., 1949.

GRUHN, WILLIAM T., and HARL R. DOUGLASS. *The Modern Junior High School.* New York: The Ronald Press Co., 1947, chaps. xi-xiii.

JOHNSTON, EDGAR, and ROLAND C. FAUNCE. *Student Activities in Secondary Schools.* New York: The Ronald Press Co., 1952.

NATIONAL ASSOCIATION OF STUDENT COUNCILS. *The Student Council in the Secondary School.* Washington, D.C.: National Association of Secondary-School Principals, 1950.

SMITH, JOE. *Student Councils For Our Times.* New York: Bureau of Publications, Teachers College, Columbia University, 1951.

ZERAN, FRANKLIN R. (ed.). *The High School Teacher and His Job.* New York: Chartwell House, Inc., 1953, chap. iv.

METHODS OF TEACHING

ASSOCIATION FOR SUPERVISION AND CURRICULUM DEVELOPMENT. *Toward Better Teaching.* Washington, D.C.: National Education Association, 1949.

BAXTER, BERNICE, and ROSALIND CASSIDY. *Group Experiences—The Democratic Way.* New York: Harper & Bros., 1943.

CUNNINGHAM, RUTH, and OTHERS. *Understanding Group Behavior of Boys and Girls.* New York: Bureau of Publications, Teachers College, Columbia University, 1951.

FAUNCE, ROLAND C., and NELSON L. BOSSING. *Developing the Core Curriculum.* New York: Prentice-Hall, Inc., 1951, chaps. vi, viii-x.

GRAMBS, J. D. "Using Group Work in High School Classes," *California Journal of Secondary Education*, XXVI (April 1951), pp. 232-36.

NOAR, GERTRUDE. *Freedom to Live and Learn.* Philadelphia: Franklin Publishing Co., 1948.

Wiles, Kimball. *Teaching for Better Schools.* New York: Prentice-Hall, Inc., 1952, chaps. v-viii.

HUMAN RELATIONS AND THE CLASSROOM

Association for Supervision and Curriculum Development. *Fostering Mental Health in the Schools.* Washington, D.C.: National Education Association, 1950.

Baxter, Bernice. *Teacher-Pupil Relationships.* New York: The Macmillan Co., 1941.

Brown, Edwin J. *Managing the Classroom.* New York: The Ronald Press Co., 1952.

Hymes, James L. *Discipline.* New York: Bureau of Publications, Teachers College, Columbia University, 1949.

Jennings, Helen Hall. *Sociometry in Group Relations.* Washington, D.C.: American Council on Education, 1948.

Langdon, Grace, and Irving W. Stout. *The Discipline of Well-Adjusted Children.* New York: The John Day Co., 1952, chaps. iii-iv.

Olson, Willard C. "Human Relationships in the Classroom." *National Education Association Journal,* XXXVI (December 1947), pp. 640-41.

Redl, Fritz, and George Sheviakov. *Discipline for Today's Children and Youth.* Washington, D.C.: National Education Association, 1944.

Wiles, Kimball. *Teaching for Better Schools.* New York: Prentice-Hall, Inc., 1952, chaps. iii-iv.

MEETING INDIVIDUAL NEEDS

American Council on Education. *Helping Teachers Understand Children.* Washington, D.C.: The Council, 1945.

Burton, W. H. *The Guidance of Learning Activities.* New York: Appleton-Century-Crofts, Inc., 1952, chap. ix.

Douglass, Harl R. *Secondary Education for Life Adjustment of American Youth.* New York: The Ronald Press Co., 1952, chap. v.

Ferguson, Evelyn B. "Getting to Know Your Pupils Quickly." *The Elementary School Journal,* L (February 1950), pp. 341-45.

National Council for the Social Studies. *Adapting Instruction in the Social Studies to Individual Differences.* Fifteenth Yearbook. Washington, D.C.: National Education Association, 1944.

Wiles, Kimball. *Teaching for Better Schools.* New York: Prentice-Hall, Inc., 1952, chaps. xi-xii.

PLANNING LEARNING ACTIVITIES

Berger, Donald. "Planning in the Core Class," *Educational Leadership,* VIII (January 1951), pp. 208-14.

Burton, W. H. *The Guidance of Learning Activities,* New York: Appleton-Century-Crofts, Inc., 1952, chap. xiii.

Douglass, Harl R., and Hubert H. Mills. *Teaching in High School.* New York: The Ronald Press Co., 1948, chap. vii.

FAUNCE, ROLAND C., and NELSON L. BOSSING. *Developing the Core Curriculum*. New York: Prentice-Hall, Inc., 1951, chap. vii.

SCHORLING, RALEIGH. *Student Teaching*. New York: McGraw-Hill Book Co., Inc., 1949, chap. vi.

PROFESSIONAL IMPROVEMENT

ANDERSON, VERNON E., PAUL R. GRIM, and WILLIAM T. GRUHN. *Principles and Practices of Secondary Education*. New York: The Ronald Press Co., 1951, chap. xix.

BROWN, EDWIN J. *Managing the Classroom*. New York: The Ronald Press Co., 1952, chaps. xvi-xviii.

WILES, KIMBALL. *Teaching for Better Schools*. New York: Prentice-Hall, Inc., 1952, chap. xiv.

PROFESSIONAL RELATIONSHIPS

ARMSTRONG, W. EARL, and T. M. STINNETT. *A Manual on Certification Requirements for School Personnel in the United States*. United States Office of Education Circular No. 290, 1951. Washington, D.C.: United States Office of Education.

BARTKY, A. JOHN. *Supervision as Human Relations*. Boston: D. C. Heath & Co., 1952.

CHAMBERLAIN, LEO M., and LESLIE KINDRED. *The Teacher and School Organization*. New York: Prentice-Hall, Inc., 1949.

ZERAN, FRANKLIN R. (ed.). *The High School Teacher and His Job*. New York: Chartwell House, Inc., 1953, chaps. iii, v, vi.

INDEX